MAKE IT
Easy

120 MIX-AND-MATCH RECIPES
TO COOK FROM SCRATCH
with **SMART STORE-BOUGHT SHORTCUTS**
WHEN YOU NEED THEM

Stacie Billis

Da Capo
LIFE
LONG

A Member of the Perseus Books Group

Copyright © 2016 by Stacie Billis
Photographs by Naomi McCullough

Editorial production by Christine Marra / Marrathon Production Services. www.marrathon.net
Book design by Lisa Diercks / Endpaper Studio. www.endpaperstudio.com
Set in Absara, Absara Sans, and Nexa Rust.

Cataloging-in-Publication data for this book is available from the Library of Congress.

First Da Capo Press edition 2016
Paperback ISBN: 978-0-7382-1886-1
Ebook ISBN: 978-0-7382-1887-8

LCCN: 2016003901

Published by Da Capo Press
A Member of the Perseus Books Group
www.dacapopress.com

Da Capo Press books are available at special discounts for bulk purchases in the U.S. by corporations, institutions, and other organizations. For more information, please contact the Special Markets Department at the Perseus Books Group, 2300 Chestnut Street, Suite 200, Philadelphia, PA, 19103, or call (800) 810-4145, ext. 5000, or e-mail special.markets@perseusbooks.com.

10 9 8 7 6 5 4 3 2 1

♥

For Isaac and Oliver for making me a hungry mama.
I love you both to the moon (pie) and back.

And for Michael for always eating with me.
No matter what, nothing beats enjoying a great meal
across the table from you.

♥

CONTENTS

Introduction

YOU REALLY CAN MAKE IT EASY

If this book is in your hands, you're probably eager for cooking to be easier than it is currently. If you're a parent, you may even be desperate for it. Cooking for a group of people night after night, each with their own tastes (and, probably, at least one picky eater) is not for the faint of heart. Doing it without completely losing your mind takes serious effort and the last thing you need is for someone to tell you that the problem is you:

You just need to relax.

You just need to make more time for cooking.

You just need to plan.

You just need to be more confident in the kitchen.

Screw that.

Don't get me wrong: I've caught myself saying these things to many frazzled home cooks because being a relaxed, confident cook who loves planning meals and being in the kitchen is what has made me a great cook. But it's also what has made me a *professional* cook. Not everyone loves cooking as much as I do, but everyone has to feed their clan. I've come to understand just how thankless a chore it is for many and, if you're one of those many, it's not your fault.

This became clear to me when I started working with personal clients, advising them on family eating, from dealing with picky eaters to helping them create personalized meal plans. I decided that it wasn't my clients' fault that they were ordering in all the time or that they were functioning as short-order cooks (talk about thankless). I convinced them to make the same shift and, together, we solved the real problem; that they didn't have flexible cooking strategies and recipe options—or they just weren't clear on how and when to use them. When we fixed that, the results were amazing.

We made cooking easy. And I'm going to make cooking easy for you, too.

HERE'S THE TRUTH: SCRATCH COOKING CAN BE EASY, EVEN ON A TIGHT SCHEDULE

For a long time before the entire country knew about *artisan food* and one of the quickest-growing fast-food joints promoted farm-to-table eating, home cooking trends were about convenience. Thirty-minute meals became fifteen-minute meals and semihomemade became a full-fledged cooking genre. We seem to have swung from one side of the pendulum to the other, and busy home cooks have been left stranded somewhere in the middle.

While I'm thrilled that the conversation has returned to scratch cooking, I hear from parents every day through my work as the managing editor at *Cool Mom Eats,* my personal blog *One Hungry Mama*, and my work advising families, that busy home cooks are more stressed than ever about getting healthy, home-cooked meals on the table.

The shift in our larger food culture has made the same people who needed those convenience tricks feel terrible about using them. In many cases, with good reasons having to do with our health and the health of our planet. But not in all cases; there's also a lot of judgment.

At the same time, the rise in popularity of scratch cooking has led many to believe that, to do it, you have to pickle, can, grow, buy entirely organic, and otherwise commit to practices that, for many of us busy home cooks, are just not practical.

We are caught in a catch-22 and it's made feeding our families hard on our schedules, on our budgets, and worst of all, on our psyches. If you don't believe me, check out some info from the US Bureau of Labor Statistics.

According to them, some families spend just less than half of their entire food budget on eating out. One survey showed that buying prepared or semiprepared meals and ordering in are two of the most popular strategies that parents use to help them ease the stress and anxiety of the relentless chore of feeding their families three times a day with already overpacked schedules. But get this: the same parents who reported using these strategies also reported that doing so didn't reduce daily stress. In fact, it often exacerbated stress and anxiety when the shortcut strategies led to meals that weren't in line with their food and eating ideals.

So, basically, busy home cooks keep applying solutions—the only practical ones they've been given—that don't solve the whole problem. Or at least the part that counts: how we feel about what we feed our families.

Sound familiar?

When I read that, I promised that I wouldn't write a cookbook until I could offer a practical solution that addresses the *whole* problem. The solution is not just about quick, easy recipes, because if they're made with the "wrong" ingredients, you still won't feel good about cooking. It's also not just about always cooking from scratch with premium ingredients, because scratch cooking can come at a high price our schedules can't afford and the best ingredients can come at a high price that our budgets can't withstand. That's stressful, too. So, why am I writing this? Because I've finally figured out that the solution is about giving busy home cooks a laid-back and flexible approach to scratch cooking that uses healthy store-bought shortcuts when you need them for maximum flexibility.

And, yes, there are healthy store-bought shortcuts. I've found them for you.

In this book, we're going to reclaim scratch cooking for busy, modern life. Sometimes scratch cooking means going all out, while other times it means using a few carefully chosen but exceedingly helpful store-bought ingredients to make a meal. And it always means cooking smart, with an eye toward mixing and matching recipes that you can combine endlessly and use repeatedly without getting bored. Because this saves time *and* money.

Make It Easy is organized in three sections

to, well, make it easy for you to use this book. We start with the basics, which are my favorite tips for how to get the most out of your time in the kitchen. Next, mix-and-match recipes that are just that: flexible dishes that fit together in varying ways to make not just one meal, but many meals. Last up, the supermarket guide, a handy reference to pantry staples and healthy cheat ingredients. You can use all three sections in tandem or not; though they complement one another, the sections are designed to stand alone.

If you're completely in the weeds and need a family cooking intervention, this book will guide you through a plan to get back on track on your terms. Hate to cook and need a handful of strategies for getting dinner on the table on busy weeknights? Hit the basics. Just need new recipes to expand the foundation of your everyday cooking repertoire? Go straight to recipes. You are in control. As it should be.

PART I

The Three
MAKE IT EASY
Basics

BASIC #1

MAKE IT EASY
On Yourself

There are a few ways that you can set yourself up so that cooking—even on a tight schedule, for picky eaters, when you don't particularly like cooking—can be easier. Just telling yourself to relax is not one of them, but feeling relaxed should happen if you follow these simple rules.

DETERMINE YOUR REAL-LIFE COOKING STYLE

It's not a complicated equation; the best place to start is simply to be honest with yourself about how you cook best in real life and how much effort you're able to put into changing that. (Spoiler alert: for most people, the answer is zero effort. And that's okay—we can still do this.)

When I worked with clients, busy home cooks just like you, I was amazed at how many said in one breath that they hated cooking and, in the next, that they wanted to cook amazing, elaborate meals for their family. Whenever they had some time and cooking inspiration struck, they took on big cooking projects that matched up with some fantasy of the domestic god or goddess they wanted to be. In reality, they were so overwhelmed that they wanted to quit halfway through cooking. The bad experience made them dread going into kitchen even more. Stop, rinse, repeat: the same thing would happen again a month later.

The trick is to set reasonable goals. Sure, stretch goals are great. But really think about yours—do you want them to be in the kitchen? If you do, are they realistic? Remember to go slow. Start by taking a brisk walk, not by trying to run a marathon.

The more your cooking expectations match your realistic cooking capacity, the more likely you are to enjoy the process and want to take things further. To get a sense of your realistic cooking capacity, answer these questions:

• Even when everything goes right, how much do I enjoy being in the kitchen?

• How much time do I really have to cook, start to finish? Is it different on some days than on others?

• How stressed out do I get by working under time constraints?

• Is it easy for me to be creative in the kitchen? Can I easily riff off recipes, or is it easier for me to follow them verbatim?

• How much do I care about having a spectacularly delicious meal at the end of every day? Are fresh, simple meals satisfying?

• Do I meal plan? (Have I ever meal planned?) Am I able to come up with meal ideas on the fly?

As you consider your answers, chase out of your head Martha Stewart or Nigella Lawson or whichever domestic icon you wish you could be. Don't be your ideal kitchen self when answering. You have to start with your *real* cooking self to successfully build your kitchen skills, if you decide that's what you want to do. And no worries if it's not.

TAKE STOCK OF WHAT YOU AND YOUR CREW LIKE TO EAT

In addition to answering the questions above, take ten minutes (or fewer!) to list the meals that make you and your entire family happy. Look at them with an eye toward finding patterns: Are they all simple? Do they all have sauce? Are they easily deconstructed so that some people are enjoying the same meal in completely different ways than others? Are they all Mexican or Italian? Do you guys like leftovers?

All of this information is already in your head, but taking time to lay it all out so that you can make meaningful connections is shockingly helpful. You only have to do it once (or, at least, once every year or two) and it doesn't take long. Then you have a sense of what you can and should take on in the kitchen.

LEARN HOW TO CHOOSE THE RIGHT RECIPES

The recipes in this book are simple. They're designed to be family-friendly and adaptable. If you're not an experienced home cook, they are easy to make, fresh, and delicious. If you're a foodie with kitchen skills, you'll be able to riff off these recipes like crazy. They leave a lot of room to play. And, no matter what kind of cook you are, the recipes in this book can be deconstructed and mix-and-matched so that one meal can feed people with several tastes (and every recipe comes with mix-and-match suggestions).

I designed this book to be a go-to resource for making cooking easy, with a handful of easy recipes that work for special occasions, too. (Because the fact that it's Junior's birthday doesn't magically clear your schedule.) But, of course, you'll look to other resources, too. When you do, you should either look for the same types of recipes or have a clear idea of how the recipes you're looking for should be different.

What are they for: Have you cleared your schedule to cook something more elaborate for a dinner party? Do you want to take on a challenging baking project to pass time on a rainy day? Are you craving a more sophisticated Sunday night meal, kids be damned?

This all goes back to knowing your real-life cooking style and understanding that it's fluid as circumstances change. You'll cook differently for that dinner party if you've set aside time to cook and have arranged for the kids to be out of the house than you will if you've got forty-five minutes to pull together a dinner for ten. It's the difference between an elegant meal and a big pot of meat sauce. Both can be great, as long as you're honest about what you can pull off and choose the right recipes.

Here are some quick guidelines to choosing the right recipe for the circumstance:

Choose recipes based on your cooking skill, as much as on appeal. Don't get attached to the *idea* of a recipe. There are millions of recipes out there and plenty will fit your style, skill, *and* crew's taste.

Look at the number of ingredients. When you need to go fast, choose recipes with fewer ingredients. Period.

Survey the number of fresh versus pantry ingredients. You can make fresh, nutritious meals using pantry ingredients, especially if you start thinking about your freezer as a part of your pantry. When you shop for a specific meal that you're sure you're going to cook, such as for a special occasion, go all out on the fresh ingredients. Otherwise, consider looking for recipes that pair a handful of fresh ingredients with affordable pantry ingredients that don't go bad, including canned chickpeas, frozen spinach or peas, tomato sauce, and rice and other dried grains.

Consider the active cooking time. Unless you have very good knife skills, recipes will always take longer than they say.

Determine how much chopping you'll need to do. Quickly scan recipes to assess the amount of chopping you'll need to do, keeping in mind that some aren't written in a way where you can tell how much chopping will be required just by looking at the ingredients. If you need to go fast, less chopping is better.

SET YOURSELF UP TO ENJOY THE KITCHEN

Once you know how you cook best, what everyone likes to eat, and what kind of recipes you should be choosing, it's time to hit the kitchen. That's where the temperature rises, even if you've set yourself up well. The most perfect plan can fall apart with a kid meltdown, a phone call, an emergency e-mail from work, or, of course, a recipe gone wrong. It happens. Making sure that your kitchen is set up so that things are easy and comfortable will help those moments roll off your back. Well, as much as they can.

Think about the things that drive you crazy every single time you cook. Do you hate rummaging for pots? Do you get annoyed every time you have to reach to the back of the pantry to grab the oil (which you use every day)? Take time to fix anything that's a constant annoyance. Including the kids.

I'm not kidding about the kids part. If the kids drive you mad while you're cooking, think of ways that you might keep them busy so that you can fit in thirty minutes of focused cooking time. Can your cooking time double as a dedicated drawing, reading, or homework time? Do you not mind having them cook alongside you? Maybe your cooking time becomes their TV time. Hey, no judgments here. If it helps you make a fresh, healthy meal, it may be a net value.

Last, but not least, do your best to turn cooking into an enjoyable moment. You have to do it one way or another, so why not pour a glass of wine and turn on your favorite album. Cooking dinner in a rush will never be a Calgon moment, but it also doesn't have to be completely hellish.

STOP FEELING GUILTY ABOUT USING SHORTCUTS

Using healthy, store-bought shortcuts—and not feeling bad about them—freed me from a tremendous amount of pressure, self-imposed of course, because how could a professional food writer not make *everything* from scratch? (She can be a busy working mom of two young kids, is how.) And, yes, there are store-bought shortcuts that are healthy, or at least healthy enough without nasty ingredients, that their convenience outweighs the small sacrifice in taste or quality (see my Supermarket Guide, pages 237–255).

On the other side of the spectrum, being discerning about shortcuts has been a revelatory change in the cooking style of my clients who once relied primarily on store-bought ingredients. With mastery of a few very easy scratch recipes for go-to staples (Everyday Pancakes, page 85; Everyday Waffles, page 87; Pizza Dough, page 191; and Peanut Butter, page 53, for example) they could let go of some of the expensive store-bought items—and also let go of the guilt that came with those purchases. And it doesn't even cost them that much extra time in the kitchen.

Determining your threshold for store-bought shortcuts is a very personal matter. What one busy cook considers a good compromise may feel like a sacrifice to another. While there are some foods and ingredients that we should all try to avoid as much as possible (check out my list on page 15), many fall in a gray area that should be considered in the context of your specific diet and budget.

Following are a few things to think about as you figure out where you want to draw the line between cooking from scratch and buying from the store.

DETERMINE WHAT YOU WANT TO BUY ORGANIC AND WHEN YOU WANT TO SAVE MONEY

The research is complicated, but I've dug though it and can tell you with confidence that organically grown produce is better for us overall and undeniably better for the planet, too. It's honestly a clear-cut issue for me, but I understand that it may not be for you. Here is a simple overview of how and why I buy organic. I hope that it helps you make buying decisions for your family that you can feel good about.

Produce

Some crops require more pesticides than others and some fruits and veggies have more permeable skin. When you cross-reference these factors, you can figure out which foods are "dirtier" than others. Every year, the Environmental Working Group (http://www.ewg.org) publishes its findings in two superuseful lists: the Dirty Dozen and the Clean Fifteen.

As a rule of thumb, I buy the organic version of any produce on the Dirty Dozen list and save my dollars by going conventional with produce on the Clean Fifteen. (See how easy we're making this?)

There's just one more thing that I want the parents of babies to consider. Beginner eaters and toddlers consume a much greater volume of fruits and vegetables compared to their body weight than do big kids and adults. For this reason, studies have shown that beginner eaters tend to have a much higher level of pesticides in their bloodstream. Babies seem to benefit most from a wholly organic diet so, whenever possible, with the exception of the Clean Fifteen, consider buying as much organic as you're able for your beginner eater.

Dairy

So much of the conversation about organic versus conventional food has centered on produce but, if you ask me, dairy is what we should be talking about. First off, in the same way that our babies and toddlers eat more produce relative to their body weight compared to older children and adults, American school-aged children eat a diet very high in dairy. Also, the labels for dairy products can be confusing.

Let's start with milk. Organic milk has been shown to contain higher levels of omega-3 fats due to the fact that cows that produce organic milk are usually fed a diet higher in omega-3 fats, including more grass. Some studies claim that the level is marginally higher (i.e., it doesn't make a difference), while a 2013 study that looked closely at four hundred samples of organic and conventional milk over eighteen months showed that the difference was quite significant. A small sample, but perhaps still food for thought.

While the omega-3 issue may be inconclusive, there are two things about dairy that are not. One is that milk does not contain antibiotics. By law, all of the milk produced for commercial consumption is tested for antibiotics and other veterinary drugs. Milk found to be contaminated is immediately pulled out of our food supply, even at conventional dairies.

The other indisputable thing about dairy is that industrially raised dairy cows are regularly injected with growth hormones (BGH, rBGH, and rBST) to increase their milk production. While some research suggest that these hormones don't survive pasteurization, other studies claim that the research is inconclusive.

Either way, whether you buy conventional or organic, the absolute latest research suggests that whole milk is best. All those good fatty acids that milk offers are carried in the fat that is removed when making 2%, 1%, and fat-free milk. And since whole-fat dairy is best, you'll want to make sure that you're not eating too much of it overall. It's been long established that a diet high in fruits and vegetables with moderate dairy intake is best for us all.

Packaged foods

Deciding whether to buy organic packaged foods is a whole separate process. I know: nothing seems easy with food anymore, but we're going to break this down and make it a cinch.

In the United States, a product made with entirely organic ingredients—from the wheat to the vanilla extract—can be labeled "100% organic." A product made with 95 percent organic ingredients can be labeled "organic," while products made with a minimum of 70 percent organic ingredients can say "made with organic ingredients."

The thing with packaged foods, organic or not, is that they are processed. So, while it may feel better to buy cookies that are "made with organic ingredients," it's important to know that they may be packed with sugar. In other words, the word *organic* is not synonymous with *healthy*.

When it comes to packaged foods, unless the product includes ingredients on the Dirty Dozen list (e.g., strawberry snack bars made with real strawberries), it's best to go back to our packaged food basics: read the nutrition and ingredients labels, stay away from foods packed with sugar, fat, and/or salt, and avoid products with ingredients that you don't like or can't pronounce. Even if the product is organic.

DECIDE WHETHER LOCAL FOOD MATTERS TO YOU

The local food movement complicates an already inscrutable food landscape, but it's also a good thing, and not just for farmers and the earth and all those other things that you wish you had more time to care about. It's also a good thing for busy home cooks, especially parents.

Local food gets from the farm to our kitchens quickly, which means fresher, better-tasting produce. Try getting a kid to fall in love with a hard peach that has been overrefrigerated to make it through the eight-day trip to your supermarket from a farm across the country. Fresh, just-picked ones, though? It takes zero effort to create a fruit—or at least a peach—lover out of your little one.

Just because food is local, does not mean that it's also organic. And just because it's not officially labeled "organic" doesn't meant that it's heavily laden with pesticides. A lot of local produce that is available direct to consumer is grown on small farms, often by struggling farmers. They may not be able to afford organic certification even if they are using organic growing processes.

If you're interested in buying local, speak to the farmers directly. Ask questions about their farming practices and decide from there. You can also consult the Dirty Dozen list. When I was still making baby food, I chose to buy organic any items on the Dirty Dozen list, even if it meant getting less tasty strawberries that had been shipped to New York from California. As my kids grew up, I decided that superfresh, local produce was just fine, even if grown conventionally, given that the rest of our diet was largely organic. You can do the same. Or not. Just learn about your options and decide what's right for your family.

KEEP IN MIND THE INGREDIENTS YOU WANT TO AVOID AT ALL COSTS

In the next chapter, we'll talk about how to read packaged food and nutrition labels. I share a list of ingredients that most experts think we should avoid as much as possible and tips on how to figure out how much salt, sugar, and fat your family should be eating. Take it all in as you're able and maybe even speak to your doctor (definitely speak to your doctor if anyone in your family has health challenges). Then, set guidelines for what you're willing to buy and stick to them, so that you don't have to reinvent the wheel every time you want to consider a new store-bought shortcut that will save you time and stress.

The key to letting go of the guilt so often associated with buying store-bought foods is to align how you *actually* feed your family with how you *want* to feed your family. Whether you realized it or not, all of the questions and considerations I've thrown your way in this chapter have been designed to help you create a flexible set of values about how you want to feed your crew. These food values will give you something to check your food decisions against.

If you see a new product that will help you make dinner easier and it fits your values, go ahead and grab it without guilt. If it doesn't fit your values, skip it. Or if it's really great or a special occasion, make an exception. The point isn't to be rigid, but to help you feel like you're doing a good job overall. Because you are.

BASIC #2

MAKE IT EASY
On Your Schedule

Time is the factor that seems to stress home cooks out more than any other. There never seems to be enough of it for us to make the kinds of meals that we want to make. In the last chapter we talked about being honest about what you can easily whip up within your schedule constraints. That's a critical part of making it easy, but there are a few other simple ways to make it easy on your schedule: meal plan, master the market, make smart use of store-bought short-cuts, and learn a few kitchen tricks.

MEAL PLAN. *I KNOW*, BUT SERIOUSLY.

Yup, the dreaded meal plan suggestion. You've heard it before and, though I've promised you a new approach, here I am saying it again. The truth is, if you can get into the habit of meal planning, it will totally and completely change your life as a busy home cook. I'm not exagger-

ating and I've seen it help clients even more than I could have ever predicted.

I've also seen that some busy cooks just can't, don't, won't meal plan. If you've tried and just can't make meal planning work, forgive yourself and move on. If you haven't given it the old college try, though, and think that you might be ready to commit, I encourage you to give it a go (another go?).

Here are some practical meal-planning tips that have helped even the most resistant of my clients. In fact, even if you're ready to accept that you're not the meal-planning type, give these tips a scan. Some can be incorporated into your routine even if you can't, don't, won't formally meal plan.

Set aside no more than ten minutes to think about meals for the week. If you allow meal planning to take twenty, thirty, or forty minutes or longer, it will become an unsustainable practice. Instead, force yourself to do it in ten minutes. Be focused, go to recipe resources you trust, and make thoughtful but quick decisions. You might even set a timer to keep you on track. Once you see what a big difference only ten minutes a week can make, you'll be motivated to continue.

Keep track of meals that work. Keeping notes on recipes that are easy to cook and meals that are a hit with the family help you from having to re-create the wheel every week. Put favorites on regular rotation so that you don't have to plan all-new meals every week.

Have other members of your crew help. Ask the rest of the people in your crew about what they want to eat. Maybe each kid gets a day of the week or every Friday is Mom's choice. Having a few meals that you don't have to think about makes meal planning easier. Plus, serving your family their favorites increases their food happiness quotient, which reduces complaining and, in turn, increases your food happiness quotient, too.

Plan a few meals around what's already in the refrigerator. Food waste can be a big source of guilt and, worse, a huge waste of money. When taking your ten minutes to make a meal plan, start with what's in the fridge. If you're not great at dreaming up meals based on one or two available ingredients, flip to the index here or in one of your other favorite cookbooks. You can also use a recipe search engine that scans by ingredient, such as www.foodily.com.

Once you get good at planning around what you have in your fridge, you can also incorporate the foods in your pantry and freezer. This will help keep you from finding four-year-old freezer burned meat or who-knows-how-old cans of beans buried in the way back.

Cook once, eat twice. While meal planning, try to double up on side dishes, veggies, or even main proteins in a week so that you can cook them once and serve them twice. So, for example, if you're making steak tacos with rice and beans one night, also plan on serving grilled chicken with a side of rice and roasted broccoli and an Asian steak salad that week, too. Then, on taco night, cook double the steak and double the rice—it takes no extra effort—and your cooking on two subsequent nights that week is significantly reduced.

Boom.

I admit that doing this masterfully is an advanced meal-planning skill, but just having the thought in your head can help, especially with sides like rice or quinoa and simple proteins like roasted chicken or pork loin.

LEARN HOW TO NAVIGATE THE SUPERMARKET LIKE A NINJA

Sometimes, making my way through the supermarket feels like trying to hack through the jungle. There are an overwhelming number of choices to begin with and, now, with brand-name companies increasingly aware of consumer desire for more natural and eco-friendly products, it's harder than ever to tell which choices are *actually* good for us.

Navigating the supermarket aisles so that you don't get overwhelmed requires you to know where to look for the healthiest options and to have a system for scanning food labels just enough to know whether a product fits your food values.

Supermarket design is fairly prescribed and has been for a long time. Perhaps you've noticed that nearly every supermarket—from the one near your house to the one by your cousin's house across the country—has a similar layout.

This is good news for us busy shoppers, since we can use the same plan of attack in any store we visit.

Shop the perimeter Start by shopping the perimeter. This is where you'll find the fresh and refrigerated food, including veggies, fruit, meat, and dairy. Once you start weaving your way through the labyrinth of aisles, make sure to look high and low. Big brands, many of which are notorious for pushing unhealthy processed foods, pay for the sweet spot at your eye level. They often pay even more for the space at your little one's eye level, so be aware of that if you've got little kids in tow.

One thing that will vary from store to store is whether it offers an organic food section and, if it does, where it is. You don't have to be a die-hard organic food buyer to start your packaged food shopping in the organic section; it's a great place for anyone who's looking for healthier options to start browsing, since all of the organic brands are concentrated in a small area instead of dispersed throughout. If you're interested, save time by asking for the organic section as soon as you walk into a new supermarket.

Speed-read food labels Even in the organic section of the market, trying to decipher labels for new food products that catch my eye is a major time suck. It's not something that I want to abandon, since reading labels is, hands down, the best way to make smarter, healthier choices.

So, I came up with a system for reading labels that makes it quick and easy. I swear: if you follow these tips you'll be speed reading labels and zeroing in on what counts most in no time.

The first rule of reading labels is to ignore everything on the front of the package, which is not regulated in the same way as the nutrition

and ingredients labels. I won't go so far as to say it's completely unregulated—it's more complicated than that—but let's just say that front-of-package claims are not very reliable.

Instead of looking at the front of a package, go straight to the nutrition label. My first move is a scan of the ingredients. I like to keep things simple so, honestly, if I don't recognize or can't pronounce an ingredient, it doesn't go into my cart. You know, as a rule of thumb. (And we all break the rules sometimes.)

When scanning ingredients on a food label, keep in mind that they are listed in order of predominance: the products contain mostly ingredient 1, then ingredient 2, et cetera, down the line. So, for example, if the ingredients list for a gummy fruit snack starts with high-fructose corn syrup and ends with fruit juice, you know that it is made with a whole lot of sugar and just a little bit of juice.

Next up: a quick scan of sugar, salt, and fat. The yum trifecta, these ingredients are what make food taste good (and even a little addictive). While cooking, you can manage the amounts and quality of sugar, salt, and fat to combine them into deliciousness that isn't terrible for you. In packaged foods, though, they are often used in obscenely unhealthy amounts to manufacture a cravable taste. And, yes, *cravable* is real food industry lingo.

The amount of salt, sugar, and fat that you want to take in varies greatly, depending on the age and health of the eaters in your family. For example, healthy sodium intake for beginner eaters and toddlers is way less than it is for an eight-year-old. The same goes for fat, plus you need to factor in activity level. Figuring out how much sugar your family should be taking in may be the most complicated calculation of all, given the various forms that sugar comes in and the

Can't Say It, Won't Eat It

For ease and quickness, the "can't say it, won't eat" rule of thumb is very helpful. That said, some naturally occurring ingredients are listed by their scientific name on food labels. Ascorbic acid, for example, is a form of vitamin C. I share this because it's important not to get hysterical; hysteria is definitely counterproductive to making it easy. Do your best and try to avoid artificial ingredients. I've put together a list of the ones I consider the worst offenders.

This list isn't exhaustive, but these are the major culprits most likely to be found in packaged foods. If you can at least avoid these things, you'll be in good shape. And to be clear: as much as I'd love for you to completely avoid these ingredients, I also want you to make it easy on yourself. Small amounts of these ingredients a few times a year will not kill your family.

So, take a breath and let it go if Grandma buys a box of Fruity Tooty cereal. Even if your child inhales every single morsel in a single weekend, he'll be fine. Complete elimination would be wonderful, but it's a steady diet of this stuff that's so bad for us.

HIGH-FRUCTOSE CORN SYRUP (HFCS). This one is controversial, I admit. You will find nutritionists that claim that our body knows no difference between HFCS and granulated sugar. But there are just as many experts, doctors, researchers, and nutritionists who disagree. And more to the point: HFCS is cheap and everywhere. Many foods made with it get a disproportionate number of calories from the sweetener and avoiding it all together makes our very tricky job of managing sugar intake—our kids' and our own!—infinitely easier. And I like easier.

ARTIFICIAL COLORS. Food dyes, including blue 1 and 2, green 3, red 3, and yellow 6, are controversial as well. The FDA has concluded that there is no clear indication of a causal relationship between food dyes and behavioral problems, such as hyperactivity in children, but has also acknowledged that artificial food dyes may exacerbate symptoms for some children. The research may not be conclusive enough for our government to mandate elimination, but these dyes are *banned* in Europe and starting to be eliminated by a growing number of major food companies.

What about when you're making your little one her fire engine birthday cake? Oh, wait: there are natural dyes for that (see pages 254–255)!

ARTIFICIAL FLAVORS. These chemicals, mixed to mimic natural flavors, are used to keep processed foods cheap. Since they can be listed simply as "artificial flavors," there isn't any way to know what you're eating. Some studies have linked these chemical flavor cocktails to allergic reactions, dermatitis, eczema, hyperactivity, and asthma. Keeping ingredients simple makes easy the job of keeping your whole crew healthy.

BENZOATE PRESERVATIVES (BHT, BHA, TBHQ). The preservative benzene is widely considered a carcinogen and endocrine disruptor. If that isn't enough, how about the fact that these preservatives are also in your makeup? I grew up with a taste for Doritos, but they're not worth eating ingredients that are also in my moisturizer. That's just gross. (Okay, but don't judge me if you catch me eating Doritos on a plane while I'm traveling alone. Like I said, we all break the rules sometimes.)

ARTIFICIAL SWEETENERS. "Sugar-free" used to be a label that parents would seek out, but these days we know better about artificial sweeteners, such as aspartame, saccharin, and sucralose. Nutritionists consider most forms of processed natural sugar comparable since they all process in the body the same way. Artificial sweeteners, on the other hand, may be harder on our metabolic system. If the worst-case scenario is that all processed natural sugars are created equal, then I figure there's no reason to choose one that was created in a lab.

fact that it's in nearly every packaged food, even ones you might not suspect (e.g., sliced whole wheat bread).

To keep things easy, I asked my pediatrician for quick salt, sugar, and fat guidelines that I could use while food shopping. I keep the three numbers in my head or, you know, in my smartphone, to help me quickly assess the nutrition label for a new food. If the salt, sugar, and fat fall in the right zone, I go for it. If not, I move on. It's a lifesaver that keeps me from stalling in the aisle, trying to decipher a label on my own while in a mad shopping rush.

If, for any reason, your pediatrician cannot do the same for you, it will probably take one Internet search for you to come up with a rough set of guidelines on your own. Bring those to the doc as a second pair of eyes, and you'll be set.

MASTER A FEW PREP HABITS

First meal planning, now prep. Am I starting to sound like the teacher in *The Peanuts*? Wah, wah, wah. Prep can be an annoying task—but it will save you time in the end, trust me. If it didn't, I wouldn't bother suggesting it.

I promise that these are the last set of tips that I'm going to share that you don't want me to repeat but, yeah, these prep tips bear repeating. If you turn even just a few of them into habit, they will make your life easier. Seriously.

• Wash greens and dry them well before storing them in produce keepers or with damp paper towels wrapped around them in plastic bags as soon as you get home from the grocery store.
• Wash tree fruit and dry well before storing in the refrigerator or on the counter.
• Although it's not ideal for cut veggies to sit for more than 24 to 48 hours, it's worth doing it ahead if it means you'll actually eat and serve

veggies. Carrots, celery, peppers, cucumber, broccoli, onion, and sweet potatoes can be washed, peeled, and prepped ahead to store in the refrigerator for up to five days. You can also trim asparagus and shred cabbage ahead of time. When I'm able, I do some of this when I get home from the market, then I'll do the rest on one easy-going night that week. Between two sessions, I can get most of my chopping for a busy week done ahead of time.
• Measure and combine rice and grains before you put a new box or bag away, so they're ready to go.
• If you have quick-cooking grains, such as rice or couscous, throw them straight into a pot and cook them as you unpack your groceries to have on hand for the week.
• Make spice blends that you use often ahead of time and store them in the freezer.
• Make dressings and quick-cook sauces in one half-hour session on the weekend, to have on hand for the week.
• If you prefer cooking with dried beans (which are, in fact, better, but also totally fine to skip for canned), always prep a double batch and store half in the freezer for next time.

TIME-SAVING TRICKS WORTH BREAKING THE RULES

Here's the truth: there is a right way and a wrong way to cook. Sure, there are variations on the right way and plenty of debate around which right way is the most right, but you are not in culinary school training to become a chef. You are a busy home cook and sometimes—often, even—learning a few tricks and breaking the rules is the only way you can get a scratch meal on the table.

While working with clients, I zeroed in on a few tricks that help even the least-experienced cooks move faster. Be warned that some of these tricks go against good technique, but they can make the different between throwing together a scratch meal and ordering in. Will the taste of your food suffer? I can't say that you'll notice if you're smart about which rules you break and how you break them. So, unless you're gunning to be on a cooking competition show, get ready to cheat.

• Chopping is the number one task that holds up home cooks. Investing in a few affordable tools that help make the task go faster—and knowing when to use them—is well worth the money:

Great knives. If there's one thing that a committed home cook should invest in, no matter what their level of skill, it's a few good knives. A 12-inch chef's knife and a paring knife are musts. From there, it depends on what you do most. Either way, avoid prepackaged sets and learn how to maintain your knives' sharpness. You may not realize it, but the only thing your dull knives are effectively skewering is your spirit. Sharp knives are easier to handle and safer, since chopping with dull ones requires a type of movement and level of pressure that can cause accidents.

Microplane. You may already own a Microplane to zest citrus, grind nutmeg, or grate cheese. The same one that you use to zest citrus can also be used to "chop" ginger, garlic, and even onion. If you use it for ginger, keep in mind that you may want to slightly reduce the amount, since Microplaned ginger is more potent. Also, a Microplane will reduce onion or garlic to a paste. Only use this shortcut with either if it is meant to be well blended and/or cooked down, as in a sauce or batter. Otherwise, stick with a knife.

Mandoline. A mandoline is a tool that will quickly slice any fruit or vegetable to a thickness that you can adjust. It makes slicing incredibly easy, and while many are very expensive, you can easily find an affordable one on Amazon that will work just fine. Look for one that's made of plastic (except for the blade, of course) and also highly rated. That's how I found mine, which is very inexpensive, and I love it.

Kitchen shears. Scissors make cutting herbs, certain veggies, and even cooked foods easier. If you have small children, they will save you a ton of time cutting dinner into the appropriate bite-size pieces for little ones. Look for a pair with stainless-steel blades, or even better, removable blades for easy cleanup.

Mini chopper. If you like using a food processor to chop veggies, such as onions, carrots, and celery, but get frustrated with how much work it takes to set it up and clean, consider investing in a mini chopper that you can keep within reach. They're popular for a reason.

Garlic press. I learned to avoid garlic presses at all cost. It was said that they break the cell wall of the garlic clove, releasing a bitter flavor. Many newfangled garlic presses are designed to cut garlic more as a knife would. If you cook with a lot of garlic but hate chopping it, put down the jarred stuff (I beg you), do a little research, and invest in one of these.

• Ever heard of *a mise-en-place*? It's a spread of all the ingredients you'll need for a recipe prepped and ready to go. Professionals always set up a *mise-en-place* before cooking, and so should you. I know that you think jumping into a recipe will save you time, but preparing all of your ingredients first will save you *more* time.

Trust me. You will also yield better results, since you won't have to scramble for ingredients at the last minute—while dinner is burning, no less.

• If your recipe calls for using two pans, but not necessarily at the same time, don't be afraid to wipe out the first pan and immediately reuse it, no matter what the recipe says. Then, there's just one pan to clean instead of two.

• Don't be afraid to mix the batter for baked goods in one bowl. It's not always possible, but for your standard everyday muffins, cakes, and cupcakes, read ahead to know the order in which you should mix everything into one bowl, to make cleaning easier.

• Don't fuss with your food. If you've got a good recipe, the timing should be laid out. Messing with the food prematurely—such as lifting to see whether a chicken breast that you are trying to brown or a steak that you want to sear is cooking properly—can cause all kinds of problems that will mess with your flavor and timing.

• Cook in batches any time you can. Double the recipe whenever you make rice, quinoa, soups, stews, chili, casseroles, and pasta sauce. It doesn't take much extra work and will give you a jump start on one or two meals in the future. Most recipes that can easily be doubled can also easily be frozen, including most rice and grains.

• Find free and in-between moments to prep ahead. I'm not talking about free moments of leisure time—relax out of the kitchen whenever possible—but, rather, those moments in the kitchen when you're waiting for something to cook or already chopping, cooking, or prepping something. For example, I often cook pasta using my make-ahead method (page 29) while packing school lunch. I'll cook hard-boiled eggs (page 32) while throwing together the boys' breakfast toast and brewing my coffee. And when I make a salad one night—or am chopping veggies to go into school lunch—I'll take an extra three minutes to chop double the amount. The extra veggies get packed up for salad another night or Cold Soba Noodle Salad (page 179) later that evening.

• Take time at some point in the week to make an all-purpose sauce that can be used in multiple ways to add quick flavor. Spinach Pesto (page 58) can be used to baste chicken legs before roasting, dress up Everyday Vinaigrette (page 124), give new life to leftover rice, couscous, or grains, and be mixed into mayo for a fancy sandwich night (or school lunch). Ginger Hoisin Sauce (page 59) can be tossed with soba noodles and quickly chopped raw veggies, served with simply grilled chicken as a dipping sauce, brushed onto broiled salmon (page 172), and thrown in a slow cooker with pork (page 165).

Other Kitchen Tools Particularly Great for Busy Home Cooks

While I could spend thousands of dollars on kitchen gear and have heard from my clients—even the ones who hate cooking!—that they could, too, I assure you that you don't need to break the bank on tons of equipment to be a great home cook.

Here is a list of really useful tools for busy home cooks, with a focus on kitchen gear that helps cut down on prep time (e.g., chopping) or that speeds up frequent, tedious jobs (e.g., washing greens). If you have most of these and a basic set of cooking gear, you'll be in good shape.

CUTTING BOARDS IN SEVERAL SIZES. I use my medium-size cutting boards most, but nothing is worse than having to clean a big board for a small task, such as chopping veggies for school lunch. I also hate managing a large roast or Thanksgiving turkey on a too-small board. So, I keep one teeny, one small, two medium-size, and one extra-large cutting board around at all times.

GOOD CHOPPING GEAR. See page 17.

SALAD SPINNER. If you prefer buying greens from your farmers' market or just would rather buy a head of lettuce and skip the packaging in which pre-washed greens come, a salad spinner is a lifesaver. Or at least a time saver.

GOOD HANDHELD STRAINER. As with the cutting boards, I find it frustrating to have to clean a big colander for a small job. Since I often do things like blanch frozen peas and make small amounts of pasta for the kids for lunch, a handheld strainer makes my life easier in addition to a full-size colander.

FISH SPATULA. This is not just a suggestion for people who cook fish a lot. Fish spatulas have a beveled edge and flexible design that make them nimbler and easier to use than regular spatulas for almost anything. I haven't touched a thick, plastic spatula in ages.

TONGS. Tongs are great for all three of my favorite cooking moves: picking up, flipping over, and tossing about. One 9- or 12-inch pair will do.

SILICONE SPATULA AND SPOON SPATULAS. These flexible, easy-to-clean tools, which come in all different shapes and sizes, are far superior to wooden spoons. I have one silicone spatula (flat head) and three spoon spatulas (curved head; two medium-size, one small) and do nearly everything with them, from stirring to pouring, mixing to spreading.

FOOD PROCESSOR. Every kitchen that will churn out homemade food, no matter how simple, should have a full-size food processor. It doesn't need to have crazy bells and whistles, but should be high-powered and come with several blade varieties.

A GOOD BLENDER AND/OR HAND BLENDER. I'm a big believer in high-powered blenders and think that, if you can afford one, it's a great thing to have even if you don't cook much. The ease with which they can make anything from baby food to soups to nut butters has made mine invaluable. That said, they are expensive. Like, *really* expensive. If you don't think that splurging on one is worth it, you can make your way through with just a food processor and either a regular blender or a hand blender, depending on what you make most (e.g., hand blenders are great for soups, regular blenders are great for smoothies and drinks).

SLOW COOKER. Slow cookers have earned a reputation for being a winter kitchen tool, but I use mine all year-round. In fact, it's great for helping to keep away from the stove in the summer heat. I love mine for stews, chilis, and pulled meat, such as Hoisin Pulled Pork (page 167), but there's a ton more that you can do with it. Although I can't quite call it an essential tool—it does take up a lot of room and can end up sitting if you don't make a habit of using it—I can tell you that you'll fall in love with yours if you make a point of cooking with it.

7¼-QUART ENAMEL-LINED DUTCH OVEN. This pot will become a go-to for everything from making soups to stews, cooking pasta, to baking bread. And, thanks to the enamel lining, it's easy to clean, too. On the high end, these can be quite expensive. More affordable brands have started to offer enamel-lined Dutch ovens, so you should be able to find one in your price range. If not, going down one size to 5½ quarts will work, though batch cooking will be more difficult.

6-QUART SAUTÉ PAN. This pan is to sautéing what the Dutch oven is to braising and stewing. Although a good skillet is great to have, a high-sided sauté pan that's big enough to fit a whole bunch of chicken cutlets or pork chops allows you to cook a large amount of food, with or without sauce, in one shot.

RIMMED COOKIE SHEETS. No longer are cookie sheets just for cookies. Nearly anything that goes into my oven can be thrown onto a rimmed cookie sheet. I used these for pizza (page 192), roasting vegetables, making Sweet and Salty Granola (page 78), baking cutlets, and even roasting meats. (If you want to use them to cook meat, too, consider getting a rack that fits well into one of your rimmed pans.) I like having at least one full-size sheet and two half-sheet pans, which gives me flexibility to cook small batches, double batches, and anything in between.

MAKE IT EASY
on Your Crew

For some home cooks, sitting at the table is often as hectic as cooking the meal—people coming in and out, the next thing on the schedule bearing down, and picky eaters exploding. If that sounds like your table, this chapter is for you.

Getting a handle on your crew at dinnertime pays dividends beyond being able to sit around a peaceful table. It also feeds back into the first Make It Easy Basic: make it easy on yourself. When your dinner table isn't a joyful—or at least an easy—place to be, there's no payoff for the work you've put into cooking. And that is not easy on anyone. An investment in a happy crew is an investment in being a happy cook.

Saying that you're going to make it easy on your crew is one thing, doing it is another. It is easier said than done, but by now you know that I have hands-on tips that will help.

CONSIDER *EVERYONE'S* TASTES

And, yes, even the one who's only willing to eat white food—everyone is allowed to have opinions about food, even picky eaters. That doesn't mean you have to be a short-order cook; you need to be a strategic cook. With a few tips and guidelines to keep in mind, my goal is to help you think about choosing and pairing recipes in a way that can accommodate everyone. (Well, mostly everyone. We'll talk in a moment about what to do with the unhappy members of your crew.)

MIX, MATCH, AND PULL APART RECIPES

As you decide what to cook for dinner—whether while making a meal plan or during a last-minute stop at the supermarket—think about meals in terms of their elements: protein, sauce, carb, and vegetable. Is there at least one component that everyone at the table can enjoy? If there is something that a bunch of people like, can it be served separately or pulled out easily? Making one meal with pull-apart components is much easier than feeling like you have to make more than one meal every night.

Also, when you discover that a recipe works for a handful of people in your family, think about how you can match it up with other components. It's critical to keep dishes that work in heavy rotation without serving them the same way over and over. For example, avocado is one of a handful of nutrient-rich foods that both of my kids enjoy. Instead of serving the same avocado salad or classic guacamole over and over, I've come up with several variations of both the salad (pages 137 and 138) and guacamole (pages 64 and 65) to make avocado a match with a wide variety of meals.

LET EVERYONE HAVE A SAY

I'm a big believer in allowing the whole crew to weigh in on what's for dinner. As I see it, having a say in what you eat goes a long way toward fostering a love of food.

If your crew has young or picky eaters, though, giving them a choice is not always simple business. Keep a list of foods that you are willing to feed the whole family that also meets your little or picky one's standards. When it's time for them to have their say, give them your limited list of options to choose from. And every once in a while (maybe once a month?), let them choose whatever they want for dinner, even if you don't love it. After all, they eat what you want most of the times—why not turn the tables?

If you have older kids in your crew who like to give you a hard time about dinner, consider letting them choose whatever they want once a week or once a month—like, really, *whatever*—and then have them do the shopping and cooking. I once read a piece by Jaden Hair of *The Steamy Kitchen* about how she lets her kids eat junk food as long as they buy it and cook it themselves. This approach keeps you from compromising your food values, which sends a clear message about what's good for you and what's not so good for you, but also avoids a fight. Plus, they get to exercise autonomy in the safety of your kitchen. It's genius.

STOP FIGHTING OVER MEALS

If you have an extremely picky eater on your hands, all of this talk about mixing and matching recipes and allowing choices probably sounds quaint—or maybe like a complete joke. I know how genuinely exhausting it can be; I also know that it can kill every ounce of joy from cooking. But there is good news (that might feel bad at first): unless there are medical, sensory, and/or emotional issues at play, picky eating is a parenting issue.

Children are in a constant state of seeking independence and control. Beginning early on, the dinner table is a comfortable place for them to try to get both. Aside from a natural ebb and flow of picky eating phases, a phenomenon explained by biology and evolution, mealtime strife is rarely more than a power struggle.

Children look to us for feedback on when and where it's appropriate for them to exercise their independence and control, and mealtime offers opportunities for both children and parents to do their part. Your child wants to feed herself or decide on her own how much to eat? Great! These are perfect ways to encourage her developing sense of self. She wants to call the shots in the kitchen or throw a fit over spinach? Not

Keeping It Easy with a Picky Eater

Mealtime is a natural place for kids to flex their independence, regardless of whether or not they are picky. Here are some tips to keep mealtime from becoming a battleground.

TRY NOT TO STRESS TOO MUCH ABOUT NUTRITION. A pediatrician once told me that she tells parents to think about what their child eats over a week, not in a day. If you have serious concerns about how your child's diet is impacting his health, speak to your doctor.

IGNORE THE HATERS. It's hard to find time to cook from scratch and very annoying when you've done so and someone in your crew won't eat. If you make something that you and at least some of the others enjoy, you will have gotten value out of your effort. Focus on that instead of on the naysayer.

PLEASE DON'T SAY, "HE WON'T EAT THAT." Try not to assume that you know what your picky eater will or will not eat. Allow yourself to be surprised, even when you're sure and of course he didn't like that. Although it happens less frequently, kids can decide to like a food as quickly as they decide to dislike it.

EXPERIMENT. Don't let your picky eater stop you from trying to introduce new foods; just do it in a way that respects his taste. Feed him new foods when he is most receptive (which may not always be at dinner at the end of a long day) and serve new foods that build on what he knows and likes. For example, if your little one loves spaghetti, try soba noodles (page 179); if he loves classic chicken soup, try feeding him an Asian-Style Chicken Soup (page 119).

KEEP IN MIND EVEN PICKY EATERS HAVE RIGHTS. Most eating challenges are a power struggle, but even picky eaters have valid tastes, however limited. You don't have to kowtow to them, but be aware and emotionally responsive. Sometimes even just a little acknowledgment goes a long way: *I made dinner with broccoli tonight because that's what I felt like eating, but I'll make your favorite string beans later this week.*

BE CLEAR ABOUT YOUR EXPECTATIONS. It's the age-old adage about parenting: although they push against them, kids thrive with clear boundaries. For me, making my expectations clear is a big part of how I keep the peace at my dinner table, or at least how I keep calm when my kids are being fussy about food. You can read about how I used calm and clear expectations to regain control of breakfast, which I, at one point, had lost to store-bought breakfast cereal (page 75). Come up with your line in the sand and know what your plan is if your kid crosses it. Having a simple plan that you can execute makes fighting unnecessary. Well, you know, for the most part.

HAVE FUN! Whether you realize it or not, your crew has a family food culture. It's defined by what you eat, what foods you bring into the home, how you talk about food, and your attitude toward cooking. It's hard to make it easy on yourself and your crew if these things are not healthy and positive. Making scratch cooking easy is a major step in the right direction toward establishing a healthier food culture in your home, and making mealtime fun is the easiest way to spread a joyous outlook on healthy eating.

When you love something, it's easy to take it seriously and also have fun with it at the same time. So, yay, for taking cooking seriously, but get silly, too. Cook hot dogs over your backyard fire pit, make fondue, serve cake for dinner every once in a while, have a once-a-month no-vegetables night, dedicate one night a month to a new cuisine, ditch the utensils every once in a while because it's weird, and order pizza. Homemade pizza (page 192) is great, but sometimes nothing beats a movie night with a freshly delivered pie from your local pizzeria.

so much, and a chance for you to let her know.

The tricky thing is that something about the kitchen disorients parents. It's as though the primal impulse to ensure that our children are well nourished causes a glitch in the parenting matrix. All of the principles we employ to impose discipline, get our kids to do their homework, promote kindness, and enforce respect, fly out the kitchen window when our little ones cry over yucky broccoli. And this becomes an opportunity for picky eaters to demand kid-menu staples or separate meals night after night.

Once you go down that road, it's very difficult to turn back. When you try, picky eaters will fight—and why wouldn't they when they know you're a sucker for making sure that they'll eat? If you engage in their fight, they will win because, well, they always have. If you have a young one and can keep from heading down that road in the first place, I encourage you to feed adventurously and never look back. It's not nearly as simple as I'm making it sound, I know, but it's easier than having to exit the picky path.

If you're already down the picky path, think about the parenting strategies that work best in your family—and not just the punitive ones. How is your child encouraged? What helps her feel confident? Empowers her to try new things?

Just as there are no magic recipes, there are also no one-size-fits-all parenting solutions, especially when it comes to food. Only you can figure out what makes sense in your home. As you suss it out, remember that you're in control of your kitchen and you can decide to stop fighting. Once you have, you can do some clear headed parenting and, hopefully, start enjoying time with your crew at the table.

PART II

Recipes

8 *Easy* THINGS EVERY COOK SHOULD KNOW HOW TO MAKE WELL

In Part I, I shared prep shortcuts that help make cooking easier. Here, we're going to go over cooking techniques—proper ones!—that are so easy you don't need to shortcut them. Once you nail them down, your cooking will be easier and your food will taste better.

When the food you serve actually tastes good, you feed back into the Make It Easy Basics. Tasty results make it easier on you because cooking is going to feel worthwhile. They make it easier on your schedule, too, because you'll find time to fit cooking in when you know it means eating well. You may still be short on time, but when you commit to something that gives you results, it's amazing how you'll find space to fit it in. And, of course, they will make it easy on your crew. Even the pickiest eaters start to come around if you are calm, consistent, and slowly urge them to eat foods that actually taste delicious. And when it's easier on your crew, they fuss less and that's easier on you.

See that? We're making it easy all around.

And by the way, even if you have a picky eater who will still make a fuss no matter how well you've cooked something, at least you've gotten to eat well yourself. You can't say that when you've made mac and cheese out of a box.

So, back to basics: learning how to turn out perfectly cooked pasta, rice, and, in my house, protein-rich quinoa (which will not taste overly bitter or smoky if you make it correctly), boil eggs, make cutlets with a quick pan sauce, skewer flavorful kebabs, and shake up a delicious vinaigrette are a few easy cooking skills that will take you further than you can imagine.

HOW TO MAKE VINAIGRETTE

My name is Stacie and I used to make horrible salad dressing. It was just something I couldn't master for a long time. I think the problem was that I always assumed it would come out fine enough and I didn't take care to, well, learn the basics. To help keep you from the same affliction, here they are: the key things you need to know to make a great vinaigrette.

1. Begin with the classic **3:1 ratio of oil to vinegar**. You can adjust per your family's taste.

2. Stick with a mild oil, such as olive, grapeseed, or vegetable. Olive oil works in nearly every dressing, even ones with Asian flavors. It can easily be your go-to oil.

3. Choose the right vinegar. I tend to use white wine vinegar for most of my dressings, but red wine vinegar is great for Italian and Greek dressings and rice vinegar is perfect for dressings made with Asian ingredients like ginger and soy sauce. Sherry vinegar is big and bold, and flavored or infused vinegars work in specific flavor combinations; while tasty, these aren't as flexible for everyday use and should be matched with the salad ingredients.

4. You can use lemon juice instead of or in combination with vinegar. If using instead of, switch to a **1:1 ratio of oil to lemon juice**. If using in combination with vinegar, combine the two acids to get to your 3:1 ratio and adjust to taste.

5. When there's time, add minced garlic or shallot. And if there is more time, begin making your dressing by allowing the minced garlic or shallot to sit in the vinegar—and only vinegar—for as few as 5 or as many as 15 minutes before you mix in the rest of the ingredients. This process, called maceration, will mellow their sharpness.

6. Once the garlic or shallot has had a chance to sit, add the oil, salt, and pepper. The only exception is when using soy sauce, in which case add the salt last, after tasting, since the soy sauce will add salt.

7. Add any other ingredients, such as:

> **Dried herbs (e.g., thyme, oregano, or herbes de Provence)**
> **Fresh herbs of nearly any kind**
> **Grated fresh ginger**
> **Dijon or another mustard**
> **Worcestershire sauce**
> **A bit of honey, agave nectar, or pure maple syrup**
> **Jam**
> **Olive tapenade**
> **Minced roasted red peppers**
> **Capers**
> **Pesto**
> **Miso paste**
> **Soy sauce**

8. Once you have all your ingredients, whisk, shake, or blend the dressing to emulsify.

❤ *Make It Tastier* The key to a great dressing is to focus on a single flavor palate. For example:

• Sherry wine vinegar pairs well with smoked paprika and a little bit of honey for a Spanish inflection.

• White wine vinegar pairs well with Dijon mustard, herbes de Provence, and/or olive or capers for an all-purpose French vinaigrette.

• Red wine vinegar combined with freshly squeezed lemon juice and fresh or dried oregano makes a simple, classic Greek dressing.

• Rice vinegar combined with freshly squeezed lemon or lime juice, miso paste, a dash of sesame oil (just a dash; use a neutral oil in the 3:1 ratio as your main oil), a dash of soy sauce, and grated fresh ginger makes a great all-purpose dressing that pairs well with Asian meals. You can add finely grated carrots to the dressing, too!

HOW TO COOK PERFECT (DRIED) PASTA

Soggy pasta is the worst! Here's a technique for cooking pasta perfectly al dente that I learned from the head chef of a global dried pasta company. This technique is the real deal and so easy to do.

1. Bring a large stockpot (ideally one with a perforated insert) of heavily salted water to a full rolling boil. Use 1 tablespoon of salt per 1 gallon of water per 1 pound of pasta (you can reduce the salt if necessary for health reasons). DO NOT add oil to the water.

2. Add the pasta, stir, then begin to measure the cooking time. Cook the pasta for 2 to 3 minutes fewer than indicated on the package.

3. Drain. If using a pot with a perforated insert, pull out the insert and leave the pot with the cooking water on the stove, which you can turn off. Otherwise, scoop the pasta out of the pot with a perforated pasta scoop. If you don't have a pasta insert or scoop, use a mug or glass measuring cup to scoop out 2 cups of the cooking water before draining the pasta. The goal is to reserve enough pasta cooking water that you can add some to your sauce (discarding the leftover water) to help it adhere better to the pasta.

4. Do not rinse the pasta!

5. Place your sauce is in a large skillet over medium heat and, once hot, add the freshly cooked and drained pasta. If you're scooping the pasta directly from the water into the skillet, allow some of the cooking water to drip into the skillet, too.

6. Toss the pasta to coat and then add one to two ladlefuls of the cooking water (depending on the desired thickness of your sauce and how much water's already made it into the skillet). Toss the pasta and sauce more to bring all of the flavors together.

7. Take the sauced pasta off the heat before adding cheese and finishing with a drizzle of high-quality olive oil.

HOW TO PRECOOK PERFECT (DRIED) PASTA

I always thought that pasta had to be cooked to order or else. I learned from the same chef who taught me how to cook pasta perfectly that pasta absolutely can be cooked ahead and still come out perfectly al dente. Here's how:

1. Bring a large stockpot (ideally one with a perforated insert) of heavily salted water to a full rolling boil. Use 1 tablespoon of salt per 1 gallon of water per 1 pound of pasta (you can reduce the salt if necessary for health reasons). DO NOT add oil to the water.

2. Add the pasta, stir, then begin to measure the cooking time. Cook the pasta for *half* of the time indicated on the package.

3. Drain the pasta, saving 2 cups of the cooking water, if possible. Seal the cooking water in a container and save for later use.

4. Do not rinse the pasta!

5. Drizzle the pasta with a tiny bit of olive oil, 1 to 2 teaspoons per pound of pasta. Toss to coat and spread the pasta on a baking or cookie sheet to cool.

6. Once completely cooled, transfer the pasta to an airtight container or resealable plastic bag for storage in the fridge. The pasta will stay good for a few days.

7. To reheat: if possible, keep your sauce a little runny. Place the sauce in a large skillet over medium heat and, once hot, add the pasta. Toss to coat and then add one to two ladlefuls of the reserved cooking water (less for thick sauces, more for runny ones). Toss more to bring the flavors together and heat the pasta through.

8. Take the sauced pasta off of the heat before adding cheese and finishing with a drizzle of high-quality olive oil.

Note To reheat a large amount of pasta (over 1 pound), dunk the precooked pasta in boiling water for 30 seconds before placing in the skillet of hot pasta sauce.

HOW TO COOK RICE PERFECTLY

Rice is one of my go-to carb sides because it's so easy to cook, stores well (even in the freezer), and goes with just about anything. Kids like it a lot, too. You can make a huge batch at the beginning of the week and scoop into it while packing your lunch or a school lunch, or and when you're short on time for making dinner. If your family eats a lot of rice, a rice cooker can be a great investment—but you should still learn how to cook it in a pot on the stovetop. It's just one of those things that's good to know how to do.

1. Measure your rice—I use ½ cup of uncooked rice per person—and rinse. (Rinsing rice washes away starch that can make your rice sticky. I used to skip this step when in a rush—sticky rice is not perfect, but also not the end of the world—but now I rinse religiously, as it's said to help reduce the arsenic by a little bit; see note.)

2. Place the rice and water in a pot. For every ½ cup of rice, I use 1 cup of water. Keep in mind that rice will expand, so use a pot big enough to accommodate the cooked amount. A 2-quart pot should be large enough for cooking 1 to 2 cups of uncooked rice. Bring the water to a boil over medium-high heat.

3. Add salt and unsalted butter (optional; I like using ¼ teaspoon of salt and ½ tablespoon of butter per cup of rice) to the boiling water, stir, lower the heat to a simmer (medium-low should do), and cover. Cook for 17 minutes.

Use a timer and restraint! You don't want to uncover the pot before 17 minutes, as the lost steam will impact the cooking. (For real: I'm not just being fussy.) You also don't want to cook for much longer than 17 minutes before checking, in case your heat is a little high or you measured a slightly too-small amount of water—then your rice might start to burn.

4. Check the rice quickly. If all of the water has absorbed, you're done. Cover the pot again (quickly!), remove it from the heat, and allow the rice to stand for 10 more minutes. Again, resist the urge to check on it; it needs to stay covered for the full duration of this rest time. And don't worry about getting lost in other things—it can rest for up to 30 minutes.

5. Uncover, fluff the rice with a fork, and serve.

6. To freeze, allow the rice to cool completely before packaging it. Then, fluff and stuff: my freezer is small so I like to freeze rice in resealable plastic bags that can lay flat, but you can use any freezer-safe container, even a muffin tin for small portions. Instead of dumping all the rice into your container, measure it into portions and, if there's a lot, freeze separately so that you can defrost in usable portions. This will help you reduce waste.

Note As you've probably heard, the problem with rice is the high level of inorganic arsenic recently reported to be found in many varieties of white and brown rice. Food scares are easily sensationalized, but this one is for real. Check out page 248 in the Supermarket Guide for more tips.

HOW TO COOK QUINOA

Quinoa had a moment—a big moment—and then it passed.

Part of the problem with quinoa is that it can be smoky and bitter, leaving home cooks wondering what the fuss is all about when it doesn't even taste good. Even I thought that it was an acquired taste until I learned how to cook it properly. With this method, you'll be able to churn out fluffy, mild-flavored quinoa that even most kids will accept if they are willing to try it.

If your family will eat it, quinoa is an ideal go-to carb: it cooks as quickly and easily as rice, it's high in protein and low in inorganic arsenic, and it's more nutritious than rice or pasta. So, yeah, it's worth a try and cooking it this way gives you the best chance for quinoa success.

1. When moving fast, it's tempting to skip the rinse, but you can't with quinoa. There's a coating on quinoa that, if not washed off, will give your cooked quinoa a bitter taste. So, break out the strainer and, as you rinse, rub the quinoa vigorously with your fingers to help shed the coating. Nearly all the bitterness can be removed with a good rinse. One cup of uncooked quinoa will yield about 3 cups of cooked quinoa.

2. Place the damp quinoa in a pot set over medium heat without any water. Toast it until it's dry and begins to pop like popcorn. If you'd like to add dried spice, such as garlic powder, cumin, curry powder, or turmeric, add it at the beginning and keep tossing the quinoa as it toasts, to keep the spice from burning.

3. Add your cooking liquid of choice to the quinoa. Be careful: it will steam, spit, and sizzle as it hits the hot pot. You'll want to add 2 cups of water or chicken or vegetable broth (pages 39 and 40) for every cup of uncooked quinoa; chicken or vegetable broth, and even a splash of white wine, go a long way to make quinoa tasty. So does salt; if you'd like to add some, now's the time. I use ¼ teaspoon for every cup of uncooked quinoa.

4. Bring the quinoa to a boil, uncovered. Lower the heat to a simmer—it's important that the quinoa is not left at a rolling boil for the duration of the cooking time—and cover. Leave covered for the entire time it cooks. One cup of uncooked quinoa cooks in 15 to 20 minutes; check quickly at 15 minutes and, if all of the liquid has absorbed, it's ready. Otherwise, cover the pot as quickly as possible and leave for another few minutes before checking again.

5. When the quinoa is done, turn off the heat and leave the pot, covered, to rest for at least 5 minutes. Then, uncover, fluff the quinoa with a fork, and serve.

6. To freeze, allow the quinoa to cool completely before packaging it. Then, just as with rice, fluff and stuff. I tend to freeze in 2-cup portions in resealable plastic bags, but you can freeze in any usable amount in any freezer-safe container.

HOW TO BOIL EGGS

Hard-boiled eggs are one of my favorite foods to always have on hand. They make a great healthy snack with nothing more than salt and pepper and can be used to throw together a healthy breakfast. I don't know how I could pack school or my lunch without hard-boiled eggs: they go into sandwiches, make egg salad, and can be packed alongside a hunk of cheese, hummus, and a handful of pretzels for a protein-rich meal. Hard-boiled eggs have even saved dinner in my house.

They are, simply put, a kitchen lifesaver. That is, when cooked properly.

It's true that boiled eggs can serve all the same purposes cooked poorly, but when cooked just the way you want them, it's hard to beat the taste and, frankly, the nutrition, too. Eggs contain almost every mineral and vitamin that the human diet requires, except for vitamin C. Also, egg proteins are said to be 97 percent digestible, making them a source of one of the highest-quality proteins in the food chain.

Over the years, some have come to think of eggs as an unhealthy choice that should be drastically limited in a healthy diet. While moderation is key—because, when is it not?—the idea that eggs can cause cholesterol or heart disease is in question. The common wisdom these days is that eggs offer great nutritional benefits that far outweigh any health drawbacks.

So, start eating them. That is, after you cook them just right.

1. Place the eggs in a single layer at the bottom of your pot; they should fit snugly, with just a little bit of room between them. Cover the eggs with cold water by 1 inch or, if your pot is full, 2 inches.

2. Set the pot over medium-high heat and bring the water to a rolling boil. Stay close because, as soon as you get that full boil, you want to put the lid on and remove the pot from the heat. Leave the eggs to sit. For how long depends on how you want them cooked:

4 minutes—**runny soft-boiled**
6 minutes—**soft-boiled**
10 minutes—**hard-boiled**

3. As soon as the time is up, drain the pot and fill it with cold water. Add a bunch of ice cubes, as well, to make sure that the water is cold enough to give the eggs a shock. This will stop them from cooking further. Sometimes, depending on how old the eggs are, it will also help make the eggs easier to peel. After a 1- to 2-minute ice-water bath, the eggs are ready to be served or can be stored in the refrigerator for up to 1 week.

HOW TO QUICK-SAUTÉ CUTLETS *with* A PAN SAUCE

This method can be used to make nearly any thin-cut chicken cutlet dinner you can imagine. Get creative: chicken with a cilantro sauce; chicken with white wine and shallots; chicken with fresh tomatoes and tarragon; chicken with tomatoes, basil, and capers; chicken with snow peas and shiitake—the possibilities are endless with this one, simple method. And what better reason to master the technique?

1. Pat the chicken cutlets dry. For four people, use 1½ to 2 pounds total, depending on your appetite.

2. Pour flour (all-purpose or gluten-free; ½ cup for every 1½ to 2 pounds of cutlets) into a wide, shallow bowl or rimmed baking sheet. Using your hands or a fork, season the flour with salt (1 teaspoon for every ½ cup of flour) and some freshly ground black pepper.

3. Dredge the cutlets in the flour, making sure to tap off any excess.

4. Heat unsalted butter and/or oil in a 12- to 15-inch high-sided sauté pan over medium heat (use 3 tablespoons of fat for every 1½ to 2 pounds of cutlets; I like using 1½ tablespoons of each). Once the butter has melted and begins to foam, swirl to coat the bottom of the pan.

5. Add the chicken and cook for 4 to 6 minutes, 2 to 3 minutes per side, depending on thickness. If the cutlets are crowded in the pan, you may need to do this in batches, keeping in mind that you may need to lower the heat to medium for the second batch to keep the butter from burning.

6. Remove the last of the cutlets from the pan and set aside. Add aromatics (e.g., onion, garlic, shallots) to the pan and sauté for 1 to 3 minutes, until softened or browned, depending on your preference.

7. Add liquid (e.g., wine, lemon juice, broth, soy sauce) to the pan (1 to 1½ cups of liquid for every 1½ to 2 pounds of cutlets).

8. Scrape the pan to get up the bits, then bring the liquid to a boil. Lower the heat and simmer to reduce liquid by one third, 3 to 5 minutes.

9. Add fresh herbs (e.g., cilantro, tarragon, oregano) and/or finishing ingredients (e.g., capers, olives, roasted red peppers). Swirl the herbs into the sauce and cook for 30 to 60 seconds before taking the pan off the heat. Immediately add 3 tablespoons of unsalted butter and keep swirling until melted.

10. Pour the sauce over the cooked cutlets and serve.

HOW TO MAKE KEBABS

Maybe it's because I'm Greek but, if you ask me, kebabs are among the easiest fool-proof meals any home cook can make. They come together just as fast as stir-fry, but are easier since there's no tricky timing or saucing.

All it takes to make kebabs is to thread quick-cooking cuts of meat, poultry, or fish with grill-friendly vegetables and throw them on the grill, in a grill pan, or even in the broiler. When you have time to plan ahead, it's a good idea to marinate the meat for extra flavor, but it's definitely not a must, especially if you're in a rush and just need a fresh, simple dinner.

So, how come so many kebabs fall flat? The primary reason is that they are dry, which is usually the result of choosing the wrong cut of meat or overcooking—or both. You want to select a meat that is tender, without too much fat and connective tissue that can make quick-cooked meat tough, but also not so lean that it doesn't have flavor.

When it comes to beef, tenderloin is wonderfully soft and tender, but can dry out quickly and lack bold flavor, especially if you don't have time to marinate it. I find that sirloin strikes a good middle ground between fatty, tasty, and tender that works well for kebabs—1½- to 2-inch cubes should cook in 10 to 12 minutes.

When making chicken, I only use boneless, skinless chicken thighs. Chicken breasts dry out quickly but, if that's all you have, you can make it work by not skipping the marinate time and watching your cook time carefully. Very carefully: 1½- to 2-inch cubes of thigh should cook in 12 to 14 minutes, and breast in 10 to 12 minutes.

Like beef, pork can be tricky, too. Pork shoul-

der has major flavor, but so much fat and connective tissue that you'll spend a lot of time trimming it. That can be worth it, but if you're a busy home cook, not for an everyday meal. Instead, opt for a boneless, center-cut pork chop or pork loin. If you go with chops, you should be able to get them 1½ to 2 inches thick, which makes cutting these up a cinch. Just be careful: this cut of pork has good flavor, but can overcook quickly—1½- to 2-inch cubes should cook in 10 to 12 minutes.

While growing up in a Greek home, for me skewers of lamb were standard fare. I've found that chunks cut from the leg of lamb are the most flavorful and easiest to cook for kebabs—1½- to 2-inch cubes should cook in 10 to 12 minutes.

Seafood kebabs are a wonderfully fun way to introduce fish to kids—or anyone—who might not otherwise be into it. I've said it before and will say it again: presentation is everything with picky eaters. Shrimp and scallops are great on skewers, as are thick and hearty fish, such as salmon (if you're concerned about mercury and/or sustainability, check pages 243–244). Shrimp should cook in 3 to 4 minutes (time will vary depending on size), scallops should cook in about 6 minutes (time will vary depending on size), and 1½- to 2-inch cubes of fish should cook in 6 to 10 minutes.

Don't forget that you can also use sausage, tofu, and even firm cubes of cheese, such as halloumi, to make kebabs. Once you get the hang of it, get creative!

1. Cut the fish, chicken, beef, pork, or lamb into 1½- to 2-inch pieces. Cut veggies into 1½- to 2-inch pieces.

2. Whip up a flavorful oil-based marinade (see ideas that follow). If marinating: be sure to separate the marinade into two batches so that you won't brush cooked meat with marinade that has touched raw. Place the loose meat and veggies into a container or resealable plastic bag and pour one portion of the marinade over the top to cover. Allow to sit for 6 hours to overnight. If using wooden skewers, soak them in water for at least 30 minutes. Then, thread the meat and veggies onto the skewers in any alternating pattern. If there's no time to marinate: thread the meat and veggies onto the soaked skewers and proceed as follows.

3. Brush the marinade over the top of the skewered meat and veggies right before cooking. Throw on the grill, in a grill pan, or in the broiler, and brush with the reserved marinade after cooking.

4. While the kebabs cook, mix together a dipping sauce; this is optional, but an especially good idea if your meat did not have time to marinate. Serve the cooked kebabs with dipping sauce on the side.

♥ *Make It Tastier* Just as when you make vinaigrette (page 124), the key to making delicious kebabs is to stick with a particular flavor profile. If you're going for Mediterranean flavors, as with my Greek-Style Kebabs (page 162), combine olive oil, freshly squeezed lemon juice, and fresh oregano for the marinade and, if making a dipping sauce, whisk together Greek-style yogurt with olive oil, freshly squeezed lemon juice, garlic, and chopped cucumber.

Prefer Asian flavors? Marinate in a neutral oil, such as grapeseed or canola, combined with a splash of sesame oil, soy sauce, fresh garlic, and ginger and serve with Ginger Hoisin Sauce (page 59) on the side.

For Mexican: marinate in a neutral oil, such as grapeseed or canola, whisked with ground cumin, dried oregano, and fresh garlic. Make Guacamole (pages 64 and 65) or Chipotle Lime Cream (page 57) for dipping.

No matter what flavor set you go for, kebabs make a tasty dinner with nothing more than a simple pile of perfectly cooked rice (page 30) and a big salad. In fact, this is even a great meal when you have people over. You can prep everything from the kebabs and dipping sauce to the rice ahead of time, which allows you to hang with your friends instead of cooking in the kitchen alone.

If you decide to feed a group with kebabs, a few extra considerations take this from simple family meal to impressive dinner party meal. Flavor your rice with a fresh herb: cilantro for Mexican, lemon zest and mint for Greek, and so on. Also, instead of defaulting to a basic green salad, match that, as well. Some fun salad options include: Country-Style Greek Salad (page 132), Avocado and Edamame Salad (page 128), Beet and Orange Salad (page 129), or Mango Slaw (page 133).

Staples

In this book, I divide staples into two categories: homemade supermarket basics and sauces, condiments, and toppings. A whole volume of books could be written on homemade versions of supermarket staples. To be included here, the recipe had to be easy and there had to be a good reason for making it at home, such as it's hard to find a store-bought version made without ingredients we'd prefer to avoid (see pages 245–255), homemade tastes significantly better, or homemade is much more cost effective. If you can find a healthy, delicious, affordable version at the market, stick with it. I do. Otherwise, these simple, quick recipes give you a better product when it's easy to make and otherwise hard to find.

As for the sauces, condiments, and toppings, the criteria were that the recipe had to be easy, possible to make ahead, and used in many endless ways. Take Quick Pickled Red Onions (page 70), for example. They take hardly twenty minutes to pull together and can be kept in a jar in your refrigerator for up to a month. Pull them out to dress up a quick and otherwise boring meal, from leftover chicken tacos to a salad that needs a little something extra. This is worth easy scratch cooking.

Please don't browse this chapter and decide, definitively, that you are or are not someone who will ever make homemade Corn Tortillas (page 45) or Peanut Butter (page 53) from scratch. Look at these recipes believing that sometimes you will and sometimes you won't—even if the sometimes you will means one time a year.

Pull out these recipes when you feel like it, whether it's for your Cinco de Mayo party or when you and the kids are looking for a great kitchen project. These recipes are a great way to show kids—and remind yourself—that cooking basic foods from scratch can be easy and fun.

However often you use this chapter, I'm just happy to give it to you.

Sweet Potatoes x 2
Red Bell Pepper
Green Bell pepper
        Limes
Red onion
        Cilantro!
String beans   DON'T F[
                                COLD B[
Olive oil

tortillas (flour)

Z-Bars
String cheese

SMALL-BATCH CHICKEN BROTH

Makes about 6 cups broth

USE THIS FOR:

RED ENCHILADA SAUCE, *page 61*

ASIAN-STYLE CHICKEN SOUP, *page 119*

LENTIL SOUP WITH SAUSAGE, *page 120*

CURRIED CAULIFLOWER AND RED LENTIL SOUP, *page 121*

VEGETABLE CHICKPEA SOUP WITH GARLIC TOASTED BREAD CRUMBS, *page 122*

CHICKEN CURRY, *page 150*

MISO AND SWEET CHILI GLAZED PORK LOIN, *page 164*

PORK CHOPS WITH MAPLE BUTTERED APPLES, *page 169*

EASY "REFRIED" BEANS, *page 205*

Chicken broth is one of those basics that is so easy to do and yields a broth much more delicious than store-bought. Also, it makes use of waste, which is both Earth-friendly and wallet-friendly, too.

Most recipes for chicken broth call for several carcasses so that you can make a big old vat of broth. As a busy home cook, I find that a little challenging. There are only four of us in my crew and we eat one chicken at a time. I don't want to be bothered to save the carcass until I have a second or third. Instead, I'd rather finish up the chicken and, that day or next, throw the bones and scraps into a pot, make a small-batch broth, and be done.

If you go through two or three chickens at a time, or perhaps you're happy to collect chicken bones and scraps in a freezer bag until you have enough for a big batch, just double or triple this recipe. Otherwise, consider making a habit of cooking up this easy, small batch of broth every time you eat a whole chicken, whether home cooked or a store-bought rotisserie. Use the broth right away or freeze it for future use.

1 chicken carcass or 2 pounds fresh bony chicken pieces (e.g., wings and thighs)

3 large carrots, washed, trimmed, and cut in half crosswise

2 medium-size onions, peeled and quartered

2 stalks celery, washed, trimmed, and cut in half crosswise

1 teaspoon peppercorns

1 bay leaf

1 teaspoon salt, plus more to taste

1. Place all the ingredients and 10 cups of water in a very large pot set over medium-high heat. Bring to a boil and skim any foam from the surface. Lower the heat to medium-low, cover, and simmer for about 2 hours.

2. If using a chicken carcass, scoop it out and discard. If using fresh chicken pieces, scoop them out and, once cool enough to handle, remove the meat and set aside; discard the bones and skin. Strain the broth, discarding the vegetables and spices.

3. Allow the broth to cool completely at room temperature. Taste and season with additional salt, if desired. Some fat will coagulate; if you want a lower-fat broth, skim and discard. Store in a sealed container, jar, or resealable plastic bag in the refrigerator for up to 5 days or in the freezer for up to 3 months. If you have chicken meat left over, store it separately or add to the broth before packing it up for storage as chicken soup.

SMALL-BATCH VEGETABLE BROTH
Makes 5 cups broth

USE THIS FOR:

RED ENCHILADA SAUCE, *page 61*

VEGETARIAN TORTILLA SOUP, *page 116*

ASIAN-STYLE CHICKEN SOUP, *page 119*

LENTIL SOUP WITH SAUSAGE, *page 120*

CURRIED CAULIFLOWER AND RED LENTIL SOUP, *page 121*

VEGETABLE CHICKPEA SOUP WITH GARLIC TOASTED BREAD CRUMBS, *page 122*

CHICKEN CURRY, *page 150*

MISO AND SWEET CHILI GLAZED PORK LOIN, *page 164*

PORK CHOPS WITH MAPLE BUTTERED APPLES, *page 169*

EASY "REFRIED" BEANS, *page 205*

There's a great trick to making homemade vegetable stock an easy DIY. As you cook, collect veggie scraps in a 1-gallon resealable plastic bag that you store in the freezer. When the bag is full—which may take a week or several, depending on how frequently you cook veggies—put all the scraps from your bag into a pot along with water and a handful of other ingredients, cook down, and—presto!—a delicious stock that you can store in the refrigerator or freezer. (I find freezing it in 2 ½-cup portions the most flexible.) You can use it for anything from cooking more flavorful rice to throwing together a quick soup. Then, start over again.

Every batch of veggie broth needs three key vegetables: onion, celery, and carrot. If your scraps bag doesn't contain much of these, you'll want to add them fresh. I also add garlic and, when I have them on hand, a few sprigs of fresh flat-leaf parsley or thyme. Make adjustments based on what's in your frozen vegetable scraps bag.

As for the veggie scraps, the whole point is that it's a no-brainer. When you trim celery, zucchini, mushrooms, or sweet potatoes; pull the ribs out of greens; or peel onion, shallots, garlic, or carrots, put the waste in a bag that you store in your freezer and keep adding to it until it's full. Beets will make your stock red and potatoes will make it cloudy and starchy. Avoid cruciferous vegetables, such as Brussels sprouts, cabbage, cauliflower, and broccoli, since those create a strong flavor. Also, keep in mind that you want the scraps to be rinsed of dirt and you don't want to include any rotten bits.

1 (1-gallon) bag full of vegetable scraps
3 cloves garlic, peeled
1 onion, peeled and quartered
2 bay leaves
Small handful peppercorns (about 20)
1 teaspoon salt
1 teaspoon white wine (optional)

1. Place the vegetable scraps, garlic, onion, bay leaves, peppercorns, and 14 cups of water in a large stockpot set over medium-high heat. Bring to a boil.

2. Lower the heat to medium, or high enough to maintain a healthy simmer, and cook for 2 hours. You can cook it longer for a more intense flavor, though your yield will go down. Remove from the heat and strain. Stir in the salt, taste, and adjust the seasoning. If you want to give it a little extra something and have an open bottle of wine lying around, add a splash. Use immediately or allow to cool completely before packing in sealed containers, jars, or resealable plastic bags in the refrigerator for up to 5 days and freezer for up to 3 months.

FRESH RICOTTA CHEESE
Makes about 1 cup ricotta

MIX-AND-MATCH WITH:
SPINACH PESTO, *page 58*
ROASTED CHERRY TOMATOES, *page 67*
CARAMELIZED ONIONS, *page 69*
GARLIC TOASTED BREAD CRUMBS, *page 72*
ALL-PURPOSE STRAWBERRY SAUCE, *page 73*
8 HEALTHY, NO-COOK BREAKFAST IDEAS,
page 76
BUTTERED PASTA WITH RICOTTA AND
PEAS, *page 186*
PASTA WITH SPINACH PESTO AND GREEN
BEANS (ADD TO TASTE), *page 188*
CLASSIC MARGHERITA PIZZA (ADD TO
TASTE), *page 192*
5 UNEXPECTED PIZZA TOPPINGS, *page 194*
ONE-BOWL LEMON RICOTTA POUND CAKE,
page 221

As much as I love to cook, I never imaged that I'd be someone who made homemade ricotta cheese on a regular basis. But after making just one batch, I was hooked. It's just, well, so easy. Sure, it's easy enough to buy ricotta, but let's just say that the supermarket kind might as well be a different cheese all together. It's not even comparable to what you'll get from this recipe. And, bonus, the homemade version won't have a weird, plastic-y taste, either.

If you have any interest in eating or cooking with ricotta cheese, I beg you to make this. But, if you just won't, well, at least splurge on fresh ricotta cheese from a cheese monger or gourmet grocery store. It's pricey, but if getting the good stuff means eating it less often, well, then, eat it less often.

3 cups whole milk

1 cup heavy cream

¾ teaspoon salt

3 tablespoons freshly squeezed lemon juice
(from about 1½ juicy lemons)

1. Place the milk, cream, and salt in a medium-size, nonreactive (i.e., glass, stainless-steel, or enamel-lined) pot set over medium-high heat. If you have one, attach a thermometer (candy or deep fry will do) to the side of the pot and heat the mixture to about 180°F, stirring occasionally to keep the dairy from scorching. If you don't have a thermometer to attach to the side of the pot, use a meat thermometer to gauge the temperature; look for early signs of bubbling to know when to check the temperature, since 180°F is the point at which the milk will begin to simmer.

2. Remove the pot from the heat and add the lemon juice. Gently stir two or three times to ensure that the lemon juice is evenly distributed, before leaving it, undisturbed, until curdled, about 5 minutes.

3. In the meantime, line a colander or strainer with two to three layers of cheesecloth and place it over a large bowl to catch the whey. Pour the curdled milk into the prepared colander and strain for 1 to 2 hours, depending on your desired consistency for the cheese. The longer the cheese strains, the thicker and more firm it will be.

♥ *Make It Easier:*
Use milk about to turn.

This may seem like a funny suggestion, but making ricotta cheese is the perfect thing to do with milk that's about to turn. (Not with milk that has turned, mind you.) The result is actually better. So, if nothing else, maybe the food savings will motivate you to make this!

Tip If, as the cheese strains, the whey fills the bowl too much, pull up the edges of the cheesecloth and hang the bundled curds somewhere where they can continue to drain without the whey soaking back in.

When done, discard the whey and serve the curds immediately or store in a sealed container in the refrigerator for up to 5 days.

FLOUR TORTILLAS
Makes 8 tortillas

USE THIS FOR:
TORTILLA CHIPS, *page 47*

MIX-AND-MATCH WITH:
GUACAMOLE: CLASSIC, TROPICAL, OR
SMOKY, *pages 64 and 65*
CHORIZO MIGAS, *page 91*
CHILI-RUBBED STEAK TACOS, *page 160*
SLOW COOKER CARNITAS, *page 165*
SLOW COOKER PULLED PORK, *page 167*
FISH TACOS, *page 175*
VEGETABLE FAJITAS, *page 180*
BEAN AND CHEESE ENCHILADAS, *page 182*

Corn tortillas may be authentic, but we're fans of flour tortillas in my house, too, and though the dough is a little fussier, these come out absolutely great. Like the real thing. It takes some effort, so I won't be surprised if you don't make these on the regular, but they are way tastier than store bought and completely wholesome. There's no reason not to make them whenever you can.

- 1½ cups all-purpose flour (see measuring tip, page 217)
- ½ teaspoon salt
- ½ teaspoon baking powder
- ½ cup very warm tap water
- 2 tablespoons neutral oil, such as grapeseed or vegetable

1. Wet two pieces of paper towel and ring dry so that they are just damp; lay them flat on a plate next to the stove. In a small bowl, whisk together the flour, salt, and baking powder.

2. Place the water in a measuring cup and measure the oil into the water. Dump the contents of the measuring cup into the bowl with the dry ingredients and, using your hands or a silicone spatula, mix until a dough forms. Knead the dough for 2 to 3 minutes, until smooth and supple.

3. Roll the dough into a ball. Using a serrated knife, cut the ball in half and then in half again. Then cut each of the four pieces in half one last time. Roll each of the resulting eight pieces into a small ball, about the size of a golf ball.

4. Line a work surface with parchment paper, place one of the small balls of dough on top, and cover with the second piece of parchment paper. Use a rolling pin to roll the dough: roll forward and backward with heavy pressure two times, then turn the dough 45 degrees and roll forward and backward two times again. Turn the dough 45 degrees once more and roll; continue this process until you've rotated the dough 365 degrees. Pull off the top piece of parchment paper and use your hands to stretch the dough even further in every direction—you're trying to get it as close to 8 inches in diameter as possible. Repeat with the remaining portions of dough.

5. Heat a lightly oiled skillet or griddle, preferably cast iron, over medium heat. Once hot, add as many tortillas as fit without touching. Cook until air pockets bubble up, about 20 seconds, flip, and cook for another 30 seconds on the other side, until the tortillas brown in spots. Stack the cooked tortillas between the two pieces of wet paper towel; they will soften by the time you're done cooking. Repeat with the remaining dough. Serve immediately or store the cooled tortillas in a resealable plastic bag in the refrigerator for up to 3 days.

♥ *Make It Easier* To reheat tortillas: tortillas are best reheated with steam. If you have a microwave, wrap them loosely in damp paper towels and microwave them on high for 10 seconds. If that's not long enough to warm them, microwave again, until warmed through, in 5-second intervals. You can also wrap them in a damp kitchen towel and place the towel inside a microwave-safe plastic bag to create a proper steamy environment. Alternatively, dampen the tortillas slightly with water, wrap them in foil, and throw the package in a preheated oven or on a grill until warmed through. If you have something already cooking in the oven, regardless of temperature, it's fine to reheat the tortillas under a watchful eye; otherwise 350°F is a good temperature for reheating the tortillas.

CORN TORTILLAS
Makes 8 tortillas

USE THIS FOR:
TORTILLA CHIPS, *page 47*

MIX-AND-MATCH WITH:
GUACAMOLE: CLASSIC, TROPICAL, OR SMOKY, *pages 64 and 65*
CHORIZO MIGAS, *page 91*
CHILI-RUBBED STEAK TACOS, *page 160*
SLOW COOKER CARNITAS, *page 165*
FISH TACOS, *page 175*
VEGETABLE FAJITAS, *page 180*
BEAN AND CHEESE ENCHILADAS, *page 182*

During my first trip to Mexico City, I visited a tortilleria (a place where they make only tortillas) expecting to learn secrets. Instead, I learned that making a world-class corn tortilla is no simple business. To do it right requires a specific kind of masa (corn flour), with a certain kind of water (minerals make a difference), and a particular type of salt.

My heart broke a little on that visit as I realized that I might never make perfect tortillas at home like the ones I ate fresh off the fire in Mexico City. And with that, I decided to riff. These may not be world class, but they are fresh, full of flavor, and healthy—none of which is easy to get at most conventional supermarkets, and certainly not all in one product.

To make these, you'll need masa harina, a finely ground flour made of corn, which is typically available in the Mexican food aisle of conventional grocery stores. When you can't find it, skip this recipe until you can; do not substitute cornmeal, which is different. I add lime to the masa harina, but if this makes you cringe or you just don't feel like zesting a lime, skip it. You'll still get a delightfully fresh tortilla that is infinitely better than anything you can buy in a bag at the store.

1 cup instant masa harina
2/3 cup plus 1 tablespoon very hot tap water
1/2 teaspoon lime zest (from 1/2 lime; optional)
1/8 teaspoon salt
Neutral oil, such as grapeseed or canola

1. Wet two pieces of paper towel and ring dry so that they are just damp; lay them flat on a plate next to the stove. Place the masa harina, water, lime zest, and salt in a medium-size bowl. Using your hands, mix the ingredients until a dough forms, then knead for about 2 minutes. The dough should feel velvety, but not too wet—like play dough.

2. Roll the dough into a ball. Using a serrated knife, cut the ball in half and then in half again. Then, cut each of the four pieces in half one last time. Roll each of the resulting eight pieces into a small ball, about the size of a golf ball.

3. Cut a plastic grocery bag into two circular pieces: if you don't have a tortilla press, make each circle 7 inches in diameter. If you do have a press, cut each circle large enough to hang over the edges.

If using a press, line the bottom with the first piece of plastic, place a ball of dough in the middle, top with the second piece of plastic, and press closed. If you don't have a tortilla press, sandwich the dough between the pieces of plastic and use a rolling pin to make a 6-inch circle of dough. Repeat with the remaining portions of dough.

4. Heat a lightly oiled skillet or griddle, preferably cast iron, over medium heat. Once hot, add as many tortillas as fit without touching. Cook for 30 seconds on one side, flip, and cook for another 30 to 50 seconds on the other side, until the tortillas brown in spots. Stack the cooked tortillas between the two pieces of wet paper towel; they will soften by the time you're done cooking. Repeat with the remaining dough. Serve immediately or store the cooled tortillas in a resealable plastic bag in the refrigerator for up to 3 days.

To reheat tortilla see Make It Easier, page 45.

TORTILLA CHIPS

Serves 4 as a small snack or side

MIX-AND-MATCH WITH:

HUMMUS, *page 50*

CHIPOTLE LIME CREAM, *page 57*

FIRE-ROASTED SALSA, *page 62*

GUACAMOLE: CLASSIC, TROPICAL, OR SMOKY, *pages 64 and 65*

10 HEALTHY SNACK IDEAS YOU CAN MAKE WITHOUT A RECIPE, *page 94*

ROASTED TOMATO HUMMUS, *page 98*

HEARTS OF PALM DIP, *page 99*

VEGETARIAN TORTILLA SOUP, *page 116*

10 TOTALLY ACCEPTABLE, NO-COOK DINNER IDEAS, *page 145*

EASY "REFRIED" BEANS, *page 205*

If you're going to make tortillas, you might as well make tortilla chips! Or, you know, even if the tortillas are not homemade, these chips are crazy easy to throw together. Since the chips are baked, they are healthier than store-bought and they're heartier, too, which is good in my house. We need anything that will slow us down on tortilla chip consumption.

Seriously. There have been genuine fights over who gets the last of the chips.

The other great thing about making tortilla chips homemade is that you can flavor them without any artificial ingredients. Keep them simple and salted, or sprinkle them with chili powder.

8 (7- to 8-inch) corn or flour tortillas, store-bought or homemade (pages 39 and 40)

1 tablespoon neutral oil, such as grapeseed or canola, for brushing, plus more for pan

Salt, to taste

1. Preheat the oven to 350°F. Using a pastry brush, lightly grease a baking sheet with oil and set aside. (Tip: Line the baking sheet with foil and brush that for easy cleanup.)

2. Brush one tortilla with oil on both sides. Place it on a work surface and stack a second tortilla on top. Brush the top side of the second tortilla with oil and stack a third on top. Repeat until all eight tortillas are piled on top of each other. Using a sharp knife, cut the tortillas into eight equal wedges (as you would a pizza).

3. Place the tortilla pieces on the prepped baking sheet in a single layer. Sprinkle with salt and bake for about 10 minutes, until golden brown and crisped. (The exact time varies depending on the brand and thickness of your tortillas, as well as the size of the chips you cut. If using a thick-style tortilla that doesn't seem golden brown at 10 minutes, leave it in for up to 5 minutes longer, checking every 2 minutes or so.) Allow to cool for at least 10 minutes before serving.

PITA CHIPS

Serves 4 as a small snack or side

MIX-AND-MATCH WITH:

HUMMUS, *page 50*

8 HEALTHY, NO-COOK BREAKFAST IDEAS,
page 76

ROASTED TOMATO HUMMUS, *page 98*

HEARTS OF PALM DIP, *page 99*

COUNTRY-STYLE GREEK SALAD, *page 132*

10 TOTALLY ACCEPTABLE, NO-COOK
DINNER IDEAS, *page 145*

Tortilla chips are delicious, but we're equally fond of pita chips. Perhaps it's my Mediterranean background or just the fact that we're obsessed with hummus. Truth be told, finding store-bought pita chips made without icky ingredients is pretty easy to do. The benefit to making them at home is that you can flavor them any way you like. Also, it's a perfect way to use up bread that's about to go stale, which is a more significant money saver than you might realize (it adds up!).

4 pita breads

3 tablespoons neutral oil, such as grapeseed or canola, for brushing, plus more for pan

¼ teaspoon salt

Spice blend (see Make It Tastier; optional)

1. Preheat the oven to 350°F. Using a pastry brush, lightly grease a baking sheet with oil and set aside. (Tip: Line the baking sheet with foil and brush that for easy cleanup.) Using a sharp knife, cut the pitas into eight equal wedges (as you would a pizza) and separate each piece at the seam (it should tear easily and cleanly).

2. Place the pieces of pita, oil, salt, and spices, if using, in a medium-size bowl and using your hands (preferable) or a silicone spatula, toss to coat pieces well and evenly. Place the pita pieces on the prepped baking sheet in a single layer and bake for 10 to 12 minutes, or until golden brown and crisped.

♥ *Make It Tastier: Pita Chips Your Way* If you're going to make pita chips, you might as well flavor them just the way you like. Here are five great flavor combinations you should try. Just don't let them stop you from finding your own favorite flavors.

- 1 teaspoon ground cumin + ½ teaspoon ground coriander + ½ teaspoon garlic powder

- 1½ chili powder + ½ teaspoon smoked paprika

- 1 teaspoon dried oregano + ⅓ cup grated Parmesan cheese

- 2 teaspoons za'atar spice blend

- 1 tablespoon granulated sugar + 1 teaspoon ground cinnamon

HUMMUS

Makes 1¼ cups hummus

USE THIS FOR:

**10 TOTALLY ACCEPTABLE NO-COOK
DINNER IDEAS**, *page 145*

MIX-AND-MATCH WITH:

TORTILLA CHIPS, *page 47*
PITA CHIPS, *page 48*
SWEET-AND-SOUR PEPPERS, *page 68*
ROASTED TOMATO HUMMUS, *page 98*

It's not that hard to find natural hummus at the market these days (page 253), but even those have added ingredients that you can skip by making homemade. And why not, when it's incredibly easy to make and so much more delicious, not to mention cheaper?

This classic Hummus could have easily gone in the snack chapter along with Roasted Tomato Hummus (page 98), but in my house, we use plain humus in so many more ways than that. My little one's favorite lunch is a plain hummus sandwich and mine is a hummus pita with leftover Giardiniera Roasted Vegetables (page 202). When I'm crazy busy, I'll grab homemade hummus out of the refrigerator and serve it topped with shredded rotisserie chicken from the store, chopped tomato, cucumbers, olives, and crumbled feta cheese with a side of pita bread. A chicken hummus bowl! It's a great dinner that takes 10 minutes.

I make this recipe without tahini, the sesame seed paste usually called for when making hummus. It's not my favorite flavor and, anyway, there aren't many more practical ways that I've found to use it up. It can be expensive, too. So, instead, I stick with pantry staples to make this rich, lemony version that my family loves more than any store-bought brand.

1 (15-ounce) can chickpeas, drained and rinsed

2 tablespoons freshly squeezed lemon juice (about 1 juicy lemon)

1 teaspoon roughly chopped garlic (from about 1 clove)

¾ cup olive oil

Salt, to taste

1. Place the chickpeas, lemon juice, and garlic in the bowl of a food processor and whiz on high speed for 10 to 20 seconds.

2. Stop the food processor, scrape down the sides, and turn on again, adding the oil in a slow, steady stream. Keep the machine running until the hummus is smooth and creamy or reaches your desired consistency. Taste and season to taste with salt, if desired; pulse two or three more times to blend in well. Transfer the hummus to a bowl and serve immediately or store in a sealed container in the refrigerator for 5 to 7 days.

NUT AND SEED BUTTER

USE THIS FOR:

8 HEALTHY, NO-COOK BREAKFAST IDEAS,
page 76

PEANUT BUTTER BANANA BITES, *page 94*

**10 TOTALLY ACCEPTABLE, NO-COOK
DINNERS,** *page 145*

**PEANUT BUTTER AND JAM THUMBPRINT
COOKIES,** *page 229*

Making your own nut and seed butter is very simple business though it can be can be confusing at moments. There's a point every time I make it I wonder, is this going to come together or is this coarse paste really it? Spoiler alert: it always comes together into something silky smooth. Always. You just need to be patient. Especially with sunflower seed butter.

I've included recipes for peanut butter and sunflower seed butter here because those are your foundations, but if you make them, I hope you'll feel that you can experiment. It's the same process every time: toast the nuts or seeds, put them in the blender with a pinch of salt and, if you want, sugar, too. You can even add spices and additional sweeteners, such as honey, maple syrup, or agave nectar. Then blend.

Blend, blend, blend.

It goes fast while making peanut butter, but you can end up blending for upward of fifteen minutes for sunflower seed (and other nut) butter, stopping to scrape down the sides along the way—sometimes every twenty to thirty seconds! Trust that this will pass. If you keep at it, the mixture will become a satisfyingly smooth spread.

The other thing to know is that, for most of the process, you want your blender to be on low speed. Once your butter goes smooth, near the very end, you can turn up the speed to move faster toward *super*smooth.

Homemade nut butters can last in the refrigerator for up to 2 months (sometimes longer) so, if you like these recipes, consider doubling them to cut down on how frequently you need to make them.

SUNFLOWER SEED BUTTER

Makes 1 scant cup sunflower seed butter

- 2 cups raw, hull-less, unsalted sunflower seeds
- 1 teaspoon granulated sugar
- ½ teaspoon salt
- 4 teaspoons pure maple syrup or honey

1. Place the sunflower seeds in a medium-size pan set over medium-high heat and toast until they just begin to turn golden brown, 5 minutes, tossing every 30 seconds or so. Remove the pan from the heat, but leave the seeds in the pan, continuing to toss, 1 more minute.

2. Place the warm, toasted seeds in a high-speed blender or food processor along with the sugar and salt. Blend on low speed, scraping down the sides frequently, until pureed into a smooth butter, about 15 minutes. (The time can greatly vary depending on your machine, from 12 to 20 minutes.) Add the maple syrup about halfway through, at the point at which the texture of the seeds goes from coarse sand to wet paste. Transfer the butter to a jar or other sealed container and store in the refrigerator for up to 2 months.

♥ Make It Tastier: 5 ways to spice up your nut and seed butters

Plain nut and seed butter is so 1990s (or, uh, whenever it was that I was young). Today, you can get a staggering array of gourmet nut and seed butters flavored with everything from artisanal cocoa to curry powder. Or you can get more bang for your buck—and customize your flavors—by making them at home.

In step 1, when you add the salt and sugar, add a little spice and maybe even some pure extract, as well. I start with about ½ teaspoon of ground spice and 1 teaspoon of extract, but adjust up or down by taste. These are my favorite combinations.

- Pure maple syrup + raisins + vanilla extract
- Pure maple syrup + ground cinnamon + extra salt
- Honey + freshly grated nutmeg
- Honey + extra salt
- Agave nectar + shredded coconut or coconut butter

PEANUT BUTTER

Makes 1½ cups peanut butter

3 cups raw, shelled, unsalted peanuts

1 teaspoon granulated sugar

½ teaspoon salt

2 teaspoons pure maple syrup or honey

3 tablespoons neutral oil, such as grapeseed or canola, plus more as necessary

1. Preheat the oven to 350°F. Place the peanuts on a parchment-lined, rimmed baking sheet and toast in the oven until golden brown, about 12 minutes, shaking the pan twice during the toasting time.

2. Place the warm, toasted peanuts in a high-speed blender or food processor along with the sugar, salt, and syrup or honey. Blend on low speed for about 30 seconds. Keep the blender or food processor running and add the oil in a slow, steady stream, blending until the butter reaches your desired consistency, 3 to 8 minutes. (The time can greatly vary depending on your machine and how you like your peanut butter, from smooth to chunky. If the butter is having a hard time smoothing out, add more oil, 1 teaspoon at a time.) Transfer the butter to a jar or other sealed container and store in the refrigerator for up to 2 months.

QUICK BERRY JAM

Makes 2 cups jam

USE THIS FOR:

8 HEALTHY, NO-COOK BREAKFAST IDEAS, *page 76*

10 HEALTHY SNACK IDEAS, *page 94*

3 DELICIOUS WAYS TO BUILD A QUICK EVERYDAY SUNDAE, *page 215*

My kids go through jam like nobody's business and I've found that the brands I like most—that aren't packed with artificial ingredients or high-fructose corn syrup—are really pricey. Don't get me wrong; so are berries. But, still, I'd rather spend more on fresh berries and make my own jam with a controlled amount of sugar and only wholesome ingredients, than to splurge on the fancy jarred stuff. Well, at least most of the time.

To keep from buying pectin, which always struck me as an unnecessary ingredient, I make this with nothing more than berries, sugar, lemon juice, and salt. Sometimes I add a splash of balsamic vinegar, which gives a little extra something (and, no, it doesn't make your jam taste like vinegar). The thing about not using pectin, though, is that this jam is a little runny.

Using a skillet will help this jam thicken in the short cooking time, since it cooks while spread in a thin layer and the liquid evaporates faster. If using a pot, you'll have to cook this for more like thirty minutes. Why not save the time, right?

Once the cooking time is up, check the thickness of the jam by using the freezer spoon trick: before you cook the jam, place a few metal spoons into the freezer. When you're ready, drizzle some jam from the pot onto a frozen spoon. Once it has cooled, after just thirty seconds or

so, run your finger through it, and if it makes a clear path, you're good to go. If not, cook for a few minutes more and test again.

One last note: one of the main reasons I make this homemade is to control the amount of sugar. I call for a relatively small measure in this recipe that works especially great during the summer when sweet berries are in season. If you're using fruit that is not sweet and/or you prefer sweet jam, use more sugar. Start with the higher amount called for here, taste, and add more as necessary before the jam cools completely.

- 2 cups halved fresh strawberries, washed and hulled
- 1 cup fresh blueberries, washed
- 1 cup fresh raspberries, washed
- ⅔ to 1 cup granulated sugar
- 2 tablespoons freshly squeezed lemon juice (from about 1 juicy lemon)
- ⅛ teaspoon salt
- 1 teaspoon balsamic vinegar (optional)

1. Place the berries in the bowl of a food processor and pulse until a textured puree results.

2. Place the berry puree in an 8- to 10-inch skillet along with the sugar, lemon juice, salt, and vinegar, if using. Turn the heat to medium-high and bring to a boil. Lower the heat to medium and simmer rapidly until thickened and bubbles cover the entire surface, 20 to 25 minutes, stirring every 5 to 10 minutes. Allow the jam to cool completely before transferring to a sealed container. Store in the refrigerator for at least 2 hours before serving and up to 15 days.

ALMOND MILK
Makes 2 cups milk

***

MIX-AND-MATCH WITH:
GET UP AND GO SMOOTHIE, *page 77*
SWEET AND SALTY GRANOLA CEREAL,
page 78
BLUEBERRY ALMOND POLENTA, *page 81*

Plant-derived milks are easy to find in most conventional markets, but many brands contain added sugar and a few other ingredients that make me uncomfortable (see pages 246–247). While I can't be sure that there's any real concern over the ingredients in most commercial almond milks, there's enough of a question for me that I prefer homemade. Plus, this recipe churns out an almond milk that is way tastier than anything you'll buy at the store.

It turns out that making almond milk is incredibly easy. It's not at all the extreme process I imagined before making it myself. If you think that you'll make this regularly, it might be worth investing in—get this—a nut milk bag. Yes, that's a real thing, and easy to find with a single search online. It's actually pretty handy. Otherwise, you can strain almond milk through a fine-mesh strainer that's been lined with a couple layers of cheesecloth.

The only catch with making almond milk is that it doesn't stay good for all that long, just a few days. If you don't drink almond milk regularly, it probably makes sense to make this when you know exactly how you'll use it. Or just keep it on hand to add to recipes where it fits as its own ingredient and isn't just a substitute for cow's milk, such as Blueberry Almond Polenta.

You'll also have almond pulp left over. I know of several vegan sites that make fun use of it, but I just save it to add to my oatmeal or Berry Almond Polenta.

1 cup raw almonds

2 cups filtered water (you can substitute any tap or bottled water), plus more for soaking

1. Soak the almonds: place the almonds in a bowl and cover with water by at least 1 inch. Soak for at least 8 hours and up to overnight for a thick, full-bodied milk. If you don't mind a thinner milk and prefer to shorten the wait, you can soak for as few as 2 to 3 hours.

2. Drain, discarding the soaking water, and place the soaked almonds in a blender along with the fresh filtered, bottled, or tap water—whatever you normally drink is fine. Blend until the almonds become a very fine pulp, 1 full minute if using a high-powered blender, 2 to 4 minutes if using a standard blender or food processor. Either way, scrape down the sides as necessary.

3. If you do not have a nut milk bag (see head-note), line a strainer with a fine-meshed cheese-cloth. Place the nut milk bag or prepared strainer over a large bowl and strain the blended almond mixture, stopping to *press hard* on the almond pulp to extract as much milk as possible.

4. Transfer the almond milk from the bowl to a jar or another sealed container and store in the refrigerator for 2 to 4 days.

CHIPOTLE LIME CREAM

Serves 4 as a fixing for a meal

MIX-AND-MATCH WITH:

TORTILLA CHIPS, *page 47*

FIRE-ROASTED SALSA, *page 62*

GUACAMOLE: CLASSIC, TROPICAL, OR SMOKY, *pages 64 and 65*

CHORIZO MIGAS, *page 91*

CHILI-RUBBED STEAK TACOS, *page 160*

SLOW COOKER CARNITAS, *page 165*

FISH TACOS, *page 175*

VEGETABLE FAJITAS, *page 180*

BEAN AND CHEESE ENCHILADAS, *page 182*

¼ cup sour cream (reduced-fat is fine)

¼ teaspoon adobo from canned chipotles in adobo

Freshly squeezed lime juice

Salt, to taste

1. Place the sour cream and adobo in a bowl and mix thoroughly. Taste and adjust the flavor with lime juice and salt. Serve immediately or store in a sealed container in the refrigerator for up to 7 days.

I have a confession: I can eat sour cream from a spoon right out of the container. That's how much I love it. In fact, any dish that goes with avocado or guacamole also goes with sour cream in my house. This takes the good stuff to a level of great.

I tend to cook with chipotles a lot, so it seems I always have an open can waiting in the refrigerator. If you don't and you don't want to buy or open a new one just for a tiny bit of adobo, I get it. Skip the chipotle and season your sour cream with salt and lime juice. Even just that little change will turn sour cream from a lazy meal addition to a seemingly fancy one—while still being lazy! You have to love that.

SPINACH PESTO

Makes 1¼ cups pesto

USE THIS FOR:
PASTA WITH SPINACH PESTO AND GREEN
BEANS, *page 188*

MIX-AND-MATCH WITH:
RICE, *page 30*
FRESH RICOTTA CHEESE, *page 41*
EVERYDAY VINAIGRETTE, *page 124*

Although I'm sure there are folks some-where in the world who don't like it much, traditional basil pesto—pesto alla genovese—seems to be a universally loved sauce. Given how easy it is to make and freeze, this is a boon for us busy home cooks. If you learn how to make one sauce, it should be pesto.

Making it isn't hard to do. You put ingredients in a food processor, whiz and, in seconds, have a sauce to toss with pasta or brush onto chicken and veggies. Simple Pasta with Spinach Pesto and Green Beans with dollops of Fresh Ricotta Cheese and pesto baked drumsticks—which are nothing more than that, no recipe needed—are two favorite last-minute dinners in my house.

Save leftovers to spread on crusty bread (or, even better, on crusty bread smeared with Fresh Ricotta Cheese), drizzle over tomatoes and moz-zarella, or whisk into a batch of Everyday Vin-aigrette for your next dinner. You can also mix pesto with mayonnaise for a delicious sandwich spread at lunch.

Spinach isn't a traditional ingredient, but I use it here for an added nutritional boost. Don't worry: thanks to its mild flavor, you can't taste the extra greens.

If you freeze your pesto, consider doing so in an ice cube tray so that you can pop out small portions to use in all kinds of glorious ways.

¼ cup pine nuts
3 cups washed fresh basil leaves
2 cups fresh baby spinach, washed and dried
1 teaspoon lemon zest (from about 1 lemon)
1 tablespoon freshly squeezed lemon juice (from about ½ juicy lemon)
1 teaspoon roughly chopped garlic (from about 1 clove)
½ teaspoon salt, plus more to taste
½ cup olive oil, plus more as needed
¼ cup grated Parmesan cheese
Freshly ground black pepper (optional)

1. Place the pine nuts in a small, dry pan set over medium-high heat and toast them until golden brown, about 3 minutes, tossing them all the while to keep from burning.

2. Place the toasted pine nuts, basil, spinach, lemon zest, lemon juice, garlic, and salt in the bowl of a food processor and puree, as far as you can, stopping the machine and scraping down the sides at least once.

3. With the food processor running, add the oil in a slow, steady stream until the mixture takes on the right texture.

4. Add the cheese and black pepper to taste, if using, and pulse three or so times, until the mixture is just combined. Season with more salt to taste, if desired. Use immediately or store in a sealed container in the refrigerator for up to 7 days or in the freezer for up to 3 months.

GINGER HOISIN SAUCE

Makes ½ cup sauce

MIX-AND-MATCH WITH:
CHICKEN CUTLETS WITH ARUGULA AND
PARMESAN (SKIP THE ARUGULA SALAD
AND USE THIS AS A DIPPING SAUCE),
page 151
SLOW COOKER HOISIN PULLED PORK,
page 167
HOISIN-GLAZED SALMON, *page 172*

Hoisin is one of those sauces that is still hard to find in the store made without preservatives, color, MSG, or other ingredients that I try to avoid. The natural options tend to be expensive and hard to get at conventional markets. Enter this superquick, tasty recipe.

It's inspired by one in Gwyneth Paltrow's *It's All Good*—but made with more easily available ingredients.

Yes, I did say easily available ingredients and there you see miso. White miso paste is increasingly available in conventional markets and, since it's a fermented food, it lasts in your fridge for literally years. So, though you might not usually buy it, I encourage you to give it a try (you can also use it to make Avocado Miso Dressing, page 126). It will be worth the money, even if it takes you months—or years—to use it all up. Chinese five-spice powder is another one that you probably don't have lying around. That said, you should be able to find it in any spice aisle.

I tried eliminating both from this recipe to make it even easier but, the truth is, with such a distinctively Chinese flavor profile, it's hard to make authentic tasting hoisin without them, unless you start adding some other seriously obscure ingredients.

If buying store-bought hoisin sauce is going to help make it easy, go for it with advice from my Supermarket Guide (pages 252–253). Otherwise, I hope you'll give this a go.

- ¼ cup pure maple syrup
- 3 tablespoons rice vinegar
- 2 tablespoons white miso paste
- 1 tablespoon neutral oil, such as grapeseed or canola (if you would like to add sesame flavor, substitute 2 teaspoons neutral oil plus 1 teaspoon sesame oil)
- 1 teaspoon minced garlic (from about 1 clove)
- 1 teaspoon Chinese five-spice powder
- ½ teaspoon minced fresh ginger

1. Place the syrup, vinegar, and miso paste in a small bowl and set aside. No need to mix them; just have them ready to go.

2. Heat the oil in a small saucepan set over medium heat for 1 minute. Add the garlic, five-spice powder, and ginger and cook until fragrant, about 30 seconds, stirring to keep the five-spice from burning.

3. Add the maple syrup mixture all at once, whisking until smooth. Bring the sauce to a boil and cook for 30 seconds, continuing to whisk all the while. Remove from the heat and use immediately or allow to cool completely before storing in a sealed container in the refrigerator for up to 5 days.

QUICKEST BBQ SAUCE

Makes 1¼ cups sauce

USE THIS FOR:
SLOW COOKER BBQ PULLED PORK, *page 167*
BBQ SALMON, *page 173*

BBQ is one of those sauces that I always have in my refrigerator. Like any sauce worth its salt, it can be used to make a quick dinner just by brushing some on top of protein before cooking the way I do for BBQ Salmon. You can also douse shredded meat to turn plain leftover chicken or the humble pork shoulder I use to make Slow-Cooker BBQ Pulled Pork into a delicious meal.

Unlike many other homemade BBQ sauce recipes, this one doesn't need to be cooked down for forty-five minutes or longer. You just simmer for a few minutes to bring the flavors together and end up with a tasty spread that has nothing more in it than the wholesome ingredients listed below.

1 cup ketchup
2 tablespoons cider vinegar
2 tablespoons light brown sugar
1 tablespoon Dijon mustard
1 tablespoon Worcestershire sauce
1 tablespoon unsulfured molasses
1 tablespoon paprika
2 teaspoon onion powder
½ teaspoon garlic powder
½ teaspoon chili powder
½ teaspoon salt
¼ to ½ teaspoon freshly ground black pepper

1. Combine all the ingredients plus ¼ cup of water in a saucepan set over medium heat. Bring to a simmer, whisking until smooth. Simmer for 2 minutes, whisking occasionally, to allow all the flavors to come together. Use immediately or allow to cool completely before storing in a sealed container in the refrigerator for up to 2 weeks.

RED ENCHILADA SAUCE

Makes 3½–4 cups sauce

USE THIS FOR:
BEAN AND CHEESE ENCHILADAS, *page 182*

Oh, Bean and Cheese Enchiladas, how we love you so. You can't go wrong with beans and other delicious ingredients wrapped in a tortilla, smothered in sauce, and baked with melty cheese. You just can't. Well, not unless your sauce doesn't taste good.

There are plenty of shelf-stable enchilada sauces on the market, but most taste more like the package they come in than the bright, tangy sauce you crave when you make enchiladas. And there's the fact that some of the tastiest store-bought options come in cans likely lined with chemicals (see page 250). If you're going to bother making enchiladas, you want them to be good, which is why homemade sauce is really the way to go. With this recipe, all it takes is a blender and twenty minutes of waiting time while the sauce simmers unattended.

Once you make this, you're likely to be game to make it again and again. In addition to using it on your enchiladas, you can also halve the recipe to flavor ground beef for taco night.

1 (28-ounce) can diced tomatoes

½ cup chicken or vegetable broth, store-bought or homemade (pages 39 and 40)

½ cup heavy cream

2 tablespoons roughly chopped fresh cilantro

½ cup roughly chopped onion (from about 1 medium-size onion)

1 teaspoon roughly chopped garlic (from about 1 clove)

1 teaspoon chili powder

1 teaspoon salt

1 teaspoon dried oregano

½ teaspoon ground cumin

1 teaspoon cider or white wine vinegar

1. Place the tomatoes, broth, cream, cilantro, onion, garlic, and spices in a blender and puree until smooth.

2. Place the tomato mixture in a medium-size saucepan set over medium heat and simmer for about 20 minutes. If, at any point, the sauce starts to boil, lower the heat to medium-low. Remove from the heat and stir in the vinegar. Use immediately or allow to cool completely before storing in a sealed container in the refrigerator for up to 7 days.

FIRE-ROASTED SALSA
Makes 3 cups salsa

MIX-AND-MATCH WITH:
TORTILLA CHIPS, *page 47*
CHORIZO MIGAS, *page 91*
CHILI-RUBBED STEAK TACOS, *page 160*
SLOW COOKER CARNITAS, *page 165*
FISH TACOS, *page 175*
VEGETABLE FAJITAS, *page 180*
EASY "REFRIED" BEANS, *page 205*
(mix a little bit into the salsa to make a dip)

I crave the fresh salsas that get plonked on the table at authentic Mexican restaurants the minute you sit down. There are usually a few, but my favorite is always the nearly smooth, fresh, mild tomato version. It has all the flavor of pico de gallo, but feels more like a sauce. You just can't get that in a jar, no matter how fancy.

In the summer, when tomatoes are sweet and juicy, I'll make this salsa with fresh tomatoes. The rest of the year, I opt for canned fire-roasted tomatoes, which have a depth of flavor and also, compared to bad winter tomatoes, a freshness that no jarred stuff can rival. To enhance the fire-roasted goodness, I also quickly pan roast the garlic and jalapeño—it adds ten minutes to the process, but is so worth it, especially since the rest of the recipe takes five minutes.

2 cloves garlic, left whole and unpeeled

1 jalapeño pepper, halved and seeded (veins removed, too, if you want this to be mild)

1 (15-ounce) can diced, fire-roasted tomatoes

½ cup roughly chopped onion (from about ½ medium-size onion)

¼ cup packed roughly chopped fresh cilantro

2 tablespoons freshly squeezed lime juice (from about 1 juicy lime)

½ teaspoon salt, plus more to taste

1. Place the unpeeled garlic cloves and jalapeño halves in a small, dry pan set over high heat and roast for about 10 minutes, turning the garlic one or two times and flipping the pepper halfway through the cooking time. Remove from the heat and allow to cool before peeling the garlic and roughly chopping both the garlic and pepper.

2. Place the garlic, pepper, and remaining ingredients in a food processor and pulse or puree until the mixture reaches your desired salsa consistency. This can be served smooth or chunky. Serve immediately or store in a sealed container in the refrigerator for up to 1 week.

GUACAMOLE, 3 WAYS

MIX-AND-MATCH WITH:

TORTILLA CHIPS, *page 47*
CHORIZO MIGAS, *page 91*
CHILI-RUBBED STEAK TACOS, *page 160*
SLOW COOKER CARNITAS, *page 165*
FISH TACOS, *page 175*
VEGETABLE FAJITAS, *page 180*
BEAN AND CHEESE ENCHILADAS, *page 182*

By now it's probably clear that my crew and I are obsessed with avocados. We love the way they taste but, really, what makes them most appealing to me is that they are nutrient dense, adaptable (you can add them to a morning Get Up and Go Smoothie, page 77, for goodness' sake!), and you don't have to cook them.

No cooking!

Our favorite way to use avocados is, of course, to make guacamole. It's so good that we can't just have one kind. The kids and I are always experimenting with ways that we can spice up our guac and these are our favorites—so far.

Sadly, there's no foolproof way to store guacamole that's been made ahead of time. I've tried so many methods and none do the job of preventing browning reliably. If you really need to make this ahead to save your sanity, pack it into a bowl, smooth out the surface, squeeze fresh lime juice to cover the surface, and press a piece of plastic wrap touching the surface to make an airtight seal. Some browning may occur, but if you've made a good seal, it should only be on top. Scrape the brown bits off and serve.

Or just make and serve fresh.

THE QUICK CLASSIC
Serves 4 as a dip, 8 as a fixing for a meal

2 ripe avocados
½ cup seeded, chopped fresh tomato (from about 1 small to medium-size tomato)
¼ cup finely chopped red onion (from about ½ small onion)
¼ cup freshly squeezed lime juice (from about 2 juicy limes)
2 tablespoons chopped fresh cilantro
1 tablespoon finely chopped and seeded fresh jalapeño pepper, plus more to taste (optional)
1 teaspoon salt, plus more to taste

1. Halve the avocados and remove the pit. Scoop out of the skin and roughly cut into 1- to 2-inch pieces. Place in a bowl and mash with a fork.

2. Add all the other ingredients and continue to mash until the mixture reaches your desired consistency. Season with more salt to taste, if desired. Serve immediately.

THE TROPICAL

Serves 4 as a dip, 8 as a fixing for a meal

2 ripe avocados

½ cup chopped fresh pineapple, mango, or a combination

¼ cup finely chopped red onion (from about ½ small onion)

¼ cup freshly squeezed lime juice (from about 2 juicy limes)

2 tablespoons chopped fresh cilantro

1 tablespoon finely chopped and seeded fresh jalapeño pepper, plus more to taste (optional)

1 teaspoon salt, plus more to taste

1. Halve the avocados and remove the pit. Scoop out of the skin and roughly cut into 1- to 2-inch pieces. Place in a bowl and mash with a fork.

2. Add all the other ingredients and continue to mash until the mixture reaches your desired consistency. Season with more salt to taste, if desired. Serve immediately.

THE SMOKY

Serves 4 as a dip, 8 as a fixing for a meal

2 ripe avocados

½ cup seeded, chopped fresh tomato (from about 1 small to medium-size tomato)

¼ cup finely chopped red onion (from about ½ small onion)

2 tablespoons freshly squeezed lime juice (from about 1 juicy lime)

1 tablespoon finely chopped and seeded fresh jalapeño pepper, plus more to taste (optional)

1 teaspoon salt, plus more to taste

¼ teaspoon ground chipotle powder

¼ cup grated sharp Cheddar cheese

1. Halve the avocados and remove the pit. Scoop out of the skin and roughly cut into 1- to 2-inch pieces. Place in a bowl and mash with a fork.

2. Add all the other ingredients and continue to mash until the mixture reaches your desired consistency. Season with more salt to taste, if desired. Serve immediately.

ROASTED CHERRY TOMATOES

Makes 1 cup tomatoes

USE THIS FOR:

ROASTED TOMATO HUMMUS, *page 98*

ZITI WITH CORN AND ROASTED TOMATOES,
page 190

5 UNEXPECTED PIZZA TOPPINGS, *page 194*

MIX-AND-MATCH WITH:

PASTA, *page 28*

FRESH RICOTTA CHEESE, *page 48*

EVERYDAY VINAIGRETTE, *page 124*

These tomatoes are nearly always in my refrigerator. Packed in a "sauce" of escaped juices and the quality olive oil in which they were cooked, these sweet tomatoes work on nearly anything. Pile them onto a piece of crusty bread (slathered with Fresh Ricotta Cheese, page 41 if you're fancy), use them as an instant sauce for pizza (page 183) or perfectly cooked pasta (page 28), add them to salad or shake them into my Everyday Vinaigrette (page 124), whiz them with chickpeas to make a Roasted Tomato Hummus—the possibilities are endless. If you keep them around, you'll see that these roasted tomatoes will find their way into so much more than you might have predicted and that your food is better for it.

1 pint cherry tomatoes, washed

¼ cup olive oil

½ teaspoon salt

1. Preheat the oven to 400°F. Combine all the ingredients on a small, rimmed baking sheet or in a small baking dish and roast for 45 minutes, or until the tomatoes are charred in spots and have popped, releasing their juices. Allow them to cool and use immediately or store in a sealed container in the refrigerator for up to 5 days.

SWEET-AND-SOUR PEPPERS

Serves 4-8

USE THIS FOR:

STEAK WITH SWEET-AND-SOUR PEPPERS,
page 159

MIX-AND-MATCH WITH:

RICE, *page 30*

QUINOA, *page 31*

HUMMUS, *page 50*

COUNTRY-STYLE GREEK SALAD, *page 132*

PARMESAN ROASTED BROCCOLI (ADD
CHOPPED TO TASTE), *page 204*

I've never been a big fan of roasted red peppers; the jarred kind, especially, taste overly sweet to me. Still, I end up using them often because, well, they're easy and pair nicely with simply cooked meat—which is to say, they pair nicely with so much.

One day, as I pulled roasted red peppers out of a jar, it occurred to me that I could dress them with red wine vinegar to give their flavor a sharp edge. It worked well—in fact, if you decide not to make these, you can use the same trick—and inspired me to make a homemade version with the same sweet-and-sour tension.

I cook the peppers in a pan instead of roasting them to save time and it works beautifully: these take all of fifteen minutes to throw together. Cook them ahead of time and keep them in the fridge for the week. You can chop and stir them into plain rice or quinoa, blend them into hummus, toss with roasted broccoli, and so much more.

¼ cup red wine vinegar

2 tablespoons granulated sugar

4 red, orange, or yellow bell peppers, or a combination

2 tablespoons olive oil

¼ teaspoon salt

1. In a small bowl, whisk together the vinegar and sugar. Set aside, giving the sugar time to dissolve.

2. Wash, seed, and cut the peppers into 1- to 1½-inch-thick strips.

3. Place the oil in a large pan set over medium-high heat. Add the peppers and salt, toss to coat the peppers in the oil, and leave them untouched to cook for a full minute, until they brown in spots. Toss again, and allow them to cook for another 5 minutes, tossing one more time before they're done.

4. Lower the heat to medium and add the vinegar mixture. Toss to coat, then cook until the peppers are tender and the vinegar reduces to a thin, syrupy coating, about 8 minutes. Serve immediately or, even better, at room temperature, or allow to cool completely before storing in a sealed container in the refrigerator for 1 week.

CARAMELIZED ONIONS

Makes 1 cup onions

USE THIS FOR:

5 UNEXPECTED PIZZA TOPPINGS, *page 194*

RICE AND LENTIL PILAF, *page 206*

MIX-AND-MATCH WITH:

FRESH RICOTTA CHEESE, *page 41*

STEAK WITH SWEET-AND-SOUR PEPPERS, *page 159*

PORK CHOPS WITH MAPLE BROWN BUTTER APPLES (ADD TO TASTE), *page 169*

BUTTERED PASTA WITH RICOTTA AND PEAS (ADD TO TASTE), *page 186*

Caramelized onions are an all-purpose condiment that makes nearly anything better. They are a quintessential part of my Rice and Lentil Pilaf and, if I have a batch waiting in the refrigerator, I stir them into Buttered Pasta with Ricotta and Peas or use them to top pizza, too. They're also great piled on burgers and dogs, any frittata, and, my favorite, bread smeared with Fresh Ricotta Cheese.

I like for these onions to tangle with other ingredients, so I cut thin slices from halved onions for this recipe. You can chop the onions any way that you want, though, and this recipe will still work.

5 tablespoons olive oil

3 medium-size to large onions, peeled, halved and thinly sliced (about 6 cups sliced onion)

½ teaspoon salt

1. Set a large pot or high-sided skillet over medium heat. Once the pan is hot, pour in the oil and swirl, allowing it to heat up, about 30 seconds. Add the onions and salt; stir to coat the onions well.

2. Cook until the onions are soft, golden, and browned in spots, for 30 minutes, stirring occasionally. If you sliced the onions thinly enough, it might even seem as if some are melting. This is good! Remove from the heat, allow to cool for 5 minutes and use immediately, or store in a sealed container in the refrigerator for up to 5 days.

QUICK PICKLED RED ONIONS

Makes 1 cup onions

USE THIS FOR:

5 UNEXPECTED PIZZA TOPPINGS, *page 194*

MIX-AND-MATCH WITH:

CHORIZO MIGAS, *page 91*

COUNTRY-STYLE GREEK SALAD, *page 132*

INDIAN-STYLE MEATBALLS, *page 157*

CHILI-RUBBED STEAK TACOS, *page 160*

SLOW COOKER CARNITAS, *page 165*

FISH TACOS, *page 175*

VEGETABLE FAJITAS, *page 180*

BEAN AND CHEESE ENCHILADAS, *page 182*

If you ask me, pickles are among the most amazing foods that you can make at home. The process turns ordinary vegetables into something extraordinarily delicious, while preserving them, too. I'm slightly obsessed with pickled onions, in particular, because they pretty much make everything you put them on better. My kids—even the little one—agree.

Serve these in tacos, alongside simply cooked meat, or even tossed into a simple potato salad, and you'll see.

You can also use this recipe to quick pickle other veggies, such as radishes, cucumber, carrots, and even grapes or raisins (both of which make a great garnish). Thicker ingredients (e.g., cucumber slices) may need more time or even overnight to take on good flavor, but I say that still counts as quick. Or, at least, quick enough!

2 cups sliced red onion, cut about ¼ inch thick (from about 1½ medium-size red onions, peeled and halved)

½ cup red wine vinegar

2 allspice berries

2 whole cloves

1 bay leaf

1 tablespoon salt

1 tablespoon granulated sugar

1. Place the onions in a medium-size, nonreactive (e.g., plastic, glass, or stainless-steel) bowl; set aside. Place the vinegar, ½ cup of water, and the spices, salt, and sugar in a saucepan set over medium heat. Bring to a boil and remove from the heat.

2. Pour the vinegar mixture over the onions and allow to cool at room temperature. Cover and refrigerate. If using right away, allow the onions to pickle for at least 1 hour, though, if you have time, 2 hours will give you the most immediate flavor. Otherwise, store in a sealed container in the refrigerator for up to 1 month.

GARLIC TOASTED BREAD CRUMBS

Makes 1 cup bread crumbs

USE THIS FOR:

VEGETABLE CHICKPEA SOUP WITH GARLIC
TOASTED BREAD CRUMBS, *page 122*
5 UNEXPECTED PIZZA TOPPINGS, *page 194*
ROASTED CAULIFLOWER WITH GARLIC
TOASTED BREAD CRUMBS, *page 197*

MIX-AND-MATCH WITH:

BUTTERED PASTA WITH RICOTTA AND
PEAS, *page 186*
ROASTED PARMESAN BROCCOLI, *page 204*

first made these bread crumbs for my Vegetable Chickpea Soup, but quickly realized that I like them for so much more, from salads to Buttered Pasta with Ricotta and Peas. In fact, they add a mouthwatering crunch to most any pasta, including a simple ziti with Marinara Sauce (page 183).

My favorite way to use these, though, is to toss them with simply roasted vegetables because, somehow, that makes the veggies more appealing to my little ones. As soon as cauliflower comes out of the oven, for example, throw it into a bowl with a handful of these garlicky bread crumbs. Or add these to the Parmesan before tossing it with roasted broccoli in my Roasted Parmesan Broccoli recipe.

2 tablespoons salted butter
**1 to 1½ teaspoons minced garlic (from
about 1 to 1½ cloves)**
1 cup panko bread crumbs

1. Place the butter in a medium-size pan set over medium heat. As soon as the last bit of butter melts, add the garlic (1 teaspoon for a mild garlic flavor, 1½ teaspoons for a stronger one). Cook until the garlic is fragrant, about 30 seconds. If your heat is even just a little too high, the garlic will start to turn a very dark golden brown before the 30 seconds is up. If this happens, immediately add the bread crumbs, lower the heat, and move on to the next step.

2. Add the bread crumbs and stir to coat well. Spread them in an even layer across the bottom of the pan and toast for 3 minutes, leaving them alone for the first minute, then tossing all the while for the remaining 2 minutes. More than watching the clock, though, I want you to watch the bread crumbs. Their exact cooking time will vary; turn off the heat as soon as you see some of the bread crumbs turn the shade of golden brown that you want.

3. Once off the heat, the crumbs will continue to toast. Leave them in the pan and keep tossing until they turn a uniform shade of golden brown; this can take up to a full minute. Use immediately or transfer them to a container to cool completely before sealing and storing at room temperature for up to 5 days.

ALL-PURPOSE STRAWBERRY SAUCE

Makes 1 cup sauce

MIX-AND-MATCH WITH:
FRESH RICOTTA CHEESE, *page 41*
YOGURT CHIA BREAKFAST PUDDING,
page 81
EVERYDAY PANCAKES, *page 84*
EVERYDAY WAFFLES, *page 87*

You might wonder why you should bother making this strawberry sauce, but if you make it once, you'll never wonder again.

You can stop buying sugary fruit yogurt and stir this into plain yogurt or Yogurt Chia Pudding (page 81).

You can mix this sauce with plain yogurt and freeze the mixture in ice pop molds.

Or skip the yogurt and mix this sauce with a little OJ for strawberry orange pops.

You can use this to sweeten your smoothies.

You can pour some over plain oatmeal.

You can mix it into milk for all-natural, pink strawberry milk.

You can switch up your waffle (page 87) and pancake (page 84) routine. (Move over IHOP.)

You can pour a little over Fresh Ricotta Cheese (page 41) smeared on toast for breakfast or an afternoon delight.

You can add a touch to Everyday Vinaigrette (page 124) to make a yummy Strawberry Vinaigrette.

You can use it to make ice-cream sundaes.

And so much more.

I like to make this when I have strawberries that are about to go bad—it's a great way to use them up. And, really, any berries will do. Mix them, even.

1½ cups chopped fresh or whole frozen strawberries, unthawed
¼ cup granulated sugar
2 tablespoons freshly squeezed lemon juice (from about 1 juicy lemon)

1. Place all the ingredients plus ⅓ cup of water in a pot set over medium heat and bring to a boil. Lower the heat to medium-low and simmer for 10 minutes.

2. Remove from the heat and transfer to a blender; puree until smooth. Strain the sauce to remove the seeds and serve immediately or allow to cool completely before storing in an airtight container in the refrigerator for up 7 days or in the freezer for up to 3 months.

Breakfast

While most people grumble about having to get dinner on the table at the end of a long day, I find it hard to make healthy breakfasts on busy weekday mornings. And, honestly, while I love making a good brunch, on half of our weekend mornings I'm angling to get more sleep and stay in bed too late to make them happen. And by "too late" I mean that I wake up at 8:30 a.m. instead of 6:30 a.m. and, by then, the boys have fed themselves, which means cereal or toast.

Most important meal of the day? Yikes.

I try not to beat myself up over my natural-born desire to get more minutes of sleep than to make a hot breakfast, but about a year ago, I'd noticed that things had gotten out of control. Without realizing it, cereal had gone from being a busy-day backup to an everyday go-to. And on mornings when I'd woken up early enough to manage more than pouring a bowl of extruded corn, I'd be faced with a fight. The boys were used to cereal and they didn't want to give it up.

Instead of fighting with them, I came up with a plan and set some clear expectations. I told the kids that they could eat cereal on three days a week—any three days that they wanted. I reminded them that they must eat fruit in the morning, too, a long-standing rule that they'd somehow been working around, and explained that ignoring the fruit rule would get cereal demoted to two days a week. The remaining four breakfasts were mine to plan and serve and theirs to eat. I'd be happy to take suggestions (*more Bacon Cheddar Waffles please*, page 89) and listen to feedback (*fine, no quinoa flakes in the oatmeal*)—but no more fighting.

It worked.

I cannot lie: some crazy busy weeks it's hard to come up with four noncereal breakfasts that I can make quickly enough. I'd die without my Get Up and Go Smoothie (page 77) and hard-boiled eggs (page 32). Some weekday mornings I can swing my Blueberry Almond Breakfast Polenta (otherwise, we gobble this quick decadence on the weekend, page 81), and I love having homemade Sweet and Salty Granola (page 78) around for cereal days. I'm always amazed at how often the kids choose to eat it over store-bought.

8 *Healthy, No-Cook* BREAKFAST IDEAS

Because let's start this chapter right—and realistically.

1. Get Up and Go Smoothie (page 77).

2. Peanut Butter (page 53) or Sunflower Seed Butter (page 52) and banana on toast or in a whole wheat pita.

3. A big, round slice of apple smeared with Peanut Butter (page 53) or Sunflower Seed Butter (page 52) and sprinkled with granola (page 78).

4. Plain yogurt with honey, maple syrup, jam (page 53) or fruit sauce (page 73), and fresh fruit. Add granola (page 78) if you're fancy.

5. Toast with Fresh Ricotta (page 41), fruit slices, and honey.

6. Yogurt Chia Breakfast Pudding (page 81).

7. Avocado toast. If you have guacamole (pages 64–65) on hand, that works, too. Feel free to add sliced cheese, tomato, cucumber, radish, smoked salmon, or anything else that you and your crew enjoy with avocado. Just oil and crunchy salt is fine, too.

8. Cream cheese swirled with jam (page 53) or fruit sauce (page 73) and served as a dip with Pita Chips (page 48) and a side of fruit.

♥ *Make It Easier*

Cereal is one of those processed foods that we, honestly, cannot live without. The kids like it, I like it, and it's just so damn easy. The problem is that it's a category of store-bought foods with some of the worst added ingredients. Most products are filled with sugar, artificial ingredients, flavors, and colors. And for a food meant to fuel our day! I did a lot of research on the best options—best being a relative term—so, if my quick breakfast suggestions here aren't enough, check them out in the Supermarket Guide (page 247).

♥ *Make It Easier: Make-ahead smoothie packs*

Making smoothies is about as easy as it gets, but in the morning, collecting and measuring the ingredients can feel like a chore. Especially if your blender doesn't live on the counter and you have to get that out, too! Some may call it lazy, but I call it reality. In fact, when you're running a household, managing a big crew, and doing all of the other stuff that you do, it's smart to conserve energy where you can.

One way that I make morning smoothies easier is to put together smoothie packs. I don't always have time to plan like this, but if I find myself with a little time to hard-boil eggs (page 32) and prep veggies for the week, I'll also premeasure the smoothie ingredients, except for the ice and liquid, and pack them together in small, individual freezer-safe resealable plastic bags. That way, come morning, all I have to do is pull out my blender, dump the contents of a single bag into it, add the liquids and ice, and blend.

GET UP AND GO SMOOTHIE

Makes 2¼ cups smoothie (serves 2-4)

MIX-AND-MATCH WITH:

HARD-BOILED EGGS, *page 32*

HUMMINGBIRD MUFFINS, *page 101*

GRANOLA BARS, *page 104*

EXTRA-THICK PEANUT BUTTER GRANOLA BARS, *page 105*

I go on these smoothie experimentation jags where I start buying crazy ingredients and throwing them together into a blender to see what happens. But, no matter what, I always come back to this one. It tastes like a super-boosted (and nonboozy) morning piña colada—its bright, sunny flavor is the perfect way to start any day.

You'll notice that this recipe calls for almond-coconut milk. I'm obsessed with this combination, which you can easily make by mixing homemade Almond Milk (page 55) with canned or carton coconut milk to taste. Alternatively, look for a premixed combination of almond and coconut milks at the market (see the Supermarket Guide, pages 246–247 and 251).

If you're thinking TWO is too much, just go ahead and substitute one or the other. Coconut milk is practical since it comes in cans that you can store in your pantry at an affordable price. You can also freeze leftovers in small portions, using an ice cube tray.

You can also use fresh fruit in this recipe, just keep in mind that you'll have to adjust the amount of ice. Altogether, you want a total of 1 to 1½ cups of frozen ingredients, including or exclusively ice.

1 cup almond-coconut milk (see headnote)

1 orange, peel and pith removed

½ avocado, pitted and peeled

½ cup fresh or frozen pineapple or mango

½ cup frozen strawberries

½ cup ice (1 cup if using fresh pineapple)

2 tablespoons freshly squeezed lime juice (from about 1 juicy lime)

1 tablespoon honey, plus more to taste

1 tablespoon chia seeds (optional)

1 tablespoon flaxseeds (optional)

1. Place all the ingredients in a high-powered blender and puree until smooth. Serve immediately.

♥ *Make It Tastier:* If you use only almond milk—or another kind of milk—add shredded unsweetened coconut and extra lime juice to amp up the tropical vibe.

SWEET AND SALTY GRANOLA CEREAL

Makes 4 cups cereal

MIX-AND-MATCH WITH:
HARD-BOILED EGGS, *page 32*
ALMOND MILK, *page 55*
YOGURT CHIA BREAKFAST PUDDING,
page 81

My boys love starting the day with cereal. So much so that I had a real problem on my hands when they started refusing oatmeal, yogurt, and my other healthy go-tos. They begged for cereal to the point where I decided to limit their cereal to three days a week. I'm no joke.

And then I introduced this granola cereal.

Since it's homemade and packed with health, I told the boys that they could eat this even on noncereal days, which felt like a win to them. As for me, well, it's true that nothing makes the morning as easy as them being able to pour themselves a big bowl of this goodness while I pack lunch. Plus, I get to eat it, too.

2 cups old-fashioned rolled oats

½ cup shredded unsweetened coconut

½ cup slivered almonds

½ cup raw, hull-less pumpkin seeds (if these are hard to find or too expensive, substitute another nut, such as chopped raw pecans)

½ cup raw, hull-less sunflower seeds

½ cup pure maple syrup

1 teaspoon salt

4 tablespoons olive oil

1. Preheat the oven to 350°F. Place all the ingredients in a large bowl. Mix thoroughly, making sure to coat all the dry ingredients with the syrup and oil. Pour the mixture onto a rimmed baking in a single layer; 17 x 12 inches works best.

2. Bake for 15 minutes, stir the granola, and return to the oven for another 5 minutes. Remove the baking pan from the oven and allow it to cool for 3 to 5 minutes. Carefully transfer the granola to a large bowl, breaking it up as you go, where it can cool for another 10 minutes before storing in an airtight container for up to 1 month.

YOGURT CHIA BREAKFAST PUDDING

Serves 4

MIX-AND-MATCH WITH:

QUICK BERRY JAM, *page 53*

STRAWBERRY SAUCE, *page 73*

SWEET AND SALTY GRANOLA CEREAL, *page 78*

This breakfast pudding isn't quite sweet enough to make a satisfying dessert, but with honey or maple syrup and vanilla, it is sweet enough to feel like a treat at breakfast.

And packed with protein from Greek yogurt and chia seeds (which help give this a thick, pudding-like consistency), it's healthy, too.

If you like fruity yogurt, top this with homemade Strawberry Sauce or a spoonful of Quick Berry Jam. You can also thin this by adding extra milk and strawberry sauce to freeze into healthy Popsicles.

- ¾ cup (6 ounces) plain Greek-style yogurt
- ¼ cup milk of choice (I love using a combo of almond and coconut; see Get Up and Go Smoothie, page 77)
- 2 tablespoons chia seeds
- 1 tablespoon honey or pure maple syrup, plus more to taste
- ½ teaspoon pure vanilla extract

1. Place all the ingredients in a medium-size bowl and whisk until the honey has dissolved and the chia seeds, which tend to clump, are evenly distributed.

2. Cover and place in the refrigerator until the mixture takes on a pudding consistency, at least 3 hours and up to overnight. Serve or store in an airtight container in the refrigerator for up to 3 days.

BLUEBERRY ALMOND POLENTA

Serves 4-6

MIX-AND-MATCH WITH:

ALMOND MILK (AND LEFTOVER ALMOND PULP, TOO), *page 55*

One of the things that I love most about polenta is that, despite its being nothing more than cornmeal, it feels luxurious. Compared to its down-home American counterpart, oatmeal, polenta is downright elegant. But don't let that fool you into thinking that it's hard to make or should be kept only as a treat. When using quick-cook polenta, you can make this breakfast just as easily on a rushed weekday morning as you can for a Sunday brunch. Splurge on crème fraiche and use it instead of Greek-style yogurt to make this fancy, sit back, and enjoy the oohs and aahs.

- 4 cups milk of choice (I like using cow's milk or homemade Almond Milk, page 55)
- ¾ cup quick-cook polenta
- ½ cup almond meal (see Make It Easier, page 83)
- 2 tablespoons unsalted butter
- 1 cup blueberries, plus more for garnish (or your favorite fresh berries or chopped stone fruit)
- ¼ to ⅓ cup honey, to taste
- ½ teaspoon pure vanilla extract
- ⅛ to ¼ teaspoon ground cardamom, to taste
- Plain Greek-style yogurt, for garnish (optional)

1. Bring the milk to a boil in a medium-size saucepan over high heat.

2. Reduce the heat to low and add the polenta, whisking constantly until smooth, 1 to 2 minutes. Add the almond meal and continue to whisk until the polenta thickens to a creamy consistency, 1 to 2 minutes. Add the butter and whisk until it melts.

3. Remove the polenta from the heat and, using a silicone spatula or wooden spoon, stir in the berries, honey, vanilla, and cardamom. Serve immediately with a dollop of Greek-style yogurt and an extra sprinkle of berries on top.

♥ *Make It Easier:* Almond meal is nothing more than almonds ground into the consistency of fine powder, almost like a flour. You can buy almond meal or make your own by throwing almonds into a food processor or high-powered blender. If you make homemade Almond Milk (page 55), you can use the leftover almond pulp instead.

OVEN-COOKED MAPLE-GLAZED BACON

Serves 4

USE THIS FOR:

BACON CHEDDAR WAFFLES, *page 89*

BACON CHICKEN PANZANELLA SALAD, *page 137*

PANZANELLA COBB SALAD, *page 138*

5 UNEXPECTED PIZZA TOPPINGS, *page 194*

MIX-AND-MATCH WITH:

EVERYDAY PANCAKES, *page 84*

EVERYDAY WAFFLES, *page 87*

There's not much to say about this recipe that the title doesn't already cover. I mean, it's crispy, sweet and salty, maple syrup–coated bacon made in the oven to avoid grease splatters. Do I really need to sell this one?

This has become the standard way that I make bacon. It's great alongside pancakes or eggs, or even layered into a sandwich. I use this to make my Bacon Cheddar Waffles when we have people over for brunch or are craving breakfast for dinner. It's also the perfect extra something in my Bacon Chicken Panzanella (page 137) and Panzanella Cobb salads (page 138).

I say that this recipe serves four because it's trouble if I don't limit us to two slices per person. Plus, the recipe calls for thick-cut bacon. If you want to make the servings bigger—a good idea if you're using a thin-cut supermarket brand—double the recipe.

As for the maple syrup, you don't honestly need to bother with a measuring spoon. If you'd rather, just pour some into a bowl and brush as necessary.

8 pieces thick-cut bacon
6 tablespoons pure maple syrup

1. Preheat the oven to 400°F. Line a baking sheet with aluminum foil and, if you have one, place a rack on top. Don't worry if you don't have a rack, though—this will still work.

2. Lay the bacon on the prepared baking sheet and use a spoon or pastry brush to slather both sides in the syrup. This should use about two thirds (4 tablespoons) of the total syrup called for.

3. Place the bacon in the oven and cook until you see that it's beginning to crisp around the edges, about 20 minutes. Remove from the oven, leaving the heat on, and carefully flip the bacon. Baste one more time with the remaining syrup and return to the oven to cook for another 5 to 10 minutes, depending on how crispy you like your bacon.

4. Remove from the oven and allow it to rest for 10 minutes; in this time, the bacon will crisp further. Halfway through the rest time, transfer the bacon to a plate to prevent it from sticking to the cooking surface. Serve immediately.

Note And speaking of thin, supermarket-style bacon, reduce your cooking time if that's what you're using or you'll end up with super-extra-crispy bacon.

EVERYDAY PANCAKES
Serves 4-6

———

USE THIS FOR:
TOTALLY ACCEPTABLE, NO-COOK DINNER IDEAS, *page 145*

———

MIX-AND-MATCH WITH:
QUICK BERRY JAM, *page 55*
STRAWBERRY SAUCE, *page 73*
OVEN-COOKED MAPLE-GLAZED BACON, *page 84*

Every family cook needs a great, go-to pancake recipe. I've tried many while looking for mine, and in the process, have learned a lot about pancakes. For example, for ethereally fluffy cakes, you need to gently fold in egg whites that have been beaten to stiff peaks.

Do you want to do that every weekend? Me, either.

I created this recipe to give you the best bang for your buck—and time. They are great and come together so quickly that you'll wonder why anyone bothers with a recipe that calls for whisking egg whites for ten minutes.

4 tablespoons (½ stick) unsalted butter
1 cup all-purpose flour (see measuring tip, page 217)
1 cup whole wheat pastry flour (or another cup of all-purpose)
¼ cup granulated sugar
2 teaspoons baking powder
1 teaspoon salt
1¼ cups milk
2 large eggs
Neutral oil, such as grapeseed or canola, for cooking

1. In a small saucepan or in the microwave, melt the butter and set aside to cool.

2. In a large bowl, whisk together the flours, sugar, baking powder, and salt; set aside.

3. In a medium-size bowl, whisk together the cooled butter, milk, and eggs.

4. Add the wet ingredients to the dry and, using a silicone spatula or wooden spoon, mix until just combined; it's okay if there are lumps and the batter will be a little thick, which is good.

5. Lightly oil a skillet or griddle and set over medium heat. Once hot, scoop the batter onto the cooking surface, using a ¼-cup measure, leaving about 1½ inches between the pancakes. Cook until bubbles appear across the surface of the pancakes, 30 to 40 seconds. Flip and cook the other side for about 1 minute, until golden brown on both sides. Repeat until all the batter is cooked. Serve immediately or allow to cool completely before packing in a sealed container or bag in the refrigerator for up to 2 days or in the freezer for up to 3 months. For more freezing tips, see the box on page 89.

❤ *Make It Easier:* Here are a few tips about making pancakes:
• The first ones will never come out perfect. It's the way of the world. Live with it.
• The key to an even, golden brown color is a perfectly greased cooking surface. How much oil you need depends on the material of your cooking surface (e.g., stainless steel, cast iron). I keep a bottle of oil and an absorbent paper towel next to the stove. Between each batch, I pour some oil onto the paper towel and carefully wipe down the cooking surface, keeping it clean and evenly greased.
• If you want to keep cooked pancakes warm while you finish cooking the batter, preheat your oven to the lowest temperature (usually 200° or 250°F) before you start cooking. Set an ovenproof plate or cookie sheet in the oven, where you can store pancakes as you move on to the next batch. Keep in mind that, if you stack them on top of each other, they will steam and get soggy.

EVERYDAY WAFFLES

Serves 4-6

USE THIS FOR:
TOTALLY ACCEPTABLE, NO-COOK DINNER
IDEAS, *page 145*

MIX-AND-MATCH WITH:
QUICK BERRY JAM, *page 55*
STRAWBERRY SAUCE, *page 73*
OVEN-COOKED MAPLE-GLAZED BACON,
page 84

Like pancakes, waffles are a delicious weekend treat that are relatively easy to make from scratch. Unlike with pancakes, I prefer waffles that are a little crispy on the outside and doughy on the inside, more like funnel cake than a traditional pancake. Hence the cornstarch in this recipe.

Make a big batch of these so that you only have to pull out the waffle iron once for every two times that you eat them. I make at least a double batch every time, allowing the extra waffles to cool completely on the counter before freezing them in a resealable plastic bag to have on hand for busy weekday mornings. Then, eating waffles is as easy as popping a few into the toaster.

Sensing a pattern here? Make a bunch, freeze the leftovers. Make this your mantra.

Note that the serving size of waffles varies greatly depending on your waffle iron and also on your appetite. This recipe makes 4 cups of batter, which feeds four in my family.

8 tablespoons (1 stick) unsalted butter

1 cup all-purpose flour (see measuring tip, page 217)

1 cup whole wheat pastry flour (or another cup of all-purpose)

½ cup cornstarch

1 tablespoon granulated sugar

2 teaspoons baking powder

1 teaspoon salt

2½ cups milk

2 large eggs, lightly whisked

1½ teaspoon pure vanilla extract

1. In a small saucepan or in the microwave, melt the butter and set aside to cool.

2. In a large bowl, whisk together the flours, cornstarch, sugar, baking powder, and salt; set aside.

3. To the flour mixture, add the cooled butter, milk, eggs, and vanilla and whisk to combine well.

4. Preheat your waffle iron according to the manufacturer's instructions, allowing the batter to sit for 5 or so minutes. When ready, cook the batter according to the manufacturer's instructions. Serve immediately, while the outside is still crispy (keeping in mind that if you stack cooked waffles while you finish cooking the batter, they will steam and get soggy), or allow to cool completely before packing in a sealed container or resealable plastic bag in the refrigerator for up to 2 days or in the freezer for up to 3 months.

BACON CHEDDAR WAFFLES

Serves 4

A variation on my classic waffles, these have a sweet and savory thing going on that I like at brunch. My kids, on the other hand, prefer plain waffles in the morning and request these for breakfast for dinner. If you want to serve these as a savory meal, consider reducing the sugar to ¼ cup to allow the salty bacon and sharp Cheddar flavors to shine.

And speaking of Cheddar, don't bother using mild for this recipe—the flavor will literally melt away. If you want this to feel different than the plain breakfast version, only sharp will do. You don't have to go crazy with an expensive, high-end Cheddar, but you also want to make sure to use something with a strong flavor.

8 tablespoons (1 stick) unsalted butter

1 cup all-purpose flour (see measuring tip, page 217)

1 cup whole wheat pastry flour (or another cup all-purpose)

½ cup cornstarch

1 tablespoon granulated sugar

2 teaspoons baking powder

1 teaspoon salt

Pinch of freshly ground black pepper

2½ cups milk

2 large eggs, lightly whisked

1½ cups shredded sharp Cheddar cheese (6 ounces)

½ cup crumbled, cooked bacon (from 2 to 4 strips cooked bacon, depending on type and whether store-bought or homemade [page 84])

1. In a small saucepan or in the microwave, melt the butter and set aside to cool.

2. In the meantime, in a large bowl, whisk together the flours, cornstarch, sugar, baking powder, salt, and pepper; set aside.

3. To the flour mixture, add the cooled butter, milk and eggs, and whisk to combine well. Add the shredded Cheddar and crumbled bacon and, using a silicone spatula or wooden spoon, stir to distribute evenly.

4. Preheat your waffle iron according to the manufacturer's instructions, allowing the batter to sit for 5 or so minutes. When ready, cook the batter according to the manufacturer's instructions. Serve immediately, while the outside is still crispy (keeping in mind that if you stack cooked waffles while you finish cooking the batter, they will steam and get soggy), or allow to cool completely before packing in a sealed container or resealable plastic bag in the refrigerator for up to 2 days or in the freezer for up to 3 months. For more freezing tips, see the box below.

♥ *Make It Easier:* Freezing home-made pancakes and waffles is one of my favorite busy cook tricks. It makes serving a hot breakfast on a busy weekday morning as easy as using the toaster. Allow pancakes or waffles to cool completely before packing them in a resealable plastic bag or freezer-safe food container. I like to place a small piece of parchment or waxed paper between each one so that they are easy to portion out, even when frozen solid. Pop frozen pancakes or waffles into a toaster or the microwave when you're ready to serve.

CORN, GREEN CHILI, *and* CHEDDAR STRATA

Serves 4-6

MIX-AND-MATCH WITH:
CLASSIC GUACAMOLE, *page 64*
AVOCADO AND HEARTS OF PALM SALAD, *page 129*

This savory bread pudding makes a wonderful make-ahead brunch dish. It's as easily served on a special occasion as it is at a casual Saturday get-together. And did I mention that it's make-ahead?

You can even make a strata for dinner. I do this sometimes when I have crusty bread about to go stale—such as when I buy fancy bread thinking I'll make French toast and then don't (sound familiar?). It takes about an hour to cook, so I prep the strata the night before and pop it into the oven the minute I walk through the door. Dinner's done by the time the boys are done with homework.

This recipe is endlessly adaptable. I've shared my favorite combination of ingredients, but feel free to riff to accommodate your favorites. Asparagus, peas, and pecorino; sausage, peppers, and provolone; bacon, mushroom, and Gruyère—the possibilities are endless. If you stick with this one, serve it with sliced avocados drizzled with my Everyday Vinaigrette (page 124) or an Avocado and Hearts of Palm Salad.

- 3 tablespoons unsalted butter, plus more for baking dish
- 1 cup chopped onion (from about 1 medium-size onion)
- 1 (4-ounce) can minced mild green chiles (½ cup)
- 2 cups fresh or 1 (10-ounce) bag frozen corn kernels
- 9 large eggs
- 3 cups milk
- ¼ teaspoon salt
- Pinch of freshly ground black pepper
- 8 cups cubed French or Italian bread, cut into 1-inch pieces (from about 1 large loaf, though this will vary greatly depending on the size and shape of loaf)
- 2 cups shredded sharp Cheddar cheese (8 ounces)

1. Melt the 3 tablespoons of butter in a medium-size pan set over medium heat. Add the onion and sauté until translucent, about 4 minutes. Add the green chiles and corn and cook for another 2 minutes. Remove from the heat and set aside.

2. In a large bowl, whisk together the eggs, milk, salt, and pepper; set aside.

3. Butter a 3-quart baking dish. Spread half of the cubed bread in the dish and top with half of the corn mixture and half of the cheese. Repeat with remaining bread, corn mixture, and cheese, pressing down to fit into the dish.

4. Pour the egg mixture over the bread and cover. Refrigerate overnight or for at least 8 hours.

5. When ready to cook, preheat the oven to 350°F. Meanwhile, remove the strata from the refrigerator and allow it to sit at room temperature for 20 minutes. Bake until the egg is set, 45 to 50 minutes. Allow the cooked strata to stand for 10 minutes to firm up before serving.

CHORIZO MIGAS

Serves 4

MIX-AND-MATCH WITH:
FLOUR TORTILLAS, *page 44*
CORN TORTILLAS, *page 45*
CHIPOTLE LIME CREAM, *page 57*
FIRE-ROASTED SALSA, *page 62*
GUACAMOLE: CLASSIC, TROPICAL OR
SMOKY, *pages 64 and 65*
QUICK PICKLED RED ONION, *page 70*
AVOCADO AND HEARTS OF PALM SALAD,
page 129
EASY "REFRIED" BEANS, *page 205*

Migas is a Tex-Mex staple that I first enjoyed in Austin, Texas. The Spanish translation is "crumbs," which is fitting, given that this is made with crispy pieces of shredded tortillas.

Although very easy to make, migas typically calls for chopped onion, tomato, and sometimes peppers. Since chopping is the last thing that I want to do in the morning—especially on weekends—I skip the veggies. Instead, I add chorizo. Because, well, can you think of a better swap? It's my favorite breakfast sausage and there's no better way to crisp tortillas than in sausage fat.

Migas is not just for breakfast; when I make it for dinner, I bother with the onions, peppers, and tomatoes. Measurements don't need to be exact: half an onion, one red bell pepper, and one seeded tomato should do the trick. Serve this with Guacamole, sliced avocados drizzled with my Everyday Vinaigrette (page 124), or an Avocado and Hearts of Palm Salad and you've got a vegetable-packed dinner in no time.

2 flour or corn tortillas, store-bought or homemade (one-quarter of either recipe, page 44 or 45)

3 to 4 links fresh chorizo

Neutral oil, such as grapeseed or canola, if necessary

3 tablespoons unsalted butter

8 large eggs, whisked

¾ cup shredded sharp Cheddar or Monterey Jack cheese

Chopped fresh cilantro, for serving (optional)

1. Using a sharp knife or kitchen shears, cut the tortillas into ½ x 2-inch strips and set aside. Remove the sausage meat from the casings and place in a pan set over medium heat. Sauté, breaking up the meat with the back of a silicone spatula or wooden spoon, until cooked through, about 5 minutes. Using a slotted spoon, transfer the sausage to a plate, leaving the rendered fat in the pan.

2. Leave the pan over medium heat and add the tortilla strips. Stir to coat in the oil and toast until crispy, tossing every few minutes, for a total of 5 to 7 minutes. Depending on how much fat you were able to render from the sausage, you may need to add a touch of oil, 1 teaspoon at a time,

Note An important note about chorizo: the fresh Mexican chorizo called for in this recipe comes raw in links, like the way you might get Italian sausage. It's different than the dried Spanish chorizo that can sit on your shelf until you're ready to eat it. Be sure to pick up the right kind and also get a mild version if you're feeding anyone who isn't into spicy food—sometimes chorizo is made hot.

to keep the tortillas from burning. Using the slotted spoon, transfer the crispy tortilla strips to a plate.

3. Wipe out the pan. If there are a lot of burned bits, you may want to carefully run a little water into it and wipe it out more thoroughly so that your eggs don't taste burnt. Melt the butter in the wiped-out pan set over medium heat. Add the eggs and cook until they are three quarters of the way to how you like your scrambled eggs set. At that point, add the reserved sausage, tortilla strips, and cheese. Finish scrambling the eggs to your desired texture and serve immediately with cilantro sprinkled over the top, if using.

Snacks

Snacking makes good sense when it's healthy fuel for an active person—kids *and* adults. Sadly, though, given the amazing quantity of snack products available at the supermarket, it's hard to find ones that fit the bill.

Snacks make up a huge part of a kid's diet, and with good reason: average, healthy children burn an amazing quantity of calories, even in a school day when they are sitting much of the time. That said, pumping them full of snacks with not much more than sugar and fat can be a recipe for disaster (for kids—and for the grown-ups).

That said, given how my family flies through snacks, it's hard to feed them exclusively homemade. I've found that a combination of snacks made from scratch and carefully selected store-bought snacks (see the Supermarket Guide, page 249) is the best way to find balance between health, budget, and my sanity.

When I go homemade, it helps to make snacks that either prep super quick or that I can whip up in a big batch ahead of time to have on hand or store in the freezer. The recipes in this chapter are divided that way, too, so that you can either whip up something in just minutes or plan ahead and stock up every other week or so.

No time for homemade? Check out my list of easy snack ideas that don't need a recipe (page 94) for quick ideas on how to throw together healthy store-bought items or pair them with simple, fresh homemade ingredients for a quick and easy snack time that you can feel good about. And maybe even share.

10 *Healthy* SNACK IDEAS YOU CAN *Make Easy* WITHOUT A RECIPE

1. A nut/seed, cheese, and fruit plate Since they can be pricey, I buy nuts and seeds in bulk, especially when they are on sale. Storing them in the freezer helps keep them from going rancid. I also keep a variety of cheeses on hand at all times and, though I typically prefer to avoid processed cheese, my fridge does always have string cheese and a bag of Babybel for convenience.

2. Smashed banana and graham cracker sandwiches This treat is particularly yummy if you freeze the sandwiches for 20 to 30 minutes before serving. I like mashing the banana with cinnamon, too, for a little extra flavor.

3. Pitted dates stuffed with cinnamon cream cheese If you've never tried dates, now's the time. The supersweet bites are hard to resist, especially stuffed with cream cheese that's been mixed with a touch of cinnamon. Dates can be pricey. If you find that to be the case, try this snack with more affordable pitted prunes instead.

4. Trail mix I use the term *trail mix* loosely to describe any combination of nuts, seeds, and fruit pieces that I find on sale and/or in the bulk bin and mix at home myself. Place your mix in a jar and you've got a grab-and-go snack for a week or two. See page 96 for tips on the easiest DIY trail mixes.

5. Chocolate-dipped fruit Easiest. Chocolate Dip. Ever: melt chocolate chips in the microwave and serve with a side of fruit, such as sliced banana or apple. Fussy fruit-free kids? The relatively small amount of chocolate helps the fruit go down without a fuss and doesn't add all that much sugar in the scheme of things. If you want to get fancy—without much extra effort—cut the fruit and place it in the freezer for a few minutes while you make Homemade Chocolate Shell (page 225). When you dip the cold fruit in the chocolate dip, it will harden. You can even do this ahead: dip a bunch of pieces of semifrozen fruit in the chocolate at once and store them in the freezer for when the kids come home from school—or you need a little pick-me-up.

6. Peanut butter banana bites Cut a banana into quarters and slice each quarter in half lengthwise. Spread Peanut Butter or Sunflower Seed Butter (pages 53 and 52) between the halves to make banana "sandwiches."

7. Hard-boiled eggs If your crew likes hard-boiled eggs (page 32), don't save them just for breakfast or lunch. They make a great, healthy snack, too. We like them with nothing more than salt and pepper, but you can also dab a little mayo on top or sprinkle with your favorite dried herb or spice. We like dill and even toasted sesame seeds.

8. Yogurt parfait I love when you can make something simple look and sound fancy with nothing more than some thoughtful presentation and a good name. This is a perfect example. Layer plain yogurt—I like to use protein-rich Greek-style—with maple syrup, honey, Strawberry Sauce (page 73), or Quick Berry Jam (page 53), sliced fresh fruit, and something crunchy, such as Sweet and Salty Granola Cereal (page 78). Suddenly you have a nutritious snack that everyone will love. Make it in a little mason jar or another glass cup for a pretty presentation.

9. Ham and cheese roll-ups Lean ham and cheese combine for a healthy hit of protein and you don't have to bother with a whole sandwich. Instead, layer a slice of ham on top of a slice of cheese and roll them up. Or, even easier, roll a slice of ham around a cheese stick. It goes down quick and gets the job done, especially with a side of pretzels or Tortilla Chips (page 47).

10. Caprese Skewers I'm sure there are folks out there who don't like fresh mozzarella, none of them live in my house. Unless you've got

one in your crew—or maybe you have a more common tomato-hater—Caprese skewers make a great savory snack that doubles as a party appetizer, too. When you make this for yourself or the kids, just throw a couple of cubes or mini balls of fresh mozzarella onto a toothpick with a couple of halved cherry tomatoes. If you're making these for a party, fold over small leaves of basil and skewer those, too, for a nice presentation. A sprinkle of crunchy sea salt is great on top, as well.

Make It Easy: DIY TRAIL MIX

Keeping trail mix easy means throwing everything in bag or jar in whatever combination you like. If it helps to have a rule of thumb, I try to make my trail mix 50 percent nuts and seeds, 30 percent dried or freeze-dried fruit (freeze-dried has much less sugar; a combination is nice, too), and 20 percent miscellaneous, including sesame sticks, sweet chips of various kinds, cereal, and so on. Here are some things that you can easily mix into a DIY trail mix:

- Dried fruit

- Freeze-dried fruit

- Banana chips

- Nuts and seeds

- Cereal bits, such as O's

- Sweet and Salty Granola Cereal (page 78)

- Toasted coconut chips

- Chocolate, white chocolate, or peanut butter chips (mini chips are perfect)

- Mini pretzels

- Popcorn (though keep in mind that it goes stale fast compared to other trail mix ingredients)

- Sesame sticks

- Dried chickpea snacks

- Dried edamame

- Rice crackers

———

♥ *Make It Tastier: 4 trail mix flavor ideas*

TROPICAL
Dried pineapple; freeze-fried mango; a touch of candied ginger; coconut and/or banana chips; macadamia nuts or, if they are too expensive, almonds and/or cashews; white chocolate chips.

SWEET AND SALTY
Sweet and Salty Granola Cereal (page 78); salted pistachios; sesame sticks; dried cherries; chocolate chips.

CARNIVAL MIX
Peanuts; pecans; popcorn; pretzels; banana chips; peanut butter and chocolate chips.

JAPANESE MIX
Plain or tamari almonds; sesame sticks; dried edamame; rice crackers.

ROASTED TOMATO HUMMUS

Makes 2 cups hummus

———

USE THIS FOR:

10 TOTALLY ACCEPTABLE NO-COOK DINNER IDEAS, *page 145*

———

MIX-AND-MATCH WITH:

TORTILLA CHIPS, *page 47*

PITA CHIPS, *page 48*

ROASTED CHERRY TOMATOES, *page 67*

Hummus is a favorite snack in my house, but since it's also a favorite lunch and dinner ingredient—in other words, since we use it all the time, in all different ways—I put the recipe for plain hummus in the Supermarket Staples section (page 50). This recipe, on the other hand, is something that you'll make from time to time to vary things up. When you do, it's a perfect snack with nothing more than pita chips. It's also a great addition to any party spread.

2 cups roasted cherry tomatoes (page 67; twice the recipe as written)

Olive oil, as necessary

1 (15-ounce can) chickpeas, drained and rinsed

2 tablespoons freshly squeezed lemon juice (from about 1 juicy lemon)

1 teaspoon roughly chopped garlic (from about 1 clove)

Salt, to taste

¼ cup grated Parmesan cheese (optional)

1. Using a slotted spoon, place the roasted cherry tomatoes in the bowl of a food processor. Pour the leftover oil and juices into a measuring cup and top with as much fresh olive oil as needed to reach ¾ cup; set aside.

2. Add the chickpeas, lemon juice, and garlic to the tomatoes in the food processor and whiz on high speed for 10 to 20 seconds.

3. Stop the food processor, scrape down the sides, and turn the food processor on again, this time adding the oil in a slow, steady stream. Keep the machine running until the hummus is smooth and creamy or reaches your desired consistency. Taste and season with salt and/or Parmesan cheese, if desired; pulse two or three more times to blend in well. Transfer the hummus to a bowl and serve immediately or store in a sealed container in the refrigerator for 5 to 7 days.

HEARTS OF PALM DIP

Makes 1 cup dip

MIX-AND-MATCH WITH:
TORTILLA CHIPS, *page 47*
PITA CHIPS, *page 48*

It's hard to beat a tasty spread that comes together this quickly and easily in your food processor. This dip was introduced to me by our beloved Nanny (one of my kids' four grand-mas!), who often includes it in the snack spread she puts out for us whenever we visit. But this is so much more than a party dip (the *easiest* party dip, to be exact); when my little one tried it and loved it, I realized that, like hummus, this makes a great everyday snack, too.

If you've never had hearts of palm, they are the edible inner part of the stem of a cabbage palm tree. They are easy to get in a can or jar at most supermarkets and taste quite a bit like canned artichokes. They usually cost the same, too.

This dip is made almost exactly like hummus, but yields a lighter, tangier dip that's super refreshing. I especially love it in the summer months. I'm not kidding about this being the easiest party dip in the world—guests ask for the recipe every time I make it.

- 1 (14-ounce) can or jar hearts of palm, roughly cut into 1- to 2-inch pieces if not already precut
- 2 tablespoons freshly squeezed lemon juice, (from about 1 juicy lemon)
- 1 teaspoon roughly chopped garlic (from about 1 clove)
- ⅛ teaspoon salt, plus more to taste
- ¼ cup plus 2 tablespoons olive oil

1. Place the hearts of palm, lemon juice, garlic, and salt in the bowl of a food processor and whiz on high speed for 10 to 20 seconds.

2. Stop the food processor, scrape down the sides, and turn on again, this time adding the oil in a slow, steady stream. Keep the machine running until the dip is smooth and creamy. Taste and season with more salt, if desired; pulse two to three times to blend in well. Transfer the dip to a bowl and serve immediately or store in a sealed container in the refrigerator for 5 to 7 days.

HUMMINGBIRD MUFFINS

Makes 16 to 18 muffins

MIX-AND-MATCH WITH:
HARD-BOILED EGGS, *page 32*
GET UP AND GO SMOOTHIE, *page 77*

I am a sucker for tropical flavors. There's something about the bright pop of pineapple, creamy taste of coconut, and warm flavor of bananas that energizes me no matter what time of day. Even though it's more southern than Caribbean, hummingbird cake has all of these flavors mingled with spices and pecans—and I love it.

Since these muffins aren't particularly low in sugar (though, for the record, they're also not particularly high in it, either), I keep the portion on the smaller side, which makes the yield more like a dozen and a half than a proper dozen. If you want oversize muffins, fill the muffin well up all the way and you'll end up with about twelve muffins.

Though I've put these in the snack section, you can easily pair one of these muffins with a perfectly hard-boiled egg or Get Up and Go Smoothie for a superquick, healthy breakfast. Allow leftovers to cool completely before placing them in a resealable plastic bag for up to three months in the freezer.

8 tablespoons (1 stick) unsalted butter

Neutral oil, such as grapeseed or canola, for pan (optional)

1 cup all-purpose flour (see measuring tip, page 217)

1 cup whole wheat pastry flour (or another cup of all-purpose)

½ cup granulated sugar

½ cup unsweetened shredded coconut

1 tablespoon baking powder

2 teaspoons ground cinnamon

1 teaspoon salt

½ teaspoon freshly ground nutmeg, or ¼ teaspoon ground

2 large eggs, ideally at room temperature

½ cup packed light brown sugar

2 teaspoons pure vanilla extract

2 ripe bananas

1 cup canned crushed pineapple, drained (but not pressed dry)

1 cup chopped pecans

1. Preheat the oven to 350°F. In a small saucepan or in the microwave, melt the butter and set aside to cool. Line a 12-well muffin tin with paper or silicone cups or lightly grease with oil.

2. In a medium-size bowl, whisk together the flours, granulated sugar, coconut, baking powder, cinnamon, salt, and nutmeg.

3. In a separate medium-size bowl, whisk together the cooled, melted butter, eggs, brown sugar, and vanilla. Add the wet ingredients to the dry and, using a silicone spatula or wooden spoon, mix until just combined.

4. Cut the bananas into ½-inch pieces and slightly mash each piece with a fork. Stir the banana pieces, pineapple, and pecans into the batter until well combined.

5. Divide the batter evenly among the prepared muffin wells and bake for 20 to 23 minutes, or until a toothpick inserted into the middle of a muffin comes out clean. Remove from the oven and allow the muffins to cool in the pan for 3 to 5 minutes before transferring them to a wire rack or the counter to finish cooling completely. Store any muffins not served the same day in a sealed container at room temperature for up to 2 days or in the freezer for up to 3 months.

BAKED CORN DOG BITES

Makes 2 dozen mini muffin-size bites

Snack time doesn't always have to be a time for sweets—it can also be a time for sweet and salty! These corn dog bites are the best of both worlds with slightly sweetened corn muffins stuffed with a small piece of salty hot dog, which, by the way, give this snack a little protein boost, too.

I make a big batch of these at once and keep the rest in my freezer for when I need them. I also pack them for school lunch sometimes, which the kids love. Nothing beats a little taste of the summer country fair in the middle of a long school day.

Neutral oil, such as grapeseed or canola, for pan
1 cup cornmeal
½ cup all-purpose flour (see measuring tip, page 217)
¼ cup granulated sugar
1 teaspoon baking powder
Pinch of salt
2 large eggs, ideally at room temperature
½ cup milk
2 tablespoons plain yogurt, regular or Greek-style
4 hot dogs, patted dry, each cut into 6 pieces

1. Preheat the oven to 350°F. Lightly oil a 24-well mini muffin tin and set aside. In a medium-size bowl, whisk together the cornmeal, flour, sugar, baking powder, and salt.

2. Make a well in the center of the dry ingredients and add the eggs, milk, and yogurt. Whisk to combine well; the batter should have a consistency similar to that of pancake batter.

3. Ladle just enough batter to cover the bottom of each well of the prepared tin. Drop a piece of hot dog into each well and then cover with more batter, filling the well three quarters of the way (½ tablespoon should do the trick). Bake for 15 minutes. Allow to cool in the pan for 5 minutes before carefully transferring the mini muffins to a wire rack or the counter to finish cooling. Serve warm or at room temperature, or allow to cool completely before storing in a sealed container or resealable plastic bag in the refrigerator for up to 3 days or in the freezer for up to 3 months.

GRANOLA BARS, 2 WAYS

MIX-AND-MATCH WITH:
GET UP AND GO SMOOTHIE, *page 77*

Hands down, my number one grab-and-go snack, for both me and the kids, is granola bars. Filling, easy to take on the go, and nutritious, they make an ideal snack (the catch is that it's not that easy to find ones that are not packed with sugar).

I know that it's hard to motivate to make homemade granola bars when there are so many tasty store-bought options. In fact, I rely on a combination of homemade and store-bought (check out the Supermarket Guide, page 249, for brands to look out for). But as much as I need to have a few boxes from the market in my pantry at all times, I also need homemade bars in my life. My kids feel the same way. These are way tastier than anything in a package, which makes them seem like a treat, and they'll make you look like parent of the year when you bring them in as a classroom snack.

I share two versions here because I couldn't decide which one should be included. One recipe is my older son's favorite: they are big, thick, and flavored with protein-rich peanut butter. The other is my younger son's favorite: they are thinner, chewier, and made without peanut butter (he doesn't like the stuff, well, except when it comes to peanut butter cups!). Both are delicious and endlessly adaptable. You can throw in chocolate chips, banana chips, different or more dried fruit—you get the picture. You can also turn these into anywhere from eight to twelve servings, depending on how you cut them up.

GRANOLA BARS
Makes one 8-inch square pan granola bars

1½ cups old-fashioned rolled oats
¾ cup sliced almonds, skin on or off
¼ cup chopped raw pecans
¼ cup unsweetened shredded coconut
¼ cup unsweetened dried cranberries
½ teaspoon salt
½ teaspoon ground cinnamon
¼ cup plus 2 tablespoons light brown sugar
¼ cup pure maple syrup
3 tablespoons unsalted butter
1 teaspoon vanilla extract
1 egg white, whisked (from 1 large egg)
Maldon sea salt, to sprinkle (optional)

1. Preheat the oven to 325°F. Line an 8-inch square baking pan with parchment paper and set aside. In a medium-size bowl, stir together the oats, almonds, pecans, coconut, cranberries, salt, and cinnamon; set aside.

2. Place the brown sugar, syrup, butter, vanilla, and 1 tablespoon of water in a medium-size saucepan set over medium heat. Cook until the sugar dissolves and the butter just melts, about 3 minutes, whisking all the while.

3. Add the wet ingredients to the dry and, using a silicone spatula or wooden spoon, stir until well combined.

4. Touch to make sure that the mixture isn't hot and, once that's the case, stir in the egg white. Place the oat mixture in the prepared pan and press down to spread it evenly across the bottom of the baking dish. (The mixture is sticky, so you may want to use a piece of parchment paper to do this.) If you want a sweet and salty snack, lightly sprinkle the top of the granola bars with crunchy Maldon salt. Bake until golden brown around the edges, 35 to 40 minutes. Allow to cool for at least 1 hour before cutting into serving-size pieces. Serve immediately or store in a sealed container at room temperature for up to 10 days or in the freezer for up to 3 months.

EXTRA-THICK PEANUT BUTTER GRANOLA BARS

Makes one 8-inch square pan granola bars

2 cups old-fashioned rolled oats

1 cup sliced almonds, skin on or off

½ cup raw or salted, roasted pepitas or sunflower seeds

½ teaspoon salt

½ teaspoon ground cinnamon

⅓ cup smooth peanut butter or sunflower seed butter, store-bought or homemade (pages 52 and 53)

¼ cup pure maple syrup

¼ cup light brown sugar

2 tablespoons unsalted butter

1 teaspoon vanilla extract

1 egg white, whisked (from 1 large egg)

1. Preheat the oven to 325°F. Line an 8-inch square baking pan with parchment paper and set aside. In a medium-size bowl, stir together the oats, almonds, pepitas, salt, and cinnamon; set aside.

2. Place the peanut butter, maple syrup, brown sugar, butter, vanilla, and 1 tablespoon of water in a medium-size saucepan set over medium heat. Cook until the sugar dissolves and the butter just melts, about 3 minutes, whisking all the while.

3. Add the wet ingredients to the dry and, using a silicone spatula or wooden spoon, stir until well combined.

4. Touch to make sure that the mixture isn't hot and, once that's the case, stir in the egg white. Place the oat mixture in the prepared pan and press down to spread it evenly across the bottom of the baking dish. (The mixture is sticky, so you may want to use a piece of parchment paper to do this.) Bake until golden brown around the edges, 35 minutes. Allow to cool for at least 1 hour before cutting into serving-size pieces. Serve immediately or store in a sealed container at room temperature for up to 10 days or in the freezer for up to 3 months.

ONE-BOWL HONEY GRAHAM CRACKERS

Makes one dozen 3-inch-square crackers

USE THIS FOR:

SMASHED BANANA; HEALTHY SNACK IDEAS YOU CAN MAKE WITHOUT A RECIPE, *page 94*

MIX-AND-MATCH WITH:

PEANUT BUTTER DIP, *page 109*

A childhood classic, graham crackers are what snack time memories are made of. Slightly sweetened with honey and, if you ask me, only done right with a touch of cinnamon, this snack—something between a cracker and a cookie—goes with anything from chocolate and marshmallow to mashed bananas (see my healthy recipe-free snack ideas, page 94). Does it get any better than that?

The graham cracker market is dominated by brands that still use artificial flavor, and though good natural options exist, they can be harder to find and more expensive. Combined with the fact that homemade is easy and cozy, I prefer to whip up a batch every so often. Because, really, that's what graham crackers are all about—cozy, homey snack times at home.

In every recipe that calls for whole wheat pastry flour, I note that you can substitute all-purpose, except for this one. Graham crackers made without graham or some form of whole wheat flour are just not graham crackers. The good news is that if you buy whole wheat pastry flour for this recipe, it's interchangeable with all-purpose and can easily be used up, especially with recipes from this book.

3 tablespoons unsalted butter

¾ cup all-purpose flour (see measuring tip, page 217)

¾ cup whole wheat pastry flour

⅓ cup granulated sugar

¼ cup dark or light brown sugar (preferably dark)

2 teaspoons baking powder

¾ teaspoon salt

½ teaspoon ground cinnamon

4 tablespoons milk

1 tablespoon honey

1. In a small saucepan or in the microwave, melt the butter and set aside to cool.

2. In a large bowl, whisk together the flours, granulated sugar, brown sugar, baking powder, and salt, and cinnamon.

3. To the dry ingredients, add the cooled butter, milk, and honey. Mix, using a silicone spatula or wooden spoon, until combined. The mixture will be crumbly; when you can't stir any longer, ditch the spoon and use your hands to knead the dough into a ball—this may take a minute or two and requires a lot of pressing and molding. Place the bowl with the ball of dough in the refrigerator for 30 minutes. If you plan to leave it in the refrigerator longer or you'd like to freeze the dough, wrap it in plastic wrap first.

4. Take the dough out of the refrigerator 30 minutes before you're ready to bake and preheat the oven to 350°F. Place a piece of parchment paper on a work surface and place the dough on top. Once the dough has warmed up enough so that you can roll it out, press down, shaping the ball into a flattened rectangle. Place another piece of parchment paper on top of the dough and roll into a 12 x 9-inch rectangle that's about

⅛ inch thick. The dough will still be a little crumbly (too much moisture and the crackers won't crisp!), but just press it back together and keep rolling.

5. Remove the top piece of parchment paper and discard. Use a sharp knife or a pizza cutter to cut the dough into twelve 3-inch-square crackers. Using a spatula, separate the crackers so that there is a little bit of space between each one. Lastly, use a fork to poke holes in each cracker and transfer the parchment paper with its crackers to a baking sheet. Place in the oven and bake until fragrant and just golden brown around the edges, about 17 minutes. Remove from the oven and allow to cool on the baking sheet for 5 minutes before transferring the crackers to a wire rack to finish cooling completely. These can be served immediately or stored in a sealed container or resealable plastic bag on the counter for up to 1 week.

FRUITY FROZEN YOGURT

Makes 2 cups yogurt

MIX-AND-MATCH WITH:
QUICK BERRY JAM, *page 53*
STRAWBERRY SAUCE, *page 73*
SAUTÉED BANANAS, *page 215*
MAPLE CINNAMON WHIPPED CREAM, *page 216*

Some kitchen magic never ceases to amaze me: making this fruity frozen yogurt is a great example. It's just so cool that a simple whizz of the food processor can give you a sweet, frozen treat that tastes as good—even better,

if you ask me—as any you'll find in the super-market. And, spoon for spoon, this costs less, too.

Follow this recipe as a basic template, but feel free to improvise. My crew isn't into super sweet, so there's a modest amount of honey. Even if you add quite a bit more, you're still likely to use less sweetener than what you'll find in packaged frozen yogurt. Just keep in mind that this is meant to be a quick, throw-it-together-now snack, as opposed to a big batch of make-ahead frozen yogurt. This simply doesn't keep as well as the kind you take time to churn.

Experiment by combining different fruits and/or adding herbs, zest, and spices. Banana mango yogurt? Or maybe minty strawberry or basil peach? Get creative or keep it simple—it's up to you. I personally like to keep it simple and douse my scoop with fresh Strawberry Sauce.

♥ *Make It Easier:* This is best served as soon as you make it. You can transfer the frozen yogurt to an airtight container and store in the freezer for up to 1 month, though like many frozen treats with high water content, this will get hard and icy. If eating this from the freezer, be sure to take it out at least 10 minutes ahead of time to allow the yogurt to soften, and be aware that it never quite gets as soft and creamy as when you first make this.

2 cups favorite frozen fruit (berries, peaches, banana, pineapple, and mango all do nicely)

½ cup plain Greek-style yogurt

2 tablespoons honey, plus more to taste

¼ teaspoon pure vanilla extract (optional)

1 tablespoon water, milk of choice, or juice, plus more as needed

1. Place all the ingredients in the bowl of a food processor and blend until smooth and the consistency of soft-serve. For some fruits, especially ones that are frozen whole, such as strawberries, you may need to stop the food processor and scrape down the sides frequently at first. Once the pieces get small, the food processor will whiz more easily. If you want to help things along, you can add 1 tablespoon of water, milk, or juice, plus more as necessary.

PEANUT BUTTER DIP
Makes 1 cup dip

MIX-AND-MATCH WITH:
SUNFLOWER SEED BUTTER, *page 52*
PEANUT BUTTER, *page 53*
ONE-BOWL HONEY GRAHAM CRACKERS,
page 106

Dipping is always a win. I'd like to say that this is true only with kids but, let's be honest, we all love a good dip. If your kids, like mine, expect something sweeter than savory at snack time, try apple slices or graham crackers paired with this sweet peanut butter dip.

Given how simple the recipe is, you might be surprised to know that I've played with it quite a bit. For a long time, I made this using cream cheese, but recently switched to using Greek-style yogurt. We all like the consistency better and I like that it adds even more protein, which is a good way to fuel up at snack time.

Oh, and if you're looking for motivation, this recipe is another great reason to make homemade nut or seed butter.

¾ cup plain Greek-style yogurt

¼ cup peanut butter, store-bought or homemade (page 53)

2 tablespoons plus 1 teaspoon honey, plus more to taste

¼ teaspoon salt

¼ teaspoon ground cinnamon (optional)

¼ teaspoon pure vanilla extract (optional, but highly recommended!)

1. Place all the ingredients in a bowl and whisk until smooth. Serve or store in a sealed container in the refrigerator for up to 7 days.

PINEAPPLE "ORANGE JULIUS"

Makes 2½ cups smoothie (serves 2-4)

———

MIX-AND-MATCH WITH:
ALMOND MILK, *page 55*

I grew up in New Jersey, the land of malls and, in those malls, was a magical place: Orange Julius. If you don't know the Orange Julius chain, all you need to know is that it made a deliciously frothy orange drink that tasted like a Creamsicle. I think that's all it sold; it's all I ever wanted.

I don't know when Orange Julius went away, but it has stayed with me all these years later and I couldn't imagine putting out a cookbook without trying to re-create this delight from my youth.

As I remember it, every Orange Julius had one of those big, industrial orange juice press machines. I'd watch through the Plexiglas front as fresh oranges rolled through the machine and were squeezed of their juice. Is it possible that their recipe called for fresh juice? It seems unlikely, especially since my early trials of this recipe using fresh OJ were so underwhelming, but maybe they had some magic mojo I don't know about (added Tang?). Either way, when making this at home, orange juice concentrate is the way to go.

It's pretty easy to find frozen orange juice concentrate without chemicals, but it's definitely higher in sugar. I guess that gets concentrated, too, so you may want to keep that in mind when deciding when to serve this.

6 ounces frozen orange juice concentrate

1 cup milk of choice

½ cup fresh pineapple chunks, cut into ½-inch pieces

1 teaspoon pure vanilla extract

1 cup ice cubes

1. Place all the ingredients in a high-powered blender and puree until smooth. Serve immediately.

FRUIT *with* CITRUS SUGAR, 5 WAYS

C alling this a recipe is almost a cheat, it's so easy. I couldn't skip it, though, since it's one of my go-to snacks.

Now, I know what you're thinking: add sugar to fruit? Not always but, yes, sometimes, why not? In most parts of the country, mine included, fruit is not great all year-round and a little bit of sugar can make the difference between eating fruit and not eating fruit. In the summer, when fruit is at peak season, citrus sugar is a treat that turns fruit into a dessert—as in, an extra serving goes down.

No matter how you think about it, the truth is that you don't need to add much sugar for this to work well. Just a touch gives extra flavor and, when needed, sweetness, too.

I make ¼ to ½ cup of sugar each time, depending on the season, and keep it sealed in my refrigerator, where it will stay good for one to one and a half weeks. You can make more or less, depending on how you use it: don't worry too much about exact measurements.

You can also use this sugar in any simple cookie recipe, to jazz it up!

¼ cup granulated sugar

½ teaspoon citrus zest from a lemon, lime, orange, or grapefruit

1. Place the sugar and citrus zest in a small bowl and, using your fingers, mix to combine well. The zest will clump at first, but keep working the sugar until the zest distributes evenly. Serve immediately or store in a sealed container in the refrigerator for 1 to 1½ weeks.

♥ *Make It Tastier: Awesome fruit + citrus sugar flavor combos*

1. Watermelon (or honeydew) with lime sugar

2. Mango with lime sugar

3. Blueberries with lemon sugar

4. Pineapple with orange sugar

5. Blackberries with grapefruit sugar (the blackberries need to be sweet for this combination to work)

Soups and Salads

Before I had kids, I thought that soup was boring. It struck me as a lot of work (I was wrong) for something that I wouldn't want to eat for dinner, at least not by itself. Before I had kids, I also single-handedly cooked elaborate dinner party meals and made Thai curry pastes with a mortar and pestle. Life changes, and so do our tastes.

As it turns out, soup can be incredibly fast and easy to make. If you keep homemade Chicken Broth or Vegetable Broth (page 39 and 40) on hand, it's incredibly tasty, too. Not that soup made with store-bought isn't tasty: buy the right kind (see the Supermarket Guide, page 245–246) and you'll be in great shape.

One vestige of my old thinking about soup is that I tend to only make really hearty soups that I'm sure will satisfy as a meal with nothing more than a salad and loaf of Garlic Bread (page 211). Even though soup doesn't take hours to make the way I used to think, I still want my efforts to serve as dinner.

I have a similar philosophy about salads, too. They either need to come together lightning fast as a side or to be packed with enough goodness to serve as the main part of a meal. Anything in between just takes up too much time.

Finding the right place for and approach to soups and salads are not the only reasons they have taken a more prominent place in my cooking since having kids. I also love that they give me great creative freedom to find new ways to serve vegetables to my crew.

Many people shy away from serving their kids soups and salads thinking that they are too vegetable forward—too obviously healthy for little eaters. In fact, their endlessly adaptable nature is what makes soups and salads the ideal dishes for experimenting with veggies for kids. Take salads, for example. You can serve them with or without leaves (it's usually the leaves that turn off young eaters); toss them with dressing or put dressing on the side; add nuts, fruit, seeds, or meat; present them on a platter with veggies carefully laid out; or toss them in a bowl with everything all mixed up.

Think about what ingredients your kid is open to—even if it's just one, lonely vegetable and, oh, bacon—and how your child likes his food presented. Is he an everything-separate kind of kid? Lay out the ingredients for my Bacon Chicken Panzanella Salad (page 137) like a salad bar and let him figure out what he wants to try without pressure. Keep doing this and I bet you'll eventually see a tomato or cucumber go down.

Soup is a little different, and perhaps more appealing to those of you who prefer to serve your crew vegetables quietly. You can pack a soup full of veggies either in chunks, pureed, or in combination, as in my Vegetarian Tortilla Soup (page 116). You can also easily add kid-friendly ingredients and garnishes that make soup more appealing—and deconstructable—to entice picky eaters. Asian-Style Chicken Soup (page 119), for example, is loaded with rice noodles, soba noodles, or angel hair pasta—whichever is easy, affordable, and most appealing. This makes it feel like more familiar chicken noodle soup, making it a great way to ease the introduction of a new cuisine. And even with all that, the best part about soup is how easy it is to make a double batch! One quick cook and you can end up with a meal for several nights.

VEGETARIAN TORTILLA SOUP

Serves 6-8

Hearty, with a little bit of spice, and topped with fried tortilla strips, tortilla soup is as satisfying as a soup gets. While I've always considered chicken—and, more to the point, a deep, rich, homemade chicken broth—to be its soul, this version is mouthwateringly good and vegetarian. Vegan, even, if you skip the grated cheese garnish. It turns out that, like so much great Mexican food, this soup is not about chicken stock but, rather, a genius blend of simple ingredients.

Instead of relying only on sautéed onions, garlic, and chili powder as the flavor base, I fortify it with sweet potato. It adds an earthy depth of flavor that lends a richness similar to that of chicken broth. I blend most of the sweet potato into the soup, which gives it a slightly thicker texture than traditional tortilla soup, but also sprinkle sautéed sweet potato and black beans over the top of every bowl, similar to the way you add shredded chicken meat to the traditional version. If you want to make this even easier, skip the sweet potato–black bean garnish and go straight for the fixings.

I like serving this with shredded Cheddar or Jack cheese, diced avocados (a must!), and a dollop of sour cream. Hot sauce, too, for those who can handle it. And, of course, fried strips of store-bought or homemade corn tortillas (page 45). Alternatively, you can use crushed up store-bought or homemade tortilla chips.

- 4 teaspoons neutral oil, such as grapeseed or canola
- 1 cup chopped onion (from about 1 medium-size onion)
- 4 teaspoons chopped garlic (from about 4 cloves)
- 2 cups chopped sweet potato, cut into ½-inch dice (from 1 large sweet potato)
- 1 (15-ounce) can black beans, drained and rinsed
- Salt, to taste
- 1½ teaspoons dried oregano
- 1 teaspoon ground cumin
- Pinch to scant ¼ teaspoon ground chipotle chile powder, to taste (optional)
- 4 cups vegetable broth, store-bought or homemade (page 40)
- 1 (15-ounce) can tomato sauce
- 1 tablespoon canned chopped mild green chiles

Optional Garnishes

- Fried strips of Corn Tortillas (page 45) or crushed Tortilla Chips, page 47
- Shredded Cheddar or Jack cheese
- Sour cream
- Diced avocado
- Fresh cilantro
- Lime wedges

1. To make the sweet potato–black bean garnish: heat 2 teaspoons of the oil in a large pot set over medium heat. Add ½ cup of the chopped onion and 1 teaspoon of the chopped garlic; sauté until just translucent, 2 to 3 minutes. Add 1 cup of the chopped potatoes; stir to coat them with the oil and cook for 1 minute. Add ½ cup of water, cover, and cook until the sweet potatoes are just tender all the way through and most of the water has cooked off, 5 to 8 minutes. (Be careful not to overcook the potatoes, or they'll get mushy.) Add the black beans and salt to taste. Stir to combine and cook for 1 to 2 minutes to bring the flavors together. Remove the sweet potato–black bean garnish from the pot and set aside. Wipe out the pot and return it to medium heat.

2. Heat the remaining 2 teaspoons of oil. Add the remaining ½ cup of onion and 3 teaspoons of garlic; sauté until translucent, 2 to 3 minutes. Add the remaining cup of sweet potato and the oregano, cumin, and as much chipotle powder as you like, if using, keeping in mind that even a scant ¼ teaspoon makes this quite spicy (when I make this with my kids in mind, I add just a small pinch). Stir to coat and cook for 2 minutes to bring the flavors together.

3. Add the broth, tomato sauce, and green chiles. Raise the heat to medium-high, bring to a boil, then lower the heat to medium, or wherever you can get it to a steady simmer, cover, and cook for 15 minutes, or until the sweet potatoes are very tender. (If you're going to fry fresh tortilla strips, now's a good time.)

4. Remove the pot from the heat and, using a hand blender, puree the soup. You can also do this with a traditional standing blender, which is best for getting a supersilky texture, though you may have to work in batches. Serve immediately topped with sweet potato–black bean garnish and any other garnishes of choice. Otherwise, allow to cool completely before storing in a sealed container in the refrigerator for up to 5 days and freezer for up to 3 months.

ASIAN-STYLE CHICKEN SOUP

Serves 6–8

MIX-AND-MATCH WITH:
SMALL-BATCH CHICKEN BROTH, *page 39*
AVOCADO AND EDAMAME SALAD, *page 128*

I find that most people have a classic chicken soup recipe that they love already. And, if not, it's pretty easy to wing it.

This not-so-classic version is just as easy and a lot more exciting, if you ask me. My family agrees. If your kids are open to Asian flavors, give this a go—they might just agree, too. And even if they don't love it better than regular chicken soup, if they like it at all, this recipe helps make serving something a little more adventurous really easy.

Also, as much as I hate to bring up cold and flu season, this gingery broth is a great meal for someone on the mend.

2 chicken breasts (you can substitute shredded leftover rotisserie chicken or, if you have it, chicken left over from when you made homemade chicken broth, page 39)

1 (16-ounce) package thin rice noodles, soba noodles, or angel hair pasta

8 cups chicken broth, store-bought or homemade (page 39)

¼ cup soy sauce

¼ cup sliced fresh ginger, smashed with the backside of a small knife or spoon

½ to 1 teaspoon sriracha or similar hot sauce, to taste

1 red bell pepper, seeded and cut into ¼-inch strips

¼ cup chopped fresh cilantro

2 tablespoons chopped fresh basil or Thai basil (optional)

2 tablespoons chopped fresh scallion (optional)

2 tablespoons freshly squeezed lime juice (from about 1 juicy lime)

Lime wedges, for serving (optional)

1. If not using already cooked rotisserie or leftover chicken, poach the chicken breasts: lay them in a single layer on the bottom of a pot and cover with cold water until it comes about 1 inch above the chicken. Bring to a boil over medium-high heat before lowering the heat to medium, covering, and simmering for about 10 minutes. Check to make sure the meat is cooked through before removing from the heat. Cool, shred, and set aside, discarding the cooking liquid.

2. In the meantime, cook the rice or soba noodles according to the package directions. If substituting angel hair pasta, see the directions on page 28 for how to cook pasta perfectly. Set aside.

3. Place the broth, soy sauce, ginger, and sriracha in a large pot set over medium-high heat. Bring to a boil, lower the heat to medium, and allow to simmer hard for 5 minutes.

4. Remove the soup from the heat and, using a slotted spoon, remove the ginger (or, at least, most pieces). Add the shredded chicken, noodles, red pepper, cilantro, basil, scallion, and lime juice, if using. Let the soup sit for 5 minutes to allow the flavors to mingle and peppers to soften. Serve immediately with lime wedges on the side or allow to cool completely before storing in a sealed container in the refrigerator for up to 5 days or freezer for up to 3 months.

LENTIL SOUP
with SAUSAGE
Serves 6-8

MIX-AND-MATCH WITH:

SMALL-BATCH CHICKEN BROTH, *page 39*

SMALL-BATCH VEGETABLE BROTH, *page 40*

COUNTRY-STYLE GREEK SALAD, *page 132*

SHAVED ASPARAGUS AND FENNEL SALAD, *page 135*

ROASTED CAULIFLOWER WITH GARLIC TOASTED BREAD CRUMBS, *page 197*

12-MINUTE SALT AND PEPPER GREEN BEANS, *page 199*

QUICKEST SAUTÉED SPINACH, *page 199*

ROASTED SQUASH WITH GINGER SHALLOT BROWNED BUTTER, *page 200*

GIARDINIERA ROASTED VEGETABLES, *page 202*

PARMESAN ROASTED BROCCOLI, *page 204*

COLD ORZO SALAD, *page 210*

GARLIC BREAD, *page 211*

CHEESY GARLIC BREAD, *page 213*

My grandmother used to make lentil soup all of the time. It was a staple in her house, which has made lentils a go-to soup ingredient for me. This is a pretty classic version, but I add sausage to make this soup a hearty, one-pot meal. If you are vegetarian, you can certainly skip it and follow the rest of the recipe as written. Either way, serve this with a salad and Garlic Bread for a warming dinner.

¼ cup olive oil

4 sprigs fresh thyme

1 cup chopped celery, cut into ¼-inch dice (from about 3 stalks)

1 cup chopped carrot, cut into ¼-inch dice (from about 3 carrots)

3 teaspoons chopped garlic (from about 3 cloves)

1 pound sweet or hot Italian sausage meat, casings removed

6 cups chicken or vegetable broth, store-bought or homemade (pages 39 and 40)

1 cup dried brown lentils, rinsed and sorted

2 bay leaves

Salt, to taste

Freshly ground black pepper, to taste

1 tablespoon red wine vinegar, to finish

1. Heat the olive oil in a large pot set over medium heat. Pull the thyme leaves off the stalks and add to the pot along with chopped celery and carrot; sauté until the celery is translucent, about 3 minutes. Add the garlic and cook until fragrant, another minute or so. Add the sausage meat and brown, breaking up the pieces with the back of a silicone spatula or wooden spoon.

2. Add the broth, lentils, and bay leaves. Bring to a boil, lower the heat to medium-low, and cover. Cook until the soup thickens slightly and the lentils are cooked through, 20 to 30 minutes. Remove from the heat and season with salt and pepper to taste and the vinegar. Serve immediately or allow to cool completely before storing in a sealed container in the refrigerator for up to 5 days or freezer for up to 3 months.

CURRIED CAULIFLOWER *and* RED LENTIL SOUP

Serves 6-8

MIX-AND-MATCH WITH:
KEBABS (SEE NOTE ABOUT MARINADE),
page 34
SMALL-BATCH CHICKEN BROTH, *page 39*
SMALL-BATCH VEGETABLE BROTH, *page 40*
CHICKEN CURRY, *page 150*
RICE AND LENTIL PILAF, *page 206*

Yes, more lentils! I love how versatile and nutrient-rich they are, plus they fill you up. This time, I swap out brown lentils for red to give this soup an ethnic vibe. With a mild curry flavor and texture similar to Indian dal soup, this recipe makes it easy for you to introduce international flavors that your crew might not otherwise be open to.

If you can find some in your freezer section, serve this with naan, an Indian flatbread served warm with butter slathered on top. (Tell me there's a better way to build interest in a new cuisine.) Otherwise, pita bread is a good choice. As with all soups, I also think that this goes well with a salad—even just greens dressed in my Everyday Vinaigrette (page 124)—and simple grilled chicken.

If you want to make a full-on Indian meal, serve this with Chicken Curry or follow my directions for making kebabs and marinate the chicken in plain yogurt whisked with oil, minced garlic, grated fresh ginger, salt, ground cumin, and either garam masala or curry powder. No need for a dipping sauce since you'll be serving soup.

2 tablespoons neutral oil, such as grapeseed or canola

1 cup chopped onion (from about 1 medium-size onion)

3 teaspoons chopped garlic (from about 3 cloves)

3 teaspoons curry powder

1 small head cauliflower, cut into florets

1 cup dried red lentils, rinsed and sorted

4 cups chicken or vegetable broth, store-bought or homemade (pages 39 and 40)

1 cup canned coconut milk

Salt, to taste

1. Heat the oil in a large pot set over medium heat. Add the onion and garlic and sauté until soft and translucent, about 3 minutes. Add the curry powder and toast for 1 minute, stirring all the while to keep the powder from burning. Add the cauliflower and lentils; stir to coat well.

2. Add the broth, stirring to incorporate all the vegetables and spice. Raise the heat to medium-high, bring to a boil, then lower the heat to medium, or wherever you can get it to a steady simmer, and cook uncovered until cauliflower is very tender, about 15 minutes.

3. Remove the pot from the heat and, using a hand blender, puree the soup. You can also do this with a traditional stand blender, though you may have to work in batches. Once the soup is fully pureed, return it to the pot and set over medium heat.

4. Stir in the coconut milk and keep the soup at barely a simmer for another 5 minutes, allowing the flavors to come together. Season with salt to taste. Serve immediately or allow to cool completely before storing in a sealed container in the refrigerator for up to 5 days or freezer for up to 3 months.

VEGETABLE CHICKPEA SOUP *with* GARLIC TOASTED BREAD CRUMBS

Serves 6-8

MIX-AND-MATCH WITH:

If you tend to find vegetable soup pretty boring this one might surprise you: it's simple, tasty, hearty, and wholesome and gets an unexpected burst of flavor from the bread crumbs, which are not to be missed. They really make this dish and are the best way that I've found to keep vegetable soup interesting.

This recipe takes more prep than most of the others in this book, but once you're done with that, the rest happens nearly on its own. And,

really, when it comes to vegetable soup, there's no way around some prep work. I try to keep this to a minimum by using squash or sweet potatoes, which are both filling and easily found precut at the market. You'll have to cut them even smaller, but most of the prep will be done for you. I also use greens, which give this soup a good nutritional boost without much more chopping. Instead, the salad spinner (page 19) does the hard part.

Make a big batch of this and keep some in your freezer for when you need a fast cold-weather meal or you are nursing someone who's under the weather.

2 tablespoons olive oil, plus more to finish

2 cups chopped butternut squash or sweet potatoes, cut into ½-inch pieces (from ½ medium-size squash, ½ [20-ounce] package precut squash, or a large sweet potato)

1 cup chopped onion, cut into ¼-inch dice (from about 1 medium-size onion)

1 cup chopped celery, cut into ¼-inch dice (from about 3 stalks)

1 cup chopped carrot, cut into ¼-inch dice (from about 3 carrots)

1 (1-pound) bunch of kale or chard, trimmed and chopped

1 tablespoon minced garlic (from about 3 cloves)

1½ teaspoons salt

½ teaspoon freshly ground black pepper

6 cups chicken or vegetable broth, store-bought or homemade (pages 39 and 40)

1 (28-ounce) can diced tomatoes, drained of their juice

1 (15-ounce) can chickpeas, drained and rinsed

¼ cup chopped fresh flat-leaf parsley

½ teaspoon lemon zest (from about ½ lemon)

1 cup Garlic Toasted Bread Crumbs (page 72), for garnish (optional, but highly recommended)

1. Heat the oil in a large, deep pot set over medium heat. Add the chopped squash, onion, celery, and carrot. Cook until the vegetables are glossy and the onion is softened, about 5 minutes. Add the kale, garlic, salt, and pepper; stir to coat and cook until the greens wilt, about 3 minutes. Stir in the broth, tomatoes, and chickpeas.

2. Raise the heat to medium-high and bring to a boil. Lower the heat to medium, or wherever you can get it to a steady simmer, and cook for 30 minutes to bring the flavors together. (If you haven't made the Garlic Toasted Bread Crumbs ahead of time, now is a good time to do so.)

3. Remove the soup from the heat and, if you are making this ahead of time, allow to cool completely before storing in a sealed container in the refrigerator for up to 5 days or freezer for up to 3 months. Otherwise, stir in the parsley and lemon zest. Taste and adjust the salt and pepper. Serve immediately, topped with Garlic Toasted Bread Crumbs, if using, and a final drizzle of good olive oil.

When serving soup that has been made ahead, warm it up all the way through before adding the parsley, zest, bread crumbs, and a final glug of olive oil.

EVERYDAY VINAIGRETTE

Makes scant 1 cup vinaigrette

MIX-AND-MATCH WITH:

AVOCADO AND HEARTS OF PALM SALAD, *page 129*

BEET AND ORANGE SALAD, *page 129*

COUNTRY-STYLE GREEK SALAD, *page 132*

SHAVED ASPARAGUS AND FENNEL SALAD, *page 135*

BACON CHICKEN PANZANELLA, *page 137*

PANZANELLA COBB, *page 138*

GREEK PANZANELLA, *page 138*

COLD ORZO SALAD, *page 210*

This is as easy as vinaigrette gets. Okay, you can make it even easier by leaving out the mustard, but I'm guessing you have some around and it makes a difference. (If you don't have some around, that's okay, too.)

The trick, if you have time, is to allow the shallots or garlic to sit in vinegar for a few minutes to macerate; this will mellow them out and keep your dressing from tasting sharp. Using good olive oil is also important: the better tasting it is, the better tasting your dressing is. I like to keep a small bottle of really delicious olive oil on hand for dressings and finishing dishes and cook with a big bottle of less expensive, all-purpose extra-virgin olive oil.

2 teaspoons minced shallot, or 1 teaspoon minced garlic (from about 1 clove) (optional, but highly recommended)

¼ cup white wine or Champagne vinegar

1 tablespoon freshly squeezed lemon juice (from about ½ juicy lemon)

½ cup olive oil

1 teaspoon Dijon or grainy mustard

½ teaspoon honey

¼ teaspoon salt, plus more to taste

Freshly ground black pepper, to taste

1. If you have time, place the shallot or garlic in a jar, top with the vinegar and lemon juice, and allow to sit 5 to 10 minutes. If you don't have time, combine the garlic or shallots, vinegar, and lemon juice in a jar and skip to step 2.

2. Add the oil, mustard, honey, and salt to the vinegar mixture. Seal the jar and shake until the dressing emulsifies. Season with pepper and more salt to taste, if desired. Use immediately or store in a sealed container in the refrigerator for up to 1 week.

♥ *Make It Easier* To measure honey smoothly, pour a small amount of oil into your measuring spoon, swirl, and discard it. Now pour in the honey, which will slip right off the spoon.

GINGER LIME VINAIGRETTE

Makes scant 1 cup vinaigrette

MIX-AND-MATCH WITH:
ASIAN STEAK SALAD, *page 141*
GREEK-STYLE KEBABS, (AS AN ALTERNATIVE MARINADE), *page 162*
AVOCADO AND EDAMAME SALAD, *page 128*
COLD SOBA NOODLE SALAD, *page 179*

I make this slightly tweaked version of my Everyday Vinaigrette for any salad paired with an Asian-inspired meal, which, in my house, is almost always an Avocado and Edamame Salad. It also makes a great marinade (think: salmon or chicken kebabs) and dressing for Cold Soba Noodle Salad, which is one of my kids' favorite make-ahead meals.

1 teaspoon minced garlic (from about 1 clove)

¼ cup rice vinegar

1 teaspoon lime zest (from about 1 lime)

1 tablespoon plus 1 teaspoon freshly squeezed lime juice (from about 1 lime)

½ cup neutral oil, such as grapeseed or canola

1 tablespoon reduced-sodium soy sauce

1½ teaspoons minced fresh ginger

1 teaspoon Dijon mustard

¾ teaspoon honey

1. If you have time, place the garlic in a jar, top with the vinegar, lime zest, and lime juice, and allow to sit for 5 to 10 minutes. If you don't have time, combine the garlic, vinegar, lime zest, and lime juice in a jar and skip to step 2.

2. Add the oil, soy sauce, ginger, mustard, and honey to the vinegar mixture. Seal the jar and shake until the dressing emulsifies. Use immediately or store in a sealed container in the refrigerator for up to 1 week.

AVOCADO MISO DRESSING

Makes about 1 cup dressing

MIX-AND-MATCH WITH:
SESAME-CRUSTED SALMON, *page 172*
COLD SOBA NOODLE SALAD, *page 179*

I often whip this up when my avocados are on the verge of going bad and use it on nights when all I can muster is hot dogs and a quick salad. There's something comforting about the fact that I'm coating a simple salad of lettuce, tomatoes, cucumber, and carrots with a dressing made with nutrient-rich miso and avocado. It makes me feel like I've done right by my crew even though I couldn't spare more than fifteen minutes on dinner.

I admit that this is not the most affordable salad dressing. Avocado can be pricey, depending on where you live, and miso can also be expensive. The good news is that miso is fermented, so it will stay good in your refrigerator for a very, very long time—like a good year or two past the use by date. And, if you're at a loss for how else to use it: warm a big pot of Chicken Broth or Vegetable Broth (pages 39 and 40), scoop some into a little bowl, whisk in miso paste, and add the miso mixture to the big pot. Suddenly, you have a comforting miso soup that you can eat plain, with cubed tofu, or even a batch of soba noodles. You can also use some to make a batch of Ginger Hoisin Sauce (page 59).

½ cup cubed avocado (about ½ large, ripe, pitted avocado)
½ small shallot, roughly chopped
2 tablespoons white wine vinegar
1 tablespoon freshly squeezed lime juice or lemon juice (from about ½ juicy lime or lemon)
2 teaspoons honey
1½ teaspoons soy sauce
½ cup extra-virgin olive oil
Salt, to taste

1. Combine the avocado, shallot, vinegar, lime juice, honey, and soy sauce in a blender and mix until combined.

2. With the blender running on medium speed, add the olive oil in a slow, steady stream until the dressing is smooth. You may have to stop once to scrape down the sides, ensuring that the shallots get completely blended. Once smooth, add enough water, up to 4 tablespoons, to achieve your desired consistency. Season with salt to taste. Use immediately or store in a sealed container in the refrigerator for up to 1 week.

BUTTERMILK DILL (OR RANCH!) DRESSING

Makes about 1 cup dressing

MIX-AND-MATCH WITH:
KEBABS, *page 34*
BEET AND ORANGE SALAD, *page 129*
COUNTRY-STYLE GREEK SALAD, *page 132*
GREEK PANZANELLA, *page 138*
GREEK-STYLE KEBABS (AS AN ALTERNATIVE MARINADE), *page 162*
COLD ORZO SALAD, *page 210*

I don't often have buttermilk around because it tends to come in containers with way more than a single recipe needs. But sometimes it's a necessity, such as for my Deep Chocolate Layer Cake (page 225). Then, I make this dressing with the leftover.

I like this dressing with just dill alone, but when I'm making BBQ chicken legs, for example, I turn it into ranch dressing by adding chives and parsley either in addition to or instead of the dill—it works either way.

You can use the dill version of this dressing for salads or to marinate chicken kebabs that will go great with a Country-Style Greek Salad. Both versions are great on cold pasta salad that makes any cookout more delicious.

½ cup buttermilk, store-bought or home-made (see Make It Easier)

¼ cup mayonnaise

¼ cup chopped fresh chives (optional; to turn this into Ranch)

2 tablespoons sour cream

2 tablespoons white or white wine vinegar

2 tablespoons chopped fresh dill (include this in the Ranch version or not; up to you)

2 tablespoons chopped fresh flat-leaf parsley (optional; to turn this into Ranch)

1 teaspoon Dijon mustard

¼ teaspoon salt

½ teaspoon Worcestershire sauce

Pinch of garlic powder

Freshly ground black pepper, to taste

1. Place all the ingredients in a jar, including black pepper to taste, seal, and shake to emulsify (make sure the honey has dissolved; you may need to shake a little longer than usual). Use immediately or store in a sealed container in the refrigerator for up to 1 week.

♥ Make It Easier: A great swap or make your own buttermilk

If you happen buy plain kefir, a good-for-you fermented dairy drink that's a lot like drinkable yogurt, use that in place of buttermilk (it might sound crazy, but totally works).

If you can't find use for a whole container of buttermilk, make your own as necessary. All it takes is 1 tablespoon of white vinegar or freshly squeezed lemon juice for every cup of cow's milk (2% or whole). Add the vinegar or juice to the milk, stir two or three times to distribute, and let stand for 10 minutes. Then, voilà, buttermilk.

AVOCADO SALAD, 2 WAYS

Avocado is the one vegetable everyone in my family eats happily, even my kids. Maybe it's because avocado is technically a fruit! Even so, I feel lucky to have a house full of fans, given how delicious and nutritious avocados are and that you can get them nearly year-round in most places. The only downside is their high cost. All I can say is that they pay off in my house: I get a lot of bang for my buck in the form of easy nutrition.

When I have to move crazy fast, I just slice an avocado, drizzle it with olive oil or my Everyday Vinaigrette (page 124), and sprinkle with salt (the good, flaky kind). That's all it takes. When I have an extra five minutes, I make one of these salads.

Between a simple avocado platter and these two salads—one that's great with anything Asian, the other with Mexican flavors—I always have a five- to ten-minute healthy side ready to go with nearly any meal. This is truly how you make it easy.

AVOCADO AND EDAMAME SALAD
Serves 4

MIX-AND-MATCH WITH:
KEBABS, *page 34*
ASIAN-STYLE CHICKEN SOUP, *page 119*
GINGER LIME VINAIGRETTE, *page 125*
THAI CHICKEN BURGERS WITH QUICK-PICKLED CARROTS, *page 147*
MISO AND SWEET CHILI GLAZED PORK LOIN, *page 164*
SLOW COOKER HOISIN PULLED PORK, *page 166*
HOISIN-GLAZED SALMON, *page 172*
SESAME-CRUSTED SALMON, *page 172*

1 to 1½ tablespoons sesame seeds, to taste

3 large, ripe avocados, peeled, pitted, and cubed into 1½-inch pieces

2 cups edamame, cooked and cooled slightly (1 [10-ounce] bag frozen)

4 tablespoons Ginger Lime Vinaigrette (page 125; one-quarter of the recipe as written), plus more to taste

Salt, to taste

1. If using raw sesame seeds, toast them first: place the seeds in an ungreased pan set over medium-high heat and cook for about 3 minutes, shaking occasionally for the first 2 minutes and constantly for the last minute, until the seeds are

golden brown and smell like popcorn. Remove from the heat and leave in the hot pan for another 30 seconds before using.

2. Place the avocado, edamame, and cooled sesame seeds in a bowl and gently toss with the dressing. Season with additional dressing and salt to taste, if desired. Serve immediately.

AVOCADO AND HEARTS OF PALM SALAD

Serves 4

MIX-AND-MATCH WITH:
VEGETARIAN TORTILLA SOUP, *page 116*
EVERYDAY VINAIGRETTE, *page 124*
CHILI-RUBBED STEAK TACOS, *page 160*
SLOW COOKER CARNITAS, *page 165*
SLOW COOKER BBQ PULLED PORK, *page 167*
BBQ SALMON, *page 173*
FISH TACOS, *page 175*
VEGETABLE FAJITAS, *page 180*
BEAN AND CHEESE ENCHILADAS, *page 182*
EASY REFRIED BEANS, *page 205*

3 large, ripe avocados, peeled, pitted, and cubed into 1½-inch pieces

1 (14-ounce) can or jar hearts of palm, drained and roughly cut into 1- to 2-inch pieces (if not precut)

4 tablespoons Everyday Vinaigrette (page 124; one-quarter of the recipe as written), plus more to taste

Salt, to taste

1. Place the avocado and hearts of palm in a bowl and gently toss with the dressing. Season with additional dressing and salt to taste, if desired. Serve immediately.

BEET AND ORANGE SALAD

Serves 4

MIX-AND-MATCH WITH:
KEBABS, *page 34*
LENTIL SOUP WITH SAUSAGE, *page 120*
VEGETABLE CHICKPEA SOUP WITH GARLIC TOASTED BREAD CRUMBS, *page 122*
EVERYDAY VINAIGRETTE, *page 124*
NO-FUSS PAN-ROASTED PAPRIKA CHICKEN, *page 146*
CHICKEN CUTLETS WITH ARUGULA AND PARMESAN, *page 151*
CHICKEN CUTLETS WITH QUICK AVOCADO-TOMATO RELISH, *page 154*
EASY ITALIAN TURKEY MEATBALLS, *page 156*
STEAK WITH SWEET-AND-SOUR PEPPERS, *page 159*
BEEF AND LENTIL SLOPPY JOES, *page 161*
SESAME-CRUSTED SALMON, *page 172*
BBQ SALMON, *page 173*
LEMONY OREGANO SHRIMP, *page 174*
FISH TACOS, *page 174*
VEGETABLE FAJITAS, *page 180*
PASTA WITH MUSHROOM AND LENTIL "BOLOGNESE" SAUCE, *pages 28 and 185*
BUTTERED PASTA WITH RICOTTA AND PEAS, *page 186*
PASTA WITH SPINACH PESTO AND GREEN BEANS, *page 188*
ZITI WITH CORN AND ROASTED TOMATOES, *page 190*
CLASSIC MARGHERITA PIZZA, *page 192*

Beets seem to have a bad rep, but roasted correctly—as I do it for this recipe—they are sweeter than earthy and very kid-friendly. Grown-up–friendly, too, if you ask me.

I often roast a big batch, peel them, and store them in the refrigerator for up to five days. Sometimes I'll make this salad; other times I'll simply drizzle slices with my Everyday Vinaigrette (page 124) or even just olive oil and flaky salt. Even if you do something different with them, keeping beets on hand is an easy way to have a vegetable ready to go the minute you walk in the door.

This is a very versatile salad that goes with nearly every main in this book, from the pizzas and pastas to Beef and Lentil Sloppy Joes (page 161). Its best matches are on the previous page.

5 to 6 medium-size to large beets, trimmed and rinsed

2 oranges

Salt, to taste

4 tablespoons Everyday Vinaigrette (page 124; one-quarter of the recipe as written), plus more to taste

Chopped fresh flat-leaf parsley, for garnish (optional)

Chopped shelled, salted pistachios, for garnish (optional)

1. Up to 5 days ahead of time, cook the beets: preheat the oven to 400°F. Pierce the beets all around with a fork and place them in an oven-safe dish that's the right size for them to fit snugly. Roast until fork-tender all the way through, 60 to 90 minutes (the exact cooking time depends on their size). Remove the cooked beets from the oven and allow them to cool completely before using a paring knife to peel them. If making them ahead, store the peeled beets whole, either wrapped individually in aluminum foil or tucked into a sealed container, in the refrigerator.

2. When ready to prepare the salad, slice beets into ½-inch-thick slices. Peel the oranges and cut crosswise into ½-inch-thick slices, removing any visible seeds. Arrange the beet and orange slices on a serving plate, sprinkle with salt, and drizzle with the dressing. Top with the parsley and pistachios, if using. Serve immediately.

COUNTRY-STYLE GREEK SALAD

Serves 4-6

MIX-AND-MATCH WITH:

SWEET-AND-SOUR PEPPERS, *page 68*

QUICK PICKLED RED ONIONS, *page 70*

LENTIL SOUP WITH SAUSAGE, *page 120*

VEGETABLE CHICKPEA SOUP WITH GARLIC
TOASTED BREAD CRUMBS, *page 122*

NO-FUSS PAN-ROASTED PAPRIKA
CHICKEN, *page 146*

STEAK WITH SWEET-AND-SOUR PEPPERS,
page 159

BEEF AND LENTIL SLOPPY JOES, *page 161*

GREEK-STYLE KEBABS, *page 162*

SESAME-CRUSTED SALMON, *page 172*

LEMONY OREGANO SHRIMP, *page 174*

There's no way a Greek girl like me can write a cookbook about simple home cooking without including a Greek salad. This is a classic dish, even in the United States, thanks to how simple and delicious it is. And thanks to feta cheese, too. (By the way, if you don't dig goat cheese, don't be afraid of feta. While some is made with goat's milk, the traditional sheep's milk version can easily be found in most supermarkets.)

You've probably had a Greek salad without lettuce before, but if you haven't, make no mistake: the omission is on purpose. In Greece, the traditional tomato–cucumber–feta cheese salad is made without leafy greens, which makes this very easy to whip up and even easier to serve.

If you want to skip the raw red onion, you can add Quick Pickled Red Onion (page 70), which is completely untraditional and totally delicious.

I also add chickpeas for extra protein and pita chips for crunch and kid appeal.

¼ cup olive oil

1 tablespoon freshly squeezed lemon juice (from about ½ juicy lemon)

1½ teaspoons red wine vinegar

¼ teaspoon salt

Freshly ground black pepper

2 cups halved cherry tomatoes (about 2 pints)

2 cups chopped cucumber, cut into ½" pieces

1 (15-ounce) can chickpeas, drained and rinsed

½ to ¾ cup crumbled feta, to taste

¼ cup thinly sliced red onion (from about ¼ small onion)

¼ cup chopped, pitted Kalamata olives

Chopped fresh flat-leaf parsley, for garnish (optional)

Crumbled pita chips, for garnish (optional)

1. Place the olive oil, lemon juice, vinegar, salt, and black pepper to taste in a jar with a lid. Seal and shake until the dressing emulsifies and set aside.

2. Place the tomatoes, cucumber, chickpeas, feta, onion, and olives in a large serving bowl. Give the dressing a few quick shakes and pour over the salad. Toss to coat well and garnish with the parsley and pita chips, if using. Serve immediately.

MANGO SLAW

Serves 4 as a side salad,
8 as a fixing for tacos

MIX-AND-MATCH WITH:

KEBABS, *page 34*

INDIAN-STYLE MEATBALLS, *page 157*

CHILI-RUBBED STEAK TACOS, *page 160*

BEEF AND LENTIL SLOPPY JOES, *page 161*
(better matched with the non-mango version)

SLOW COOKER CARNITAS, *page 165*

SLOW COOKER BBQ PULLED PORK, *page 167*
(better matched with the non-mango version)

BBQ SALMON, *page 173*
(better matched with the non-mango version)

FISH TACOS, *page 175*

VEGETABLE FAJITAS, *page 180*

BEAN AND CHEESE ENCHILADAS, *page 182*

I've never been a big fan of traditional coleslaw, but this version with lime juice and mango speaks to me. Fish Tacos are my favorite thing to serve with this slaw—sometimes I pile it on top of the fish, while other times I serve it on the side. It's also good with burgers, BBQ chicken and, strangely, even on top of hot dogs, which makes a fun, everyone-loves-it summer dinner. This can easily be your go-to cookout slaw.

If you ever feel that you want to get more green veggies into your meals, grab a bag of broccoli slaw and use it in this recipe instead of cabbage. It tastes just as great and—broccoli! Another way that you can change up this slaw is to omit the mango for more traditional uses. That's how I make this when I serve it on top of Beef and Lentil Sloppy Joes.

¼ cup plain, Greek-style yogurt

¼ cup freshly squeezed lime juice (from about 2 juicy limes)

2 tablespoons sour cream or mayonnaise

½ teaspoon honey

¼ teaspoon salt, plus more to taste

4 cups shredded purple cabbage (from about ½ small head)

2 cups thinly sliced mango (from about 2 large mangoes)

¼ cup chopped fresh cilantro (optional, but recommended)

1. Place the yogurt, lime juice, sour cream, honey, and salt in a jar with a lid. Seal and shake until the dressing emulsifies and set aside.

2. Place the cabbage, mango, and cilantro, if using, in a serving bowl. Shake the dressing a few times and toss with the vegetables. Serve immediately or store, covered, in the refrigerator for up to 3 hours. Keep in mind that the cabbage will soften if you dress this ahead.

SHAVED ASPARAGUS AND FENNEL SALAD

Serves 4

This salad is spring perfection, though you can make it anytime you can find good asparagus and fennel in the market. It's easiest to make this with a mandoline (see page 17). In fact, unless you have killer knife skills, you might want to invest in one for this. Part of what makes this very simple combination of ingredients work so well is that the veggies are cut into deliciously paper-thin slices.

When I have my Everyday Vinaigrette ready to go, I'll use that, but this salad is best with an even simpler dressing that you can make on the spot (recipe follows). It's also great tossed with cubed fontina cheese. In the fall, when apples are abundant in my neck of the woods, I also add thinly shaved apple.

> 2 tablespoons olive oil
>
> 1 tablespoon white wine or Champagne vinegar
>
> 1 tablespoon freshly squeezed lemon juice (from about ½ juicy lemon)
>
> Salt
>
> 1 bunch of fresh asparagus (about 12 stalks), washed but not trimmed
>
> 2 small to 1 medium-size bulb fresh fennel
>
> ½ medium-size to large red onion

1. Place the olive oil, vinegar, lemon juice, and salt in a jar with a lid. Seal and shake until dressing emulsifies and set aside.

2. Holding the back end of an asparagus spear, run a vegetable peeler from just above your fingers to the tip, moving away from your body. Keep doing this, rotating the spear as necessary, until the entire thing has been shaved into very thin slices. Repeat with remaining spears, placing the thinly shaved slices in a serving bowl.

3. Trim the bottom and outer leaves of the fennel. Cut the bulb in half through the root and use a mandoline to shave thinly, or place each half on a cutting board, cut side down, and use a knife to cut very thin slices. Add the thinly shaved fennel to the shaved asparagus.

4. Use a mandoline to shave the red onion very thinly, or place on a cutting board, cut side down, and use a knife to cut very thin slices. Add the thinly shaved onion to the other shaved vegetables.

5. Give the dressing a few shakes and pour over the vegetables. Sprinkle with salt to taste and toss well. Serve immediately.

PANZANELLA SALAD, 3 WAYS

MIX-AND-MATCH WITH:

KEBABS (VEGGIE ONLY OR SKIP THE CHICKEN IN THE SALAD), *page 34*

EVERYDAY VINAIGRETTE, *page 124*

NO-FUSS PAN-ROASTED PAPRIKA CHICKEN (SKIP THE CHICKEN IN THE SALAD), *page 146*

EASY ITALIAN TURKEY MEATBALLS (SKIP THE CHICKEN IN THE SALAD), *page 156*

STEAK WITH SWEET-AND-SOUR PEPPERS (SKIP THE CHICKEN IN THE SALAD), *page 159*

SESAME-CRUSTED SALMON (USE IN PLACE OF CHICKEN), *page 172*

P anzanella is a popular Tuscan salad made with chunks of stale bread and tomatoes. Although the bread remains crunchy, it soaks up the vinegary dressing in that perfect way that you try to achieve when you drag a piece of crusty bread along the bottom of your salad bowl. Imagine: a whole salad of that goodness.

With such easy fundamentals—tomato, bread, and vinaigrette—and satisfying flavor, it's hard not to riff off the traditional recipe. There are endless ways to vary panzanella, and why not when the result is a light, but totally satisfying meal?

All three of these versions call for chicken to make this a one-bowl meal that's especially perfect in the summer months or whenever you're craving a light, refreshing dinner. You can easily adapt any of these to be made without meat or with just a touch of bacon if you prefer to serve this as a side salad. Just keep in mind that it's filling, with plenty of bread; when you serve this, take it easy on yourself and skip a carb side, since this serves as both your carb and veggie.

BACON CHICKEN PANZANELLA
Serves 4

3 tablespoons olive oil

4 cups cubed French or Italian bread, cut into 1-inch pieces (from about ½ large loaf, though this will vary greatly depending on exact size)

⅛ teaspoon salt, plus more to taste

Freshly ground black pepper, to taste

1 clove garlic, thinly sliced

1 pound chicken tenders or breast cut into strips

4 medium-size tomatoes, seeded and cut into wedges

2 cups sliced cucumber (from about 1 large English cucumber)

½ cup thinly sliced red onion (from about ½ small onion)

4 fresh basil leaves, cut into chiffonade (see Make It Easier)

4 strips cooked bacon, such as Maple-Glazed Bacon (page 84; one-half of the recipe as written), crumbled to bits

½ to ¾ cup Everyday Vinaigrette (page 124)

1. Toast the bread: heat 2 tablespoons of the oil in a large skillet set over medium-high heat. Add the bread in a single layer and sprinkle with the ⅛ teaspoon of salt and black pepper to taste. Toast until dark golden brown all around, 8 to 10 minutes, tossing every 2 minutes or so. Transfer the toasted bread to a plate and set aside.

2. Cook chicken: carefully wipe out the hot pan and return it to stove, this time over medium

♥ *Make It Easier: How to chiffonade*

As you've figured out by now, I'm not one for thinking that busy home cooks need to be schooled in proper culinary technique. There are a few useful technical approaches, though, that help you get a better result. And by better, I don't mean proper, but more flavorful.

Cutting an herb, such as basil, into chiffonade produces long, very thin strips (it means "ribbons" in French) that allow you distribute the flavor of the herb throughout without anyone getting stuck with a big, leafy piece. It's an easy thing to do:

Stack the basil leaves (or any leaves, such as sage or even spinach), one on top of the other, and roll them tightly into a log. Using a sharp knife, slice the leaves perpendicular to the roll. That's it. Or, you know, just tear the herb into pieces instead!

heat. Add the remaining tablespoon of oil and garlic. Season the chicken on both sides with salt and black pepper and, once the oil and garlic are fragrant, 30 to 60 seconds, add chicken and cook, untouched, until browned, 4 to 5 minutes. Flip and cook until the other side browns and the chicken is cooked through, another 4 to 5 minutes. Remove the chicken from the pan and allow to cool to the touch before cutting into bite-size pieces.

3. In the meantime, place the tomatoes, cucumber, onion, basil, and crumbled bacon in a large serving bowl.

4. Add the chopped chicken and cubed bread to the bowl as well and toss with dressing. Taste and adjust the salt and pepper to taste. Serve immediately or leave at room temperature and serve within the hour.

PANZANELLA COBB
Serves 4

Follow directions for Bacon Chicken Panzanella and add four medium- to hard-boiled eggs (page 137), each cut into quarters; place the pieces on top of the salad before serving. You can also add cubed avocado from 1 to 1½ avocados in step 4.

You can also substitute Sesame-Crusted Salmon (page 172) for chicken.

GREEK PANZANELLA
Serves 4

Follow the directions for Bacon Chicken Panzanella, but omit the bacon from recipe and add scant ½ cup of crumbled feta cheese in step 4.

You can also substitute Sesame-Crusted Salmon (page 172) for chicken.

ASIAN STEAK SALAD

Serves 4

MIX-AND-MATCH WITH:
GINGER LIME VINAIGRETTE, *page 125*
COLD SOBA NOODLE SALAD, *page 179*

Flank steak has a bad reputation and I understand why. It's a tough cut of meat that, when used improperly, seems impossible to cook well. The truth is that it just needs to be matched with the right recipe—any that cooks fast and calls for thin cuts.

Although flank steak has a delicious beefy flavor, it's relatively low in fat and tastes best when marinated or paired with other bold flavors that complement savory beef. That makes flank steak a great match for this salad, which is packed with tons of flavor from the Ginger Lime Vinaigrette and fresh herbs.

Because marinating flank steak does wonders for the cut, try to plan ahead when making this. Allowing the steak to soak in flavor overnight will make a big difference in both taste and texture. If you forget to plan ahead, though, even just thirty minutes to marinate will help.

♥ *Make It Easier* It's worth knowing when flank steak will do you good, since it is more affordable than interchangeable cuts such as skirt steak. I especially like using it when I'm feeding a crowd, since it's an easy, cheaper way to serve steak to a big group of people. In fact, though I love using fatty skirt steak to make fajitas or my Chili-Rubbed Steak Tacos (page 160) for the family, I use flank instead to save money when serving them at a dinner party or cookout.

For the steak:

3 tablespoons neutral oil, such as grapeseed or canola oil

2 tablespoons freshly squeezed lime juice (from about 1 juicy lime)

1 tablespoon soy sauce

2 teaspoon minced fresh ginger

½ teaspoon sriracha or similar hot sauce (optional)

¼ teaspoon rice vinegar

1½ pounds flank steak

For the salad:

½ large head napa cabbage, chopped

4 ounces watercress (optional, but worth it)

2 cups sliced cucumber (from about 1 large English cucumber)

1½ cups chopped snow peas

1 red bell pepper, seeded and cut into thin strips

1 cup chopped peanuts (also optional, but worth it)

¼ cup chopped fresh cilantro

¼ cup chopped fresh mint

1 scant cup Lime Ginger Lime Vinaigrette (page 125)

1. Begin by marinating the steak: in a medium-size bowl, whisk together the oil, lime juice, soy sauce, ginger, sriracha, if using, and vinegar. Add the steak to the bowl, making sure that the marinade covers it well, and cover with plastic wrap or transfer the marinade and steak to a large, resealable plastic bag. Place in the refrigerator to marinate for several hours or up to overnight, or leave on the counter for 30 minutes.

2. When ready to serve, cook the steak: remove the steak from the marinade and broil, grill, or pan fry for 6 minutes, untouched. Flip the steak and, for medium doneness, cook for another 6 minutes. Use a thin-blade knife to check if it's at medium or, preferably, check for doneness by using a meat thermometer. You want the temperature to read about 140°F for medium. Allow the meat to rest for at least 5 to 10 minutes before slicing thinly.

3. While the steak cooks, make the salad: toss cabbage, watercress, if using, cucumber, snow peas, pepper, peanuts, if using, cilantro, and mint with the dressing to taste in a large serving bowl. Add the meat and toss a couple more times or serve with the sliced meat placed over the top. Serve immediately.

Dinner

Poor dinner: it carries such a heavy burden. In talking with busy cooks, which I've done endlessly over the last eight years, I've found that most make do however they can for breakfast, lunch, and snack time with the expectation that they'll make up for it at dinner. That's when they'll serve a well-rounded, homemade meal with veggies and all the other good stuff that a meal is supposed to have. The problem is that dinner is at the end of the day. The long, *long* day.

This approach can work if you plan ahead and have the time and energy to cook at night. Many of us don't, though, and, instead, we end up swallowing our expectations—and food values—with a big helping of guilt and sense of failure. I find it easier to spread the responsibility of feeding my crew nutritious food across meals, and with the right shift in approach, so have the busy home cooks who have worked with me.

Even though I know this Dinner section is the one you've been waiting for, don't forget to peruse the other chapters. There are tons of recipes, ideas, and advice around other meals

of the day that can help alleviate the pressure of making a spectacularly complete dinner. For example:

If you love the idea of making a big family meal every Sunday night, skip one Sunday a month and instead use your time to make big batches of hard-boiled eggs (page 32), Sweet and Salty Granola Cereal (page 78), Hummingbird Muffins (page 101), and Yogurt Chia Breakfast Pudding (page 81). Pack your pantry, fridge, and freezer with these healthy breakfasts.

You can do the same thing for snacks. One evening, when you have time to make dinner, order a pizza instead and treat the kids to a movie night while you pour a big glass of wine, turn on some good music, and enjoy your slice while whipping up a big batch of Hummus (page 50), Granola Bars or Extra-Thick Peanut Butter Granola Bars (pages 104 and 105), and Baked Corn Dog Bites (page 102) that can help ensure healthier snacking during the week.

Okay, I know. But still, this chapter is the linchpin.

These dinner recipes are designed to be simple and easy to throw together. They are full of simple, fresh flavor that, if you don't cook often, will help you impress yourself and your family, too. If you're big into cooking, these are your go-to recipes when you're super busy and don't have enough time to make that Thai curry paste that you've been dying to make by hand. And, either way, they are a foundation you can build on and riff off of. They are simple enough for you to customize or break apart so that you can feed your crew easily, to taste.

10 *Totally Acceptable, No-Cook* DINNER IDEAS

———

Because some nights, that's how we have to roll. And it's okay. Save money, skip the take-out, and try one of these quick, nutritious meals.

1. Bowl of hummus (page 50) topped with feta and whatever else you have around (think: cucumbers, chopped tomato, olives, capers, left-over chicken) served with Pita Chips (page 48).

2. Yogurt, nut, and fresh fruit parfaits. Add granola (page 78), if you have it, for extra heft.

3. Peanut Butter (page 53) or Sunflower Seed Butter (page 52) and banana sandwiches.

4. Get Up and Go Smoothie (page 77) blended with oats for extra heft and nutrition with some whole-grain toast.

5. Everyday Waffles (page 87) or Everyday Pancakes (page 84) from the freezer with fresh fruit.

6. Tomato, cheese, and pickle sandwich with raw veggie sticks.

7. Tuna salad sandwich with raw veggie sticks and Pita Chips (page 48) or Tortilla Chips (page 47) on the side.

8. Deli meat Cobb salad with a side of toast.

9. Roasted Tomato Hummus (page 98) and avocado on crusty bread. Add a smoothie on the side if you have time.

10. A quick bean salad made with drained and rinsed canned beans, any veggies you have on hand (e.g., cucumber, chopped tomato, thawed peas, or corn), and crumbled or cubed cheese, dressed with oil and vinegar. Add leftover or deli meat, if you have some.

MEAT

NO-FUSS PAN-ROASTED PAPRIKA CHICKEN
Serves 6

MIX-AND-MATCH WITH:

In his book *Cooking By Hand*, renowned chef Paul Bertolli described his method of laying chicken, skin side down, in a pan for thirty minutes and flipping it only once, as delivering flavor only beaten by wood-fire-cooked chicken. The method has since been adopted, refined, and riffed off by many talented cooks and, with this recipe, I humbly throw my hat in the ring, too.

This method turns out juicy meat and impossibly crispy skin. And it's easy. So, so easy. Like any pan-roasted chicken recipe, it can create some splatter, but other than that, this is effortless. The chicken nearly cooks itself. All you do is season it and turn it over after fifteen minutes. Then dinner's done.

If you don't like paprika, skip it and season the chicken with nothing more than salt and pepper, or add other dried spices, such as garlic, onion powder, curry powder, or a combination of coriander and cumin. Also, you can follow the directions on pages 33–34 and make a pan sauce—just pick up at step 7. A combination of broth and sherry vinegar would be great with this paprika version. If you try it, throw in pitted green olives at the end.

1 teaspoon sweet paprika

1 teaspoon smoked paprika (or another teaspoon sweet paprika, though the extra flavor smoked gives is worthwhile)

8 bone-in, skin-on chicken thighs (about 2¾ pounds)

Salt

2 teaspoons olive oil

1. In a small bowl, combine the sweet and smoked paprika; set aside. Pat the chicken dry with paper towels on both sides and lay, skin side up, in a single layer on a work surface. Season generously with salt, then sprinkle the skin with the paprika mixture, pressing to make it stick, dividing it equally among the chicken thighs.

2. Heat the oil in a large skillet over medium heat and swirl to coat. Place the chicken in the pan, skin side down, just as the oil begins to ripple. Be careful not to overcrowd; you may need to work in batches. Press the chicken to make sure that it is lying as flat as possible on the bottom of the pan. Season the side of the chicken facing up with salt and cook for 15 minutes.

3. Flip the chicken and press to make sure that the chicken is lying as flat as possible, given the bones. Cook for another 15 minutes. Remove from the heat and allow the chicken to rest for 5 minutes. Season with more salt to taste, if desired. Serve immediately.

THAI CHICKEN BURGERS *with* QUICK PICKLED CARROTS

Serves 4

MIX-AND-MATCH WITH:

AVOCADO AND EDAMAME SALAD, *page 128*

12-MINUTE SALT AND PEPPER GREEN BEANS, *page 199*

QUICKEST SAUTÉED SPINACH, *page 199*

ROASTED SQUASH WITH GINGER SHALLOT BROWNED BUTTER, *page 200*

I have a soft spot for recipes that gently introduce selective eaters to global flavors. They're usually familiar in some way—burgers, meatballs, some form of noodle or pasta—and lightly flavored. They are just barely new, but with enough of a twist to make eaters curious for more. These burgers are like that.

To make this extra fast, I often use preshredded carrots from the store. Start by making them and in the twenty minutes that it takes for them to soak up plenty of flavor, you'll be able to prep and cook the burgers. If you have an extra ten minutes, you can also whip up a side of 12-Minute Salt and Pepper String Beans to have a complete meal in half an hour.

For the carrots:

3 tablespoons rice vinegar

2 tablespoons Asian fish sauce

2 tablespoons freshly squeezed lime juice (from about 1 juicy lime)

2 tablespoons granulated sugar

2 tablespoons chopped fresh cilantro

1 tablespoons chopped fresh mint

Heavy sprinkle of salt

1½ cups shredded carrots

For the burgers:

1 pound ground chicken, dark meat preferable

¼ cup chopped scallions

¼ cup chopped fresh cilantro

2 tablespoons Thai sweet chili sauce

2 teaspoons Asian fish sauce

1 teaspoon chopped garlic (from about 1 clove)

Burger buns, potato rolls preferable

Mayonnaise, for topping (optional)

Sriracha or other similar hot sauce, for topping (optional)

1. To prepare the carrots: In a medium-size bowl, whisk together all the ingredients, except the carrots, until the sugar and salt dissolve. Add the carrots, mixing to coat well, and allow to sit for at least 20 minutes or as long as overnight. Drain the liquid before serving.

2. To make the burgers: preheat a grill, grill pan, or broiler. Place all the ingredients in a medium-size bowl and, using your hands, a silicone spatula, or a wooden spoon, mix to combine well.

3. Portion the burgers—you can divide the meat into four quarter-pound burgers or make the grown-up burgers slightly larger and the kid burgers slightly smaller—and cook over medium-high heat until cooked all the way through, 5 to 7 minutes per side, though the exact cooking time will vary depending on thickness. Serve on a roll with the quick-pickled carrots on top and mayonnaise mixed with sriracha to taste.

♥ *Make It Easier for everyone at the table* The flavors in this recipe are quintessentially Thai, but mild enough that my kids love them—even my picky eater. For him, I skip the carrots and serve the burger plain on a roll. For the big one, who's more adventurous, I add the tangy quick-pickled carrots. The grownups get the burger, carrots, and mayo with sriracha swirled in for spice.

CHICKEN CURRY

Serves 4

MIX-AND-MATCH WITH:

RICE, *page 30*

QUINOA, *page 31*

CURRIED CAULIFLOWER AND RED LENTIL
SOUP, *page 121*

12-MINUTE SALT AND PEPPER GREEN
BEANS, *page 199*

QUICKEST SAUTÉED SPINACH, *page 199*

ROASTED SQUASH WITH GINGER SHALLOT
BROWNED BUTTER, *page 200*

Curry powder is such an easy way to add flavor to anything from hard-boiled eggs (page 32) to sweet potatoes, to excite still-developing palates. If you're intimidated by the thought of making your own curry spice blend, let me reassure you. At first blush, the ingredients list may seem intimidatingly long, but really it's not much more than a list of fairly common spices. Turmeric is the one thing that you may not have on hand and, in a pinch, you can leave it out. Also, not everyone has ground cardamom around, but I suggest you give it a go. The rest of the ingredients are standard quick-dinner fare.

- 5 tablespoons unsalted butter
- 1½ pounds boneless, skinless chicken breast, cut into 2-inch chunks
- 1½ teaspoons salt, plus more to season chicken
- Freshly ground black pepper
- ½ cup finely chopped onion (from about ½ medium-size onion)
- 1 tablespoon minced fresh ginger
- 1 teaspoon chopped garlic (from about 1 clove)
- 1 tablespoon ground coriander
- 1 teaspoon ground cumin
- ½ teaspoon sweet paprika
- ½ teaspoon ground nutmeg, preferably freshly grated
- ¼ teaspoon ground cardamom
- ¼ teaspoon ground turmeric
- ¼ teaspoon ground cloves
- 1 (6-ounce) can tomato paste (a heaping ½ cup)
- 1 (13.5-ounce) can coconut milk (scant 1 ¾ cups)
- ½ cup water or chicken or vegetable broth, store-bought or homemade (pages 39 and 40)
- 1 (15-ounce) can chickpeas, drained and rinsed
- 1 tablespoon freshly squeezed lemon juice (from ½ juicy lemon), plus more to taste

1. Melt 1 tablespoon of the butter in a large, deep skillet set over medium-high heat. In the meantime, season the chicken generously with salt and pepper. Add the chicken to the skillet in a single layer, being careful not to overcrowd; you may have to work in batches. Cook until

♥ *Make It Easier: Make the sauce for a superquick weeknight meal*
I usually make the sauce for this dinner in real time, but you can make it up to 5 days ahead, just follow steps 2 through 4. Then, when you want this for dinner, brown the chicken, add the sauce and chickpeas, and simmer until the chicken cooks through and the sauce is thoroughly reheated. You can also make this with cauliflower and chickpeas for a vegetarian, or even vegan, version.

Using cardamom Cardamom is one of my favorite spices and is especially great paired with fruit. If you're wondering how else to use this lovely spice, you can find it in Almond Berry Polenta (page 81), Indian-Style Meatballs (page 157), and Cherry Clafoutis (page 224). You can also throw it into any fruity muffin batter (it's a great addition to simple blueberry muffins) or simple vanilla cake batter. Only a pinch is necessary to give a mild yet exotic background flavor that will help set simple recipes apart.

browned, about 3 minutes on one side and 2 minutes on the other. Transfer the chicken to a plate and set aside.

2. Melt the remaining 4 tablespoons of butter in the pan. Add the onion, ginger, garlic, and spices. Toss to coat well and sauté until fragrant, 1 to 2 minutes.

3. Add the tomato paste and stir; cook for another minute or so to toast the paste.

4. Stir in the coconut milk and water or broth, stirring or whisking until smooth. Bring to a boil, then lower the heat and cook until thickened slightly, 7 to 10 minutes.

5. Return the chicken to the pan and add the chickpeas and the 1½ teaspoons of salt. Stir to incorporate and simmer until the chicken is cooked through, another 5 minutes. Adjust the salt and finish with lemon juice to taste. Serve immediately or allow to cool completely and store in a sealed container in the refrigerator for up to 5 days or in the freezer for up to 3 months.

CHICKEN CUTLETS, 2 WAYS

In my house, breaded chicken cutlets are the ultimate comfort food. To my kids, they are like chicken fingers (or their favorite dining-out meal, Japanese chicken katsu). To my husband and me, they are home-cooking at its coziest. Although tasty on their own, they can be a little boring, which is why I'm all about serving them with simple garnishes that elevate the dish without adding significant time or effort. Also, the garnishes double as veggies, so there's that.

CHICKEN CUTLETS *with* ARUGULA AND PARMESAN
Serves 4

MIX-AND-MATCH WITH:

This is my favorite way to serve chicken cutlets, with very lightly dressed arugula and Parmesan shavings. It's a common Italian preparation that I like to imagine is a staple in homes with children throughout the country. It makes me feel worldly even though my kids are probably thinking, "Yay, chicken fingers for dinner!" A win-win, I guess.

You can certainly serve this with a soup or side veggie, but if you're in a rush, skip it—an arugula salad is built in, after all. Instead, put your energy toward making Garlic Bread, or even better, Cheesy Garlic Bread.

For the chicken:

½ cup all-purpose flour, plus more as necessary (see measuring tip, page 217)

1 teaspoon salt

Freshly ground black pepper

2 large eggs

2 cups panko bread crumbs

¼ cup grated Parmesan cheese

1½ to 2 pounds boneless, skinless, thin-cut chicken cutlets

6 to 8 tablespoons olive oil, plus more as necessary

For the salad:

5 ounces baby arugula

3 tablespoons olive oil, or to taste

2 tablespoons freshly squeezed lemon juice (from about 1 juicy lemon)

Salt, to taste

Freshly ground black pepper, to taste

Parmesan shavings

1. To prepare the chicken: place the flour, salt, and pepper in a wide, shallow bowl. Beat the eggs in a second wide, shallow bowl along with 2 teaspoons of water. Combine the bread crumbs and grated Parmesan in a third wide, shallow bowl.

2. Lay out the chicken in a single layer and pat dry. Dredge each cutlet in the flour, shaking off any excess. Dip it in the egg mixture, turning to coat both sides, allowing any excess to drip back into the bowl. Lastly, dip in the bread crumbs, turning to coat both sides and pressing to help the bread crumbs adhere. Repeat with all the cutlets; I find it easiest to dredge all of the cutlets in flour, then all of them in egg, and lastly, all of them in bread crumbs, rather than taking one breast through the whole process and repeating it.

3. Set a paper towel–lined plate next to the stove. Heat 6 tablespoons of the oil in a large pan set over medium-high heat. Add the cutlets to the pan, being careful not to overcrowd; you may need to work in batches. Cook, untouched, until one side turns golden brown, about 4 minutes; flip and cook the second side for another 3 to 4 minutes. Transfer the chicken from the pan to the paper towel–lined plate and add an additional 2 tablespoons of oil to the pan before cooking

♥ **Make It Easier:** The breading process can seem arduous at first but, once you get going, it's simple business. Still, maximize your effort by breading a double batch at once. Cook half of the chicken and freeze the other half by placing the uncooked, breaded cutlets on a cookie sheet in a single layer and freezing them solid. Then, transfer them to a resealable plastic bag to grab and thaw cutlets as you need them for a quick meal. They'll last in the freezer for up to 3 months.

the next batch of chicken. Continue until all the cutlets are cooked. Season with more salt to taste, if desired.

4. To prepare the arugula salad: place the arugula in a large bowl and toss with the oil, lemon juice, salt, pepper, and Parmesan shavings to taste. Serve the cutlets on top of the salad or top each cutlet with salad; either way, serve immediately.

CHICKEN CUTLETS *with* QUICK AVOCADO-TOMATO RELISH

Serves 4

MIX-AND-MATCH WITH:
RICE, *page 30*
VEGETABLE CHICKPEA SOUP WITH GARLIC TOASTED BREAD CRUMBS, *page 122*
BEET AND ORANGE SALAD, *page 129*
SHAVED ASPARAGUS AND FENNEL SALAD, *page 135*
12-MINUTE SALT AND PEPPER GREEN BEANS, *page 199*
QUICKEST SAUTÉED SPINACH, *page 199*
GREEN CHILE CHEESY RICE, *page 209*
COLD ORZO SALAD, *page 210*
GARLIC BREAD, *page 211*
CHEESY GARLIC BREAD, *page 213*

This simple avocado-tomato relish is nothing more than cubed avocado gently tossed with grape tomatoes, basil, and lemon juice. Given that avocado is nutrient-dense, I often serve this with nothing more than a big side of rice or buttered orzo. And for the record, this relish goes great on salmon, too. It's a perfect way to dress up otherwise too-simple grilled or broiled meat or fish.

For the chicken:

½ cup all-purpose flour, plus more as necessary (see measuring tip, page 217)
1 teaspoon salt
Freshly ground pepper
2 large eggs
2 cups panko bread crumbs
1½ to 2 pounds boneless, skinless, thin-cut chicken cutlets
6 to 8 tablespoons olive oil, plus more as necessary

For the relish:

2 avocados, peeled, pitted, and cubed
1½ cups grape tomatoes, halved or quartered, depending on size
8 large fresh basil leaves, washed and cut into a thin chiffonade (see Make It Easier on page 138)
2 tablespoons freshly squeezed lemon juice (from about 1 juicy lemon)
Salt, to taste

1. To prepare the chicken: place the flour, salt, and pepper in a wide, shallow bowl. Beat the eggs in a second wide, shallow bowl along with 2 teaspoons of water. Place the bread crumbs in a third wide, shallow bowl.

2. Lay out the chicken in a single layer and pat dry. Dredge each cutlet in the flour, shaking off any excess. Dip it in the egg mixture, turning to coat both sides, allowing any excess to drip back into the bowl. Lastly, dip in the bread crumbs, turning to coat both sides and pressing to help the bread crumbs adhere. Repeat with all the cutlets; I find it easiest to dredge all of the cutlets in flour, then all of them in egg, and lastly, all of them in bread crumbs, rather than taking one breast through the whole process and repeating it.

3. Set a paper towel–lined plate next to the stove. Heat 6 tablespoons of the oil in a large pan set over medium-high heat. Add the cutlets to the pan, being careful not to overcrowd; you may need to work in batches. Cook, untouched, until one side turns golden brown, about 4 minutes; flip and cook the second side for another 3 to 4 minutes. Transfer the chicken from the pan to the paper towel–lined plate and add an additional 2 tablespoons of oil to the pan before cooking the next batch of chicken. Continue until all the cutlets are cooked. Season with more salt, if desired.

4. To make the Avocado-Tomato Relish: place the avocado, tomatoes, and basil in a bowl and gently toss with the lemon juice and salt to taste. Top each cutlet with the relish and serve immediately.

MEATBALLS, 2 WAYS

Some people are advocates for world peace, others for animal rights. While I'm for both, I'm most known for my meatball advocacy. And proud of it.

Meatballs are easy to throw together in just one bowl, forgiving, endlessly adaptable to almost any cuisine, kid- and grown-up-friendly, and just plain delicious. They can be served on skewers, wrapped in lettuce, nestled on pasta or rice, smothered in sauce, or tucked into a crusty roll. They can be fried, grilled, stewed, or baked. Meatballs hold up well if you make them ahead of time and freeze beautifully. You can make them with any type of ground meat that you have on hand and even make them taste good with only pantry ingredients added. In other words, keep ground meat in your freezer and you always have a meal in meatballs.

It's true that not all meatballs are created equal. It can be hard for inexperienced cooks to make a meatball with perfect flavor, a crispy outside, and super tender inside. But an imperfect meatball can still be totally delicious, so don't be afraid to experiment or think that you have to take on some painstaking process to cook up an easy, tasty meal.

These are two of my family's favorite meatball recipes. The first, Easy Italian Turkey Meatballs, is a great example of how you can move fast, use nontraditional ground turkey, and (gasp) even ketchup, and still end up with a delicious, tender meatball.

The second recipe, Indian-Style Meatballs, is to demonstrate how easy it is to vary meatballs to suit whatever cuisine your crew likes most. As long as you have ground meat, a binder (e.g., eggs, bread crumbs), and something like fresh herbs or dried spices to add flavor, you've got everything you need.

EASY ITALIAN TURKEY MEATBALLS

Serves 4-6

MIX-AND-MATCH WITH:

PASTA, *page 28*

VEGETABLE CHICKPEA SAUCE WITH
GARLIC TOASTED BREAD CRUMBS, *page 72*

BEET AND ORANGE SALAD, *page 129*

SHAVED ASPARAGUS AND FENNEL SALAD,
page 135

MARINARA SAUCE, *page 183*

5 UNEXPECTED PIZZA TOPPINGS, *page 194*

ROASTED CAULIFLOWER WITH GARLIC
TOASTED BREAD CRUMBS, *page 197*

12-MINUTE SALT AND PEPPER GREEN
BEANS, *page 199*

QUICKEST SAUTÉED SPINACH, *page 199*

GIARDINIERA ROASTED VEGETABLES,
page 202

PARMESAN ROASTED BROCCOLI, *page 204*

COLD ORZO SALAD, *page 210*

GARLIC BREAD, *page 211*

CHEESY GARLIC BREAD, *page 213*

Yep, I use ketchup here. I know it may seem gauche to some, but the point of this recipe is to make something irresistibly delicious with everyday pantry items so that it can become a no-brainer, go-to recipe. That's also why I often don't brown these meatballs. You can just cook them in your sauce—even if it's jarred—to make succulent meatballs an easy endeavor. These are THE match for your perfectly cooked pasta with Marinara Sauce.

- 1 pound ground dark meat turkey
- 1 large egg, beaten
- ¼ cup plain Italian-style bread crumbs
- ¼ cup grated Parmesan cheese
- 2 tablespoons ketchup
- 2 teaspoons chopped garlic (from about 2 cloves)
- ⅛ teaspoon ground onion powder
- 2 tablespoons olive oil (optional)

1. Place all the ingredients, except the oil, in a large bowl and, using your hands, a silicone spatula, or a wooden spoon, mix together thoroughly. Lightly wet your hands before rolling the meat mixture into golf ball–size meatballs (about 1½ inches).

2. To brown (optional): heat the oil in a large pan set over medium-high heat. Add the meatballs, being careful not to overcrowd; you may need to work in batches. Fry until browned and cooked through, 10 to 15 minutes total, turning them two or three times along the way. Alternatively, cook for 8 to 10 minutes, turning them two or three times to brown all the way around, and transfer the meatballs to a simmering sauce to finish cooking, 2 to 3 more minutes.

To cook without browning: add the pasta sauce to a pot with enough room that the sauce level can rise at least 2 inches without an issue. Bring to a simmer, add the raw meatballs, cover, and cook until the meatballs are cooked through, about 12 minutes.

Keep in mind that the exact cooking time will vary depending on the exact size of the meatballs and that poultry should be cooked well done.

Serve immediately or allow to cool completely and store in a sealed container in the refrigerator for up to 5 days or in the freezer for up to 3 months.

INDIAN-STYLE MEATBALLS
Serves 4-6

MIX-AND-MATCH WITH:

RICE, *page 30*

QUINOA, *page 31*

QUICK PICKLED RED ONIONS, *page 70*

CURRIED CAULIFLOWER AND RED LENTIL
SOUP, *page 121*

MANGO SLAW, *page 133*

12-MINUTE SALT AND PEPPER GREEN
BEANS, *page 199*

QUICKEST SAUTÉED SPINACH, *page 199*

ROASTED SQUASH WITH GINGER SHALLOT
BROWNED BUTTER, *page 200*

RICE AND LENTIL PILAF, *page 206*

serve these alongside a big salad and either store-bought flatbread, Rice and Lentil Pilaf, or Quinoa flavored with some of the same dried spices and tossed with drained, canned chickpeas. Quick Pickled Red Onions are also great on the side, or pick up your favorite Indian-style pickle or chutney at the supermarket.

⅓ cup canned coconut milk

½ cup panko bread crumbs

1 pound ground lamb

1 pound 85% to 90% lean ground beef

2 teaspoons minced garlic (from about
   2 cloves)

1 teaspoon ground coriander

1 teaspoon ground cumin

¾ teaspoon salt

½ teaspoon ground turmeric

½ teaspoon freshly ground black pepper

½ teaspoon minced fresh ginger

⅛ teaspoon ground cinnamon

⅛ teaspoon ground cardamom

½ tablespoon salted butter

1. Set a paper towel–lined plate next to the stove. In a large bowl, combine the coconut milk and bread crumbs; allow to sit for 5 minutes. Add the rest of the ingredients, except the butter, and, using your hands, a silicone spatula, or a wooden spoon, mix together thoroughly. Lightly wet your hands before rolling the meat mixture into golf ball–size meatballs (about 1½ inches).

2. Heat the butter in a large pan set over medium-high heat. Add the meatballs, being careful not to overcrowd; you may need to work in batches. Fry until browned on the outside, 3 to 5 minutes, turning them two or three times along the way.

3. Place ¼ cup of water in the pan, cover, and allow the meatballs to cook through, 3 to 5 more minutes, keeping in mind that the cooking time will vary, depending on the size of your meatballs. Transfer the cooked meatballs to the paper towel–lined plate and repeat the process as necessary. Enough fat should have rendered from the first batch to brown subsequent batches without adding more butter. Serve immediately or allow to cool completely and store in a sealed container in the refrigerator for up to 5 days or in the freezer for up to 3 months.

STEAK *with* SWEET-AND-SOUR PEPPERS

Serves 4

MIX-AND-MATCH WITH:

SWEET-AND-SOUR PEPPERS, *page 68*

CARAMELIZED ONIONS, *page 69*

VEGETABLE CHICKPEA SOUP WITH GARLIC TOASTED BREAD CRUMBS, *page 122*

BEET AND ORANGE SALAD, *page 129*

COUNTRY-STYLE GREEK SALAD, *page 132*

SHAVED ASPARAGUS AND FENNEL SALAD, *page 135*

ROASTED CAULIFLOWER WITH GARLIC TOASTED BREAD CRUMBS, *page 197*

12-MINUTE SALT AND PEPPER GREEN BEANS, *page 199*

QUICKEST SAUTÉED SPINACH, *page 199*

ROASTED SQUASH WITH GINGER SHALLOT BROWNED BUTTER, *page 200*

GIARDINIERA ROASTED VEGETABLES, *page 202*

PARMESAN ROASTED BROCCOLI, *page 204*

COLD ORZO SALAD, *page 210*

GARLIC BREAD, *page 211*

CHEESY GARLIC BREAD, *page 213*

Given health and cost factors, steak is far from an everyday meal in my house. That said, every once and a while, it's the only thing that will do. When I'm treating myself and other grownups, I'll splurge on a strip, T-bone, or rib eye, which need nothing more than salt, butter, and lots of heat to cook well. When I'm feeding the whole crew, though, I use tender boneless sirloin steaks. The only catch is the price but, then again, steak dinners like this are a once-in-a-while occasion worthy of splurge.

2½ pounds (1- to 1¼-inch-thick) boneless sirloin steak

Salt, to taste

Freshly ground black pepper, to taste

2 tablespoons salted butter, plus more as necessary

Sweet-and-Sour Peppers (page 68)

1. Remove the steak(s) from the refrigerator and, ideally, allow them to sit at room temperature for 10 to 20 minutes. When ready to cook, season the steak(s) generously with salt and pepper on both sides.

2. Melt the butter in a large pan set over medium-high heat. As soon as the foam subsides, add the steak(s), being careful not to overcrowd; you may need to work in batches, adding more butter between each batch as necessary. Cook for 6 minutes, untouched, until nicely browned on one side. Flip, and for medium doneness, cook for another 6 to 7 minutes, untouched. Use a thin-blade knife to check if it's at medium or, preferably, check for doneness by using a meat thermometer. You want the temperature to read about 140°F for medium. Remove the steak(s) from the pan and allow them to rest for at least 5 to 10 minutes before slicing thinly.

3. Arrange the sliced steak on a serving platter or divided among four plates and serve immediately with Sweet-and-Sour Peppers over the top.

♥ *Make It Tastier* It's easy enough to make the peppers ahead or while you whip up your sides. Or, though they're not quite as tasty, you can use some from a jar. If you can't find the sweet-and-sour kind, grab a jar of roasted red peppers and dress them with red wine vinegar.

CHILI-RUBBED STEAK TACOS

Serves 4

MIX-AND-MATCH WITH:

FLOUR TORTILLAS, *page 44*

CORN TORTILLAS, *page 45*

CHIPOTLE LIME CREAM, *page 57*

FIRE-ROASTED SALSA, *page 62*

GUACAMOLE: CLASSIC, TROPICAL, OR SMOKY, *pages 64 and 65*

QUICK PICKLED RED ONIONS, *page 70*

VEGETARIAN TORTILLA SOUP, *page 116*

AVOCADO AND HEARTS OF PALM SALAD, *page 129*

BEET AND ORANGE SALAD, *page 129*

MANGO SLAW, *page 133*

12-MINUTE SALT AND PEPPER GREEN BEANS, *page 199*

QUICKEST SAUTÉED SPINACH, *page 199*

EASY "REFRIED" BEANS, *page 205*

GREEN CHILE CHEESY RICE, *page 209*

I don't know what makes easier tacos: this recipe or Slow Cooker Pork Carnitas (page 165), so it's a good thing that they serve different purposes with a similar delicious end. These tacos are what you make when you haven't had time to plan ahead and are left with only twenty minutes to pull dinner together.

More good news: skirt steak is perfect for a quick cook and the fat will combine to make the rub, which is nothing more than chili powder and salt, way more flavorful than you could ever expect. This is truly a time when the less expensive option is best. If you can't find skirt steak, flank is a suitable substitute but, unless you're cooking for a crowd, I'd say you're better off waiting until you can get your hands on skirt steak.

Serve thin slices of this meat tucked into warm Flour or Corn Tortillas with Cheddar and Chipotle Guacamole and Quick Pickled Red Onions. Or top your tacos with nothing more than Mango Slaw. If you want to go all out—which you may have time to do, given how quick the steak cooks—make an Avocado and Hearts of Palm Salad and/or Green Chile Cheesy Rice, too.

2 pounds skirt steak

2 tablespoons chili powder

½ teaspoon salt

8 warmed flour tortillas, store-bought or homemade (page 44)

Fixings of choice (see headnote)

1. Preheat a grill, grill pan, or broiler. Remove the steak from the refrigerator and, ideally, allow it to sit at room temperature for 10 to 20 minutes. In the meantime, in a small bowl, combine the chili powder and salt.

2. Rub the steak with the chili powder mixture, dividing it evenly between the front and back. For medium, broil or grill for about 8 minutes, 4 minutes per side, keeping in mind that the cooking time will vary depending on the thickness of the steak. Use a thin-blade knife to check if it's at medium or, preferably, check for doneness by using a meat thermometer. You want the temperature to read about 140°F for medium. Allow the steak to rest for at least 5 to 10 minutes before slicing thinly. (If you need to reheat the tortillas, see Make It Easier, page 45.) Serve the steak tucked into warm tortillas with fixings of choice.

BEEF AND LENTIL SLOPPY JOES

Serves 4-6

MIX-AND-MATCH WITH:

VEGETABLE CHICKPEA SOUP WITH GARLIC
TOASTED BREAD CRUMBS, *page 122*

BEET AND ORANGE SALAD, *page 129*

COUNTRY-STYLE GREEK SALAD, *page 132*

MANGO SLAW (WITH OR WITHOUT
MANGO), *page 133*

SHAVED ASPARAGUS AND FENNEL SALAD,
page 135

ROASTED CAULIFLOWER WITH GARLIC
TOASTED BREAD CRUMBS, *page 197*

12-MINUTE SALT AND PEPPER GREEN
BEANS, *page 199*

QUICKEST SAUTÉED SPINACH, *page 199*

GIARDINIERA ROASTED VEGETABLES,
page 202

PARMESAN ROASTED BROCCOLI, *page 204*

I didn't grow up with American classics like sloppy joe sandwiches and even had an aversion to them. Sloppy joes never seemed to offer enough of their own value. And then I had kids.

When you feed children and making dinner every night becomes a necessity (they need to eat *again*?!), even the most creative cooks get tapped out. You'll try anything and new presentations of their favorite foods become a kitchen lifeline. So, are sloppy joes just a variation on burgers? Who cares? My kids like them.

Never one to completely abandon my personal tastes for my children (sorry, guys), I decided to give the sloppy joe a makeover. Because of the sauce, this recipe offers a unique opportunity to mix in other healthy ingredients, such as lentils. (You can also pack it full of vegetables, such as chopped bell pepper, carrot, or even spinach, by the way.)

The beans bulk up and stretch a pound of beef, making a big batch of relatively lean, high-protein sandwich filling that tastes like the classic. And, now, suddenly, I dig sloppy joes. Who knew?

- 4 teaspoons neutral oil, such as grapeseed or canola
- 1 pound lean ground beef
- ½ cup chopped onion (from about ½ medium-size onion)
- 2 teaspoons minced garlic (from about 2 cloves)
- 2 tablespoons chili powder
- 1 teaspoons dried oregano
- 1 teaspoon ground yellow mustard or prepared mustard
- 1 teaspoon salt, plus more to taste
- ½ teaspoon onion powder
- ½ teaspoon garlic powder
- 5 tablespoons tomato paste
- 1 (8-ounce) can tomato sauce
- 1 cup dried lentils, cooked according to the package instructions, or 1 (15-ounce) can lentils, drained and rinsed
- Freshly ground black pepper, to taste
- Rolls, for serving
- Mango Slaw (page 133, made without mango)

1. Heat 1 teaspoon of the oil in a large, deep skillet set over medium heat. Swirl to coat the bottom and add the ground beef. Cook, breaking up the beef with a silicone spatula or wooden spoon, until browned, 6 to 8 minutes. Using a slotted spoon, transfer the beef to a bowl and set aside. Pour out and discard the grease from the pan.

2. Return the pan to medium heat and add the remaining 3 teaspoons of oil. Swirl to coat the bottom and add the onion and garlic. Cook until the onion is translucent and garlic is fragrant, 2 to 3 minutes. Add the chili powder, oregano, mustard (if using ground; otherwise, hold off), 1 teaspoon of salt, the onion powder, and garlic powder; stir to coat the onion and garlic with the spices and cook for about 1 minute.

3. Add the tomato paste and, if using, the prepared mustard; stir to combine and toast for 1 minute. Add the tomato sauce to the pan. Fill the emptied tomato sauce can with water and add the water to the pan, as well. Stir to combine. Bring to a low simmer and cook for 2 to 3 minutes.

4. Return the meat and add the cooked lentils to the pan. Stir to combine and heat through, 2 to 3 minutes. Add more salt and pepper to taste. Serve immediately on toasted hamburger rolls, topped with the mango slaw, or store in a sealed container in the refrigerator for up to 5 days or in the freezer for up to 3 months.

GREEK-STYLE KEBABS
Serves 4-6 (makes 6 skewers)

MIX-AND-MATCH WITH:

RICE, *page 30*

QUINOA, *page 31*

VEGETABLE CHICKPEA SOUP WITH GARLIC TOASTED BREAD CRUMBS, *page 122*

BUTTERMILK DILL (OR RANCH!) DRESSING (AS AN ALTERNATIVE MARINADE), *page 127*

BEET AND ORANGE SALAD, *page 129*

COUNTRY-STYLE GREEK SALAD, *page 132*

SHAVED ASPARAGUS AND FENNEL SALAD, *page 135*

GREEK PANZANELLA (WITHOUT CHICKEN), *page 138*

ROASTED CAULIFLOWER WITH GARLIC TOASTED BREAD CRUMBS, *page 197*

12-MINUTE SALT AND PEPPER GREEN BEANS, *page 199*

QUICKEST SAUTÉED SPINACH, *page 199*

RICE AND LENTIL PILAF, *page 206*

GARLIC BREAD, *page 211*

CHEESY GARLIC BREAD, *page 213*

If you read my instructions on How to Make Kebabs (page 34), you already know that I consider making delicious skewers an essential skill for any busy home cook. Once you get the hang of making them, you'll find that you don't need a recipe to make your own signature kebabs. These are mine.

These make a delicious meal served on a bed of Rice and Lentil Pilaf or buttered orzo with a Country-Style Greek Salad (page 132). When I have time or there is already some in my refrigerator, I dress plain orzo with Buttermilk Dill (or Ranch!) Dressing instead of just butter. In fact, if you have enough dressing at the ready, you can use it as the marinade, too.

6 to 8 tablespoons freshly squeezed lemon juice (from 3 to 4 juicy lemons)

3 tablespoons olive oil

2 tablespoons chopped fresh oregano

½ teaspoon salt, plus more to taste

½ teaspoon freshly ground black pepper, plus more to taste

2 pounds boneless beef sirloin, cut into 1½- to 2-inch cubes (see pages 34–35 about other cuts of meat or seafood that you can substitute)

2 red and/or green bell peppers, seeded and cut into 1½- to 2-inch pieces

1 red onion, peeled and cut into 1½-inch chunks

1. In a small bowl, whisk together the lemon juice, olive oil, oregano, the ½ teaspoon of salt, and the ½ teaspoon of black pepper. If you have time to marinate, add the meat and vegetables to the bowl, making sure that the marinade covers everything well. Alternatively, transfer the marinade, meat, and vegetables to a large, resealable plastic bag. Place the bowl or bag in the refrigerator for at least 3 hours or up to overnight, or leave on the counter for 30 minutes.

Alternatively, divide the marinade evenly between two bowls, one for brushing the raw meat and the other for brushing the cooked meat.

2. If using wooden skewers, soak them in water for 30 minutes while you preheat a grill, grill pan, or broiler

3. Thread the marinated meat and veggies onto prepped skewers, alternating the meat, onion, and peppers. If you did not marinate the meat and veggies, thread the meat and vegetables onto the prepped skewers and brush generously with the marinade from the for-raw-meat bowl.

4. Cook for 10 to 12 minutes, flipping halfway through. If you did not marinate the meat, brush the kebabs with the raw-meat marinade one or two times during cooking and, then, from the other bowl, as soon as they are off the heat. Season with more salt and pepper to taste. Allow the kebabs to rest for 5 to 10 minutes before serving immediately.

♥ *Make It Easier: You don't even need the sticks.* Wooden or metal skewers help keep everything together and they are a fun way to serve food, but here's a little secret: you can skip them. If you're really in a rush, cut the vegetables large enough that they don't need the extra support and throw everything on the grill or on a pan that can go in the broiler, loose. It works, and it's not as if everything doesn't just come off the stick anyway.

MISO AND SWEET CHILI GLAZED PORK LOIN

Serves 4-6

MIX-AND-MATCH WITH:

RICE, *page 30*

QUINOA, *page 31*

SMALL-BATCH CHICKEN BROTH, *page 39*

SMALL-BATCH VEGETABLE BROTH, *page 40*

AVOCADO AND EDAMAME SALAD, *page 128*

12-MINUTE SALT AND PEPPER GREEN BEANS, *page 199*

QUICKEST SAUTÉED SPINACH, *page 199*

ROASTED SQUASH WITH GINGER SHALLOT BROWNED BUTTER, *page 200*

This recipe is a great example of how simple roast meats can be made special with an easy, but well-thought-out marinade and sauce. In that way, the beauty of this recipe is similar to that of kebabs (page 34). Pick a cuisine—in this case, I chose Asian flavors—and combine sauce ingredients that taste great together. Marinade or brush while cooking and save some as a sauce to serve on the side.

Neutral oil, such as grapeseed or canola, for pan

¼ cup white miso paste

¼ cup white wine vinegar

2 tablespoons Thai sweet chili sauce

2 tablespoons honey

1 teaspoon minced garlic (from about 1 clove)

1 teaspoon finely minced fresh ginger

2 trimmed pork tenderloins (about 1 pound each)

Salt, to taste

Freshly ground black pepper, to taste

½ cup chicken or vegetable broth, store-bought or homemade (pages 39 and 40)

1. Preheat the oven to 425°F. Remove the pork loins from the refrigerator and, ideally, allow them to sit at room temperature for 10 to 20 minutes. In the meantime, coat a small roasting pan or medium-size rimmed baking sheet with oil. If you have a rack that fits, grease that, too, and nestle it inside the pan; set aside.

2. In a small saucepan set over medium heat, combine the miso paste, vinegar, sweet chili sauce, honey, garlic, and ginger. Whisk until smooth and cook until the mixture just begins to bubble and thickens, 2 to 3 minutes. Spoon 4 tablespoons of the sauce into a small bowl, leaving the rest of the sauce in the pan.

3. Pat the pork loins dry and season generously with salt and pepper. Lay them side by side in the prepped pan, on top of the rack, if using. Brush the loins all over with about half of the sauce reserved in the bowl and place in the oven. Roast the pork for 15 minutes before carefully flipping the loins and brushing with the remaining sauce in the bowl. Return to the oven to roast for about 20 more minutes, or until the meat registers 130°F on a meat thermometer (see Make It Tastier, next page). Remove from the oven and allow the meat to rest for at least 5 minutes.

4. In the meantime, add the broth to the sauce reserved in the saucepan. Set over medium heat and cook until simmering, then lower the heat to low and cook, stirring occasionally, until reduced to about ½ cup, 5 to 7 minutes.

5. Cut the rested pork loins into ½-inch-thick slices and serve immediately with the sauce spooned over top.

♥ *Make It Easier* A quick note about cooking pork, especially if you're sharing with young eaters: USDA guidelines say that it should be cooked to 145°F. Because the internal temperature of the meat will go up as it rests, the pork will be dry if you cook it up to the point where your thermometer reads 145°F. Depending on the thickness of your pork loins, cooking for 35 minutes, per this recipe, will get you to about 130 to 135°F, which will raise to 145°F with rest time and keeps the pork at a juicy, just-medium doneness. If you have any concerns at all, especially if using pork from an unknown source, consider cooking for a little longer. And no matter how long you cook the meat, allow it to rest at least 5 minutes (10 is ideal) before cutting into it.

PULLED PORK, 3 WAYS

Making pulled pork in a slow cooker is one of the most satisfying cooking experiences a busy home cook can have. You put meat into a slow cooker, add sauce, cover, and come home to a finger-licking good pile of meat that has been cooking for hours without your help. It's genius, really.

Pulled pork can be adapted in many ways, across many cuisines from Mexican to Asian to American. No matter what set of flavors you go for, you want to start with a fatty hunk of pork, such as shoulder. In most stores, the shoulder will be trimmed of the thick outer layer of skin and fat. But if you prefer not to buy meat from conventional markets, you may need to ask the butcher to do this for you or do it yourself. Either way, don't go too crazy trimming the fat, since it's what makes pulled pork juicy and delicious. If you make it too lean, you'll end up with dry pork—and sauce won't disguise that.

SLOW COOKER CARNITAS
Serves 6

MIX-AND-MATCH WITH:
FLOUR TORTILLAS, *page 44*
CORN TORTILLAS, *page 45*
CHIPOTLE LIME CREAM, *page 57*
FIRE-ROASTED SALSA, *page 62*
GUACAMOLE: CLASSIC, TROPICAL, OR SMOKY, *pages 64 and 65*
QUICK PICKLED RED ONIONS, *page 70*
VEGETARIAN TORTILLA SOUP, *page 116*
AVOCADO AND HEARTS OF PALM SALAD, *page 129*

Carnitas has great, meaty flavor that serves as a tasty backdrop for many dishes. Although I make it most for tacos—I serve it taco-bar style with Flour Tortillas, Easy "Refried" Beans, Guacamole or Fire-Roasted Salsa, Quick Pickled Red Onions, and sour cream—it's also great with a side of scrambled eggs, tortillas, and guacamole, or even added to an Avocado and Hearts of Palm Salad.

3 pounds boneless pork shoulder

½ cup freshly squeezed orange juice (from about 2 juicy oranges)

2 teaspoon salt

1 bay leaf

1. Trim the pork of some of the excess fat around the outside, being sure to leave some on to aid in the cooking. Keep in mind that carnitas is pork cooked in its own fat, so you don't want to get rid of it all. Cut into 2-inch-thick strips.

2. Put the meat in a slow cooker along with the orange juice, salt, and bay leaf. Toss to coat the meat with the juice, cover, and cook on LOW for 8 hours.

3. When the cooking is done, use two forks to shred the pork. Serve immediately or allow to cool completely and store in an airtight container in the refrigerator for up to 5 days or in the freezer for up to 3 months.

SLOW COOKER HOISIN PULLED PORK

Serves 6

This recipe is a little unexpected and totally delicious, especially if you make it with Ginger Hoisin Sauce. I'm partial, but think that the homemade sauce makes all the difference and it only takes an extra ten minutes. You can serve this piled onto a soft roll to make a delicious dinner sandwich or with Flour Tortillas, moo shu style. You can also throw Mango Slaw into the wrap; when I do that, I make the slaw without mango, but add chopped scallion, a dash of soy sauce, and squirt of sriracha. Either way, pair this dinner with an easy "salad" of avocado halves topped with Ginger Lime Vinaigrette (page 125).

3 pounds boneless pork shoulder

2 cups hoisin sauce, store-bought or home-made (page 59; four times the recipe as written)

Warmed flour tortillas, store-bought or homemade (page 44) or soft rolls, for serving (optional)

1. Trim the pork of some of the excess fat around the outside, being sure to leave some on to aid in the cooking, and cut into 2-inch-thick strips.

2. Put the meat in a slow cooker with about 1½ cups of the hoisin sauce, setting ½ cup aside. Toss to coat the meat with the sauce, cover, and cook on HIGH for 6 hours.

3. When the cooking is done, use two forks to shred the pork. Add the reserved hoisin sauce and toss to coat. Serve immediately—I like to serve this in warm flour tortillas (page 44), moo shu style, or piled onto a soft roll—or allow to cool completely and store in an airtight container in the refrigerator for up to 5 days or in the freezer for up to 3 months.

SLOW COOKER BBQ PULLED PORK
Serves 6

MIX-AND-MATCH WITH:
QUICKEST BBQ SAUCE, *page 60*
AVOCADO AND HEARTS OF PALM SALAD,
page 129
MANGO SLAW (WITHOUT THE MANGO),
page 133
ROASTED CAULIFLOWER WITH GARLIC
TOASTED BREAD CRUMBS, *page 197*
12-MINUTE SALT AND PEPPER GREEN
BEANS, *page 199*
QUICKEST SAUTÉED SPINACH, *page 199*
COLD ORZO SALAD, *page 210*
GARLIC BREAD, *page 211*
CHEESY GARLIC BREAD, *page 213*

This is my easy take on classic American pulled pork. The success of this dish will come entirely from your BBQ sauce, so use a good one or take a few extra minutes to make it homemade—it's worth it.

I like to pile this pork on top of soft rolls and top it with Mango Slaw, which, in this case, I make without the mango. A side of pickles and green beans are the only other things you need to make this a complete and totally mouthwatering meal.

3 pounds boneless pork shoulder
1¼ cups BBQ Sauce, store-bought or
homemade (page 60)

1. Trim the pork of some of the excess fat around the outside, being sure to leave some on to aid in the cooking, and cut into 2-inch-thick strips.

2. Put the meat in a slow cooker with about 1 cup of the BBQ sauce, setting ¼ cup aside. Toss to coat the meat with the sauce, cover, and cook on HIGH for 6 hours.

3. When the cooking is done, use two forks to shred the pork. Add the reserved BBQ sauce, toss to coat, and serve immediately or allow to cool completely and store in an airtight container in the refrigerator for up to 5 days or in the freezer for up to 3 months.

PORK CHOPS *with* MAPLE BUTTERED APPLES

Serves 4

MIX-AND-MATCH WITH:

SMALL-BATCH CHICKEN BROTH, *page 39*

SMALL-BATCH VEGETABLE BROTH, *page 40*

CARAMELIZED ONIONS (TO TASTE), *page 69*

SHAVED ASPARAGUS AND FENNEL SALAD, *page 135*

ROASTED CAULIFLOWER WITH GARLIC TOASTED BREAD CRUMBS, *page 197*

12-MINUTE SALT AND PEPPER GREEN BEANS, *page 199*

QUICKEST SAUTÉED SPINACH, *page 199*

ROASTED SQUASH WITH GINGER SHALLOT BROWNED BUTTER, *page 200*

RICE AND LENTIL PILAF, *page 206*

GARLIC BREAD, *page 211*

CHEESY GARLIC BREAD, *page 213*

When you want a taste of fall, this is your recipe. You'll love it so much that you'll make it all year-round—except maybe when summer fruits make it too hard to fathom apples. Then, make it using peaches instead. (It works!)

This recipe may have just a handful of ingredients, but they carefully balance sweet and tangy, savory and bright. It's that tension—particularly between the maple syrup and cider vinegar—that makes this so irresistibly delicious. If you make these pork chops frequently, you'll get adept enough to improvise this pan sauce when cooking more affordable chicken cutlets, too. You might also start riffing: sometimes I increase the amount of black pepper in the sauce for more bite, while other times I throw in chopped, fresh sage or thyme in step 4.

4 (1-inch-thick), bone-in pork chops (about ¾ pound each)

½ teaspoon salt, plus more to season chops

½ teaspoon freshly ground black pepper, plus more to season chops

4 tablespoons olive oil

1 cup white wine, apple cider, or chicken or vegetable broth, store-bought or home-made (pages 39 and 40)

4 tablespoons unsalted butter

2 tablespoons pure maple syrup

4 medium-size apples, peeled, cored, and cut into eighths

2 tablespoons cider vinegar

1. Remove the pork chops from the refrigerator and, ideally, allow them to sit at room temperature for 10 to 20 minutes. Pat them dry on both sides with paper towels. Season very generously with salt and pepper.

2. Heat the oil in a large, deep skillet over medium-high heat. Add the pork chops, being careful not to overcrowd them; you may need to work in batches. Cook, untouched, until browned, 3 to 4 minutes. Flip and continue to cook for another 3 minutes, untouched, on the other side. Transfer the pork chops to a plate and allow them to rest for at least 5 to 10 minutes.

3. Leave the pan over medium-high heat and add the wine to the pan, stirring to scrape up any browned bits. Lower the heat to medium-low and add the butter, syrup, apples, and the ½ teaspoon each of the salt and pepper. Cover and cook until the apples are tender, about 7 minutes

4. Uncover and add the cider vinegar to the sauce; swirl to incorporate. Return the chops to the pan, and cook for 1 more minute, spooning the sauce over the meat. Serve immediately.

SALMON RICE BOWL
Serves 4

MIX-AND-MATCH WITH:
RICE, *page 30*
GINGER LIME VINAIGRETTE, *page 125*
SESAME-CRUSTED SALMON, *page 172*
12-MINUTE SALT AND PEPPER GREEN
BEANS, *page 199*
QUICKEST SAUTÉED SPINACH, *page 199*

If you want to practice loosely following recipes, start with this one. Nothing more than a simple bowl of rice topped with fish, some veggies, and a dressing, it is very forgiving.

The point is to cook a big mess of rice and fill people's bowls as full as they want. This is the main heft of the meal, so don't skimp. Top with fish or flake it in. I use Sesame-Crusted Salmon, but salmon roasted with nothing more than salt, pepper, and olive oil will do just as well.

I love the way avocado pairs with the Ginger Lime Vinaigrette that I use to dress these Salmon Rice Bowls and, even more, that it's a nutrient-dense food that doesn't require cooking. If you're not into avocado, though, you can swap in—or add—edamame, broccoli, or even humble green peas. If you aren't fixed on Asian flavors, this is just as good with my Everyday Vinaigrette (page 124).

2 cups uncooked rice
¼ cup mirin (optional)
Salt, to taste
4 fillets Sesame-Crusted Salmon (page 172)
2 ripe avocados, halved, pitted, and cut into ½-inch cubes or ½-inch-thick slices
1 cup chopped watercress (from about 1 bunch), or baby arugula
Chopped fresh cilantro for garnish (optional)
Ginger Lime Vinaigrette (page 125)

1. Cook the rice according to the package instructions or the directions on page 30. While still hot, toss with the mirin, if using, and season with salt to taste. If you've cooked the rice ahead of time, add the mirin to the cold rice before reheating it and salt to taste once it's hot.

2. Divide the seasoned rice among four large bowls. Top with the salmon fillets, one for each bowl. Alternatively, flake the fillets and mix into the rice.

3. Top with the avocado, watercress, and cilantro. Drizzle with dressing to taste and serve immediately.

ROASTED SALMON, 3 WAYS

The easiest healthy meal that you can make is broiled fish. My mom used to make it for me all the time, but with nothing on the fish! Not a good move if you're trying to get your kids to develop a taste for seafood—or enjoy your own dinner. The simple act of brushing fish with a tasty sauce is all it takes to go from a dinner dud to one that you'll add to heavy rotation.

The great thing about roasting a hearty piece of salmon is that it's easy to customize without extra effort. If you have a picky eater who isn't into sauces, roast one piece with nothing more than a quick sprinkle of salt and pepper and brush of olive oil. Or maybe there's one rogue salmon hater in your crew. For him, cook a flounder fillet or some other mild, white, flaky fish alongside the salmon. No harm, no, uh, foul.

HOISIN-GLAZED SALMON
Serves 4

MIX-AND-MATCH WITH:
RICE, *page 30*
GINGER HOISIN SAUCE, *page 59*
AVOCADO AND EDAMAME SALAD, *page 128*
12-MINUTE SALT AND PEPPER GREEN BEANS, *page 199*
QUICKEST SAUTÉED SPINACH, *page 199*
ROASTED SQUASH WITH GINGER SHALLOT BROWNED BUTTER, *page 200*

4 (6-ounce) salmon fillets
Salt, to taste
Freshly ground black pepper, to taste
½ cup hoisin sauce, store-bought or home-made (page 59)
1 tablespoon freshly squeezed lime juice (from about ½ juicy lime), to finish
Chopped fresh cilantro, for garnish (optional)

1. Preheat the oven to 425°F. Pat the salmon fillets dry with paper towels and place, skin side down, on a baking sheet. Season generously with salt and pepper.

2. Set aside 1 tablespoon of the hoisin sauce and brush the remaining sauce over the salmon fillets, dividing equally among all four pieces.

3. Roast the salmon for 13 to 15 minutes, depending on their thickness and your desired doneness.

4. Lightly brush the cooked fillets with the reserved tablespoon of hoisin sauce and sprinkle with the lime juice. Garnish with cilantro, if using, and serve immediately.

SESAME-CRUSTED SALMON
Serves 4

MIX-AND-MATCH WITH:
RICE, *page 30*
AVOCADO MISO DRESSING (A NICE DIPPING SAUCE), *page 126*
AVOCADO AND EDAMAME SALAD, *page 128*
COUNTRY-STYLE GREEK SALAD, *page 132*
SHAVED ASPARAGUS AND FENNEL SALAD, *page 135*

I've seen toasted sesame seeds sold in packages at Japanese supermarkets, but don't believe they are readily available in conventional markets. If you only have raw sesame seeds, you can use them as is or toast them yourself. Although both ways work in this recipe, I prefer the flavor of toasted seeds.

To toast, throw the raw seeds in an ungreased pan set over medium-high heat. Cook them for about 3 minutes, shaking occasionally for the first 2 minutes and constantly for the last minute, until the seeds are golden brown and smell like popcorn. Remove the pan from heat, but leave the sesame seeds untouched for another 30 seconds before using.

4 (6-ounce) salmon fillets
Salt, to taste
Freshly ground black pepper, to taste
½ cup toasted sesame seeds (see headnote)
All-natural cooking oil spray

1. Preheat the oven to 425°F. Pat the salmon fillets dry with paper towels and season generously with salt and pepper.

2. Pour the sesame seeds onto a plate and press the salmon, flesh side down, onto them. Repeat as necessary to coat the entire surface of the

fillet. Place, skin side down, on a baking sheet and lightly spray the sesame seed crust with cooking oil.

3. Roast the salmon for 13 to 15 minutes, depending on their thickness and your desired doneness. Serve immediately.

BBQ SALMON
Serves 4

Oliver, a once die-hard salmon lover, suddenly declared one day that he didn't like it anymore. Flummoxed, I stopped making it for him until I realized that BBQ sauce could lure him back in.

Salmon is a bold flavored fish that can stand up to BBQ sauce, a favorite condiment in my house. Feeding Oliver plain roasted salmon with BBQ sauce on the side doesn't work as well as brushing it over the top this way, so now this is how we do it. And though I'm still frustrated that he won't eat salmon other ways, at least we have this, which goes perfectly with a side of Mango Slaw and fresh corn on the cob.

4 (6-ounce) salmon fillets

Salt, to taste

Freshly ground black pepper, to taste

½ cup BBQ sauce, or to taste, store-bought or homemade (page 60; about half of the recipe as written)

1. Preheat the oven to 425°F. Pat the salmon fillets dry with paper towels and season generously with salt and pepper. Place, skin side down, on a baking sheet.

2. Set aside 2 tablespoons of the BBQ sauce and brush the remaining sauce over the salmon fillets, dividing equally among all four pieces.

3. Roast the salmon for 13 to 15 minutes, depending on their thickness and your desired doneness.

4. Lightly brush the cooked fillets with the reserved BBQ sauce. Serve immediately.

LEMONY OREGANO SHRIMP
Serves 4

MIX-AND-MATCH WITH:

RICE, *page 30*

QUINOA, *page 31*

BEET AND ORANGE SALAD, *page 129*

COUNTRY-STYLE GREEK SALAD, *page 132*

SHAVED ASPARAGUS AND FENNEL SALAD, *page 135*

ROASTED CAULIFLOWER WITH GARLIC TOASTED BREAD CRUMBS, *page 197*

12-MINUTE SALT AND PEPPER GREEN BEANS, *page 199*

QUICKEST SAUTÉED SPINACH, *page 199*

PARMESAN ROASTED BROCCOLI, *page 204*

COLD ORZO SALAD, *page 210*

GARLIC BREAD, *page 211*

CHEESY GARLIC BREAD, *page 213*

Shrimp is an underused protein in busy home kitchens. It keeps in the freezer for months at a time and, depending on whether you buy it pre-cooked or raw, when you defrost it, it's either ready to eat or ready to cook, which can happen in just minutes. When you're crunched for time, you just can't get better.

I always keep a bag of uncooked, cleaned, and peeled shrimp to make some version of this quick sauté when a thirty-minute meal isn't fast enough. When you make this, be sure to use fresh oregano. If you don't have any, skip dried and used another fresh herb instead—parsley, tarragon, or even cilantro will do.

As is, this make a tasty Greek-style meal with none other than my Country-Style Greek Salad and a side of orzo tossed with butter or Buttermilk Dill (or Ranch!) Dressing (page 127).

1 pound medium shrimp, thawed if frozen, cleaned and peeled

¼ teaspoon salt, plus more to taste

Pinch of freshly ground black pepper, plus more to taste

1 tablespoon olive oil

2 teaspoons chopped garlic (from about 2 cloves)

Pinch of red pepper flakes (optional)

¼ cup white wine

3 tablespoons freshly squeezed lemon juice (from about 1½ juicy lemons)

1 tablespoon salted butter

3 tablespoons chopped fresh oregano

1. Season the shrimp with ¼ teaspoon of salt and pinch of pepper. Heat the oil in a large skillet set over medium heat. Add the garlic and red pepper flakes, if using. Cook until the garlic turns golden brown, about 2 minutes.

2. Add the shrimp in a single layer and cook until opaque all the way through, 2 to 3 minutes, flipping the shrimp halfway through the cooking time. Transfer to a plate and set aside.

3. Return the pan to medium heat and add the wine; cook until reduced by half, 30 to 60 seconds. Add the lemon juice, butter, and oregano, swirling the pan to mix in the butter as it melts. Cook until the sauce thickens just a little bit, 1 to 2 minutes, and return the shrimp to the pan. Toss to coat well and remove from the heat. Season with more salt and pepper to taste. Serve immediately.

FISH TACOS
Serves 4

MIX-AND-MATCH WITH:

FLOUR TORTILLAS, *page 44*

CORN TORTILLAS, *page 45*

CHIPOTLE LIME CREAM, *page 57*

FIRE-ROASTED SALSA, *page 62*

GUACAMOLE: CLASSIC OR TROPICAL, *pages 64 and 65*

QUICK PICKLED RED ONIONS, *page 70*

VEGETARIAN TORTILLA SOUP, *page 116*

AVOCADO AND HEARTS OF PALM SALAD, *page 129*

BEET AND ORANGE SALAD, *page 129*

MANGO SLAW, *page 133*

12-MINUTE SALT AND PEPPER GREEN BEANS, *page 199*

QUICKEST SAUTÉED SPINACH, *page 199*

EASY "REFRIED" BEANS, *page 205*

GREEN CHILE CHEESY RICE, *page 209*

I have a fish taco problem. It's really a taco problem, but fish tacos are the best of them all. Warm tortillas filled with healthy fish that still tastes great with lots of fixings? Who wouldn't have a problem eating too much of that?

At home, I keep it easy and healthy; rather than fry, I marinate an affordable white fish such as pollock (cod works, too) and cook it in a pan without any oil other than the little bit in the marinade. It's amazing how flavorful the fish comes out with so little added fat.

Because the fish has such great flavor on its own, you don't have to go crazy with toppings. That said, we are talking tacos: naked is not allowed. I serve these with Flour Tortillas and either just Mango Slaw or a selection of fixings,

including Tropical Guacamole, Quick Pickled Red Onions, Chipotle Lime Cream, and plain shredded cabbage or thinly sliced radish.

- 1½ pounds pollock fillet or other flaky, white fish fillet, such as Dover sole
- 1 jalapeño pepper
- 6 tablespoons freshly squeezed lime juice (from about 3 juicy limes)
- 3 tablespoons neutral oil, such as grapeseed or canola
- 1 teaspoon ground coriander
- ½ teaspoon salt, plus more to taste
- ½ teaspoon ground cumin
- ½ teaspoon chili powder
- ¼ cup chopped fresh cilantro, plus more for serving
- 8 warmed flour tortillas, store-bought or homemade (page 44)
- Fixings of choice (see headnote)

1. Cut the fish fillets into 2 x 4-inch strips. If you want the fish to be mild, trim, seed, and devein the jalapeño before cutting it into thin slices. Set both the fish and pepper aside.

2. In a medium-size bowl, whisk together the lime juice, oil, coriander, the ½ teaspoon of salt, cumin, chili powder, and cilantro. Add the fish and sliced jalapeño to the bowl, making sure that the marinade covers them well. Alternatively, transfer the marinade, fish, and jalapeño to a large, resealable plastic bag. Place in the refrigerator to marinate for several hours or up to overnight, or leave on the counter for 20 minutes.

3. When ready to cook, heat a large pan over medium-high heat. Once the pan is hot, add the fish, allowing a small amount of the marinade to drip in. Be careful not to add too much marinade or the fish won't brown. If you don't add enough, the pan will start to burn; you can add more marinade as necessary so that there is just enough to grease the pan. Cook the fish until thoroughly opaque, 8 to 9 minutes, flipping halfway through. Season with more salt to taste. Meanwhile, if you need to reheat the tortillas, see Make It Easier, page 45. Serve immediately, tucked into the flour tortillas with additional cilantro and other fixings of choice.

COLD SOBA NOODLE SALAD

Serves 4

MIX-AND-MATCH WITH:
GINGER LIME VINAIGRETTE, *page 125*
AVOCADO MISO DRESSING, *page 126*
ASIAN STEAK SALAD, *page 141*

As with the Salmon Rice Bowl (page 170), you can very loosely follow the recipe for this easy, go-to dinner. It's what I make when I need a dinner in twenty minutes or have nothing but raw veggies in the refrigerator. You know, the ones that I also use to pack lunch. Cut up bell peppers, carrots, and cucumber, cook soba, and toss with dressing. Honestly, it's that easy.

Feel free to get fancier if you have time—you can throw in green peas, thawed frozen edamame, or avocado and top with toasted sesame seeds—or go even simpler. Just soba, red peppers, and dressing is a great, healthy dinner. Make this your own however you want . . . or can.

1 pound soba noodles
4 scallions, trimmed and chopped
1 cup shredded carrot
1 red, orange, or yellow bell pepper, seeded and cut into ¼-inch-thick strips
1 English cucumber, peeled, cut into 4-inch sections, and then ¼-inch-thick strips
1 cup Ginger Lime Vinaigrette (page 125) or Avocado Miso Dressing (page 126)

1. Cook the soba noodles according to the package instructions. Drain, rinse with cold water, and drain some more before placing in a large serving bowl.

2. Add the scallions, carrot, pepper, cucumber, and dressing to the noodles and, using tongs, toss well to combine and coat everything with dressing. Serve immediately or store in a sealed container in the refrigerator for up to 3 days.

VEGETABLE FAJITAS

Serves 4–6

MIX-AND-MATCH WITH:

FLOUR TORTILLAS, *page 44*

CORN TORTILLAS, *page 45*

CHIPOTLE LIME CREAM, *page 57*

GUACAMOLE: CLASSIC, TROPICAL, OR SMOKY, *pages 64 and 65*

QUICK PICKLED RED ONIONS, *page 70*

AVOCADO AND HEARTS OF PALM SALAD, *page 129*

BEET AND ORANGE SALAD, *page 129*

MANGO SLAW, *page 133*

12-MINUTE SALT AND PEPPER GREEN BEANS, *page 199*

QUICKEST SAUTÉED SPINACH, *page 199*

EASY "REFRIED" BEANS, *page 205*

GREEN CHILE CHEESY RICE, *page 209*

For some reason, Mexican meals can be vegetarian and still make everyone happy—not easy to do in a house of omnivores. Maybe all the fixings compensate for a lack of animal protein? Whatever it is, as much as we love our steak tacos, Mexican food makes reducing meat in our diet easier and these veggie fajitas are a great example of why.

Thick, roasted wedges of sweet potato make sure that these fajitas satisfy, especially when paired with guacamole. When I don't have time to make proper guacamole, I serve this with avocado that's been quickly mashed with a squeeze of lime and heavy sprinkle of salt.

1 teaspoon ground cumin

1 teaspoon dried oregano

½ teaspoon sweet paprika

¼ teaspoon chili powder

⅛ teaspoon salt, plus more to taste

2 large sweet potatoes, peeled, halved, and cut into 1½-inch-thick wedges

1 red bell pepper, seeded and cut into 1½-inch-thick strips

1 green bell pepper, seeded and cut into 1½-inch-thick strips

1 red onion, peeled, trimmed, and cut into 1-inch-thick wedges (see Make It Tastier)

4 tablespoons neutral oil, such as grapeseed or canola

8 warmed flour tortillas, store-bought or homemade (page 44)

Lime wedges, for serving (optional)

Guacamole, store-bought or homemade (pages 64–65), for serving

Chopped fresh cilantro, for serving (optional)

1. Preheat the oven to 425°F. In a small bowl, combine the cumin, oregano, paprika, chili powder, and salt.

2. Place the vegetables on a rimmed baking sheet, drizzle with the oil, and sprinkle with the spice mixture. Toss to coat the vegetables evenly. Roast in the oven until the potatoes are tender throughout and the edges of some of the onion and pepper are charred, 25 to 30 minutes. Season with more salt to taste, if desired. Serve immediately with warm flour tortillas (page 44), lime wedges, guacamole, and cilantro.

♥ *Make It Tastier: Cut thick, not thin* Very thin pieces of onions will nearly disappear in the time that it takes to roast the other vegetables. Instead, to get thick wedges, trim the top of the onion and cut it in half through the root. Peel each half and place them on your cutting board cut side down. Cut each in half again and then into ½-inch wedges, slicing through the root each time.

BEAN AND CHEESE ENCHILADAS

Serves 4-6

MIX-AND-MATCH WITH:

FLOUR TORTILLAS, *page 44*

CHIPOTLE LIME CREAM, *page 57*

RED ENCHILADA SAUCE, *page 61*

GUACAMOLE: CLASSIC, TROPICAL, OR SMOKY, *pages 64 and 65*

QUICK PICKLED RED ONIONS, *page 70*

VEGETARIAN TORTILLA SOUP, *page 116*

AVOCADO AND HEARTS OF PALM SALAD, *page 129*

BEET AND ORANGE SALAD, *page 129*

MANGO SLAW, *page 133*

12-MINUTE SALT AND PEPPER GREEN BEANS, *page 199*

QUICKEST SAUTÉED SPINACH, *page 199*

EASY "REFRIED" BEANS, *page 205*

GREEN CHILE CHEESY RICE, *page 209*

If you're trying to shift your family to more frequent meatless meals, this is a great place to start. These enchiladas are hearty and full of flavor that anyone—meat eater or vegetarian, alike—will love. The great taste comes mostly from the Enchilada Sauce so, if you're not making it from scratch, be sure to choose a good brand (see the Supermarket Guide, page 252). The beans you use are also important.

Making my Easy "Refried" Beans takes barely any extra time and ensures a tasty filling made without chemicals or additives. If it makes the difference between trying a meatless meal or not, use canned. There are decent all-natural options (see the Supermarket Guide, pages 250–251). Just promise you'll try making these from scratch at least once. It's worth it.

3½ to 4 cups enchilada sauce, store-bought or homemade (page 61)

8 flour tortillas, store-bought or homemade (page 44)

2 to 2½ cups refried beans, store-bought or homemade (page 205)

3½ cups shredded Cheddar or Jack cheese (12 ounces), or a combination

Chopped fresh cilantro, for garnish (optional)

Sliced avocado or guacamole (pages 64–65), for garnish (optional)

Quick Pickled Red Onions (page 70) or thinly sliced red onion, for garnish (optional)

1. Preheat the oven to 350°F. Cover the bottom of a 12 x 9-inch baking dish with a thin layer of enchilada sauce; set aside.

2. Pour about ½ cup of the enchilada sauce into a wide, shallow bowl. Dip in a tortilla to cover both sides with sauce, allowing the excess to drip back into the bowl. Spoon black beans into the middle of the tortilla and top with shredded Cheddar. Roll up the tortilla and place, seam side down, in the baking dish. Repeat with the remaining seven tortillas, dividing the beans and about 1½ cups of the shredded Cheddar equally among all eight enchiladas.

3. Pour the remaining 2½ cups of sauce and any leftover in the wide, shallow dipping bowl on top of the rolled-up enchiladas. Top with the remaining 2 cups of shredded Cheddar. Bake until the Cheddar is melted and bubbly, 30 to 35 minutes. Top with chopped cilantro, avocado slices, and pickled or raw red onions, if using, and serve immediately.

MARINARA OR PIZZA SAUCE

Makes 3 cups for 1 pound of pasta or 3 pizzas

MIX-AND-MATCH WITH:

PASTA, *page 28*

EASY ITALIAN TURKEY MEATBALLS, *page 156*

CLASSIC MARGHERITA PIZZA, *page 192*

GARLIC BREAD (AS A DIPPING SAUCE), *page 211*

CHEESY GARLIC BREAD (SPREAD UNDER THE CHEESE OR SERVED ON THE SIDE AS A DIPPING SAUCE), *page 213*

Y ou know how to make it easy in the kitchen? Find recipes that can be used in multiple ways. Is there *technically* a difference between marinara and pizza sauce? There it. Is there *practically* a difference between the two? There doesn't have to be. In fact, I prefer both to be simple and full of nothing more than bright tomato flavor.

This sauce is as easy as sauce gets and can be used to toss perfectly cooked pasta, dress Italian Turkey Meatballs, or top a round of Pizza Dough (page 191). No matter how I use it, I prefer my sauce to be a little chunky or, more elegantly put, *home style*. If you like a smooth, silky sauce, you'll need to whip out the blender for a little help.

1 (28-ounce) can whole peeled tomatoes

¼ cup olive oil

¼ cup thinly sliced garlic cloves (from about 5 large cloves)

1 (15-ounce) can tomato sauce

5 fresh basil leaves

¾ teaspoon salt

1. Place the whole peeled tomatoes and their juices in a bowl. If you like your sauce a little chunky, as I do, use your hands to break up the tomatoes, removing the tough bits. If you prefer a smooth sauce, remove the tough bits and use a stand or immersion blender to break up the tomatoes to your desired consistency.

2. Place the oil and garlic in a large pot set over medium heat. Cook until the garlic just starts to brown around the edges, about 2 minutes.

3. Add the prepped tomatoes, tomato sauce, 1 cup of water (either pasta cooking water or tap water that's been used to clean out the tomato can), basil, and salt. Bring to a boil, then lower the heat to medium-low and simmer until the sauce reaches your desired consistency, about 25 minutes, stirring occasionally and using the back of a spoon to break up any tomato chunks. Serve immediately or allow to cool completely before storing in a sealed container or resealable plastic bag in the refrigerator for up to 1 week or in the freezer for up to 3 months.

MEAT SAUCE

Serves 4-6, makes enough for 1 pound pasta

MIX-AND-MATCH WITH:

PASTA, *page 28*

ROASTED CAULIFLOWER WITH GARLIC
TOASTED BREAD CRUMBS, *page 197*

12-MINUTE SALT AND PEPPER GREEN
BEANS, *page 199*

QUICKEST SAUTÉED SPINACH, *page 199*

GIARDINIERA ROASTED VEGETABLES,
page 202

PARMESAN ROASTED BROCCOLI, *page 204*

GARLIC BREAD, *page 211*

CHEESY GARLIC BREAD, *page 213*

There are innumerable approaches to meat sauce. As a busy home cook, my objective is always to get the most flavor out of the least effort and number of easily acquired ingredients. After a lot of testing, this is what I've come up with for meat sauce and, in my house, it's a major hit. In fact, if my crew could eat only one recipe from this book forevermore, it would be this richly flavored pasta sauce. Try it and see if you agree.

Serve it over perfectly cooked pasta with a side of Parmesan Roasted Broccoli, Giardiniera Roasted Vegetables, or a salad dressed with Everyday Vinaigrette (page 124). A side of Cheesy Garlic Bread never hurts, either.

- **1 (28-ounce) can whole peeled tomatoes**
- **2 tablespoons olive oil, plus more to finish**
- **1 cup chopped onion (from about 1 medium-size onion)**
- **1 tablespoon chopped garlic (from about 3 cloves)**
- **1½ pounds ground beef**
- **1 teaspoon salt, plus more to taste**
- **¼ teaspoon garlic powder**
- **½ cup red wine (optional)**
- **1 (15-ounce) can tomato sauce**

1. Place the whole peeled tomatoes and their juices in a bowl and use your hands to break up the tomatoes, removing the tough bits; set aside.

2. Pour the 2 tablespoons of olive oil into a large pot set over medium-high heat. Add the onion and garlic and sauté until fragrant and translucent, 2 to 3 minutes.

3. Add the ground beef, the teaspoon of salt, and garlic powder and cook, breaking the meat up with a silicone spatula or wooden spoon, until browned, 4 minutes. Add the wine, if using, and cook until evaporated, 2 minutes; otherwise skip to step 4.

4. Add the prepped tomatoes, tomato sauce, and 1½ cups of water (either pasta cooking water or tap water that's been used to clean out the tomato can) to the pot. Bring the sauce to a boil, then lower the heat to medium-low and simmer until the sauce reaches your desired consistency, about 30 minutes. Remove from the heat and stir in a hearty glug of olive oil. Season with more salt to taste, if desired. Serve immediately or allow to cool completely before storing in a sealed container or resealable plastic bag in the refrigerator for up to 5 days and in the freezer for up to 3 months.

MUSHROOM AND LENTIL "BOLOGNESE" SAUCE

Serves 4-6, makes for 1 pound pasta

MIX-AND-MATCH WITH:

PASTA, *page 28*

ROASTED CAULIFLOWER WITH GARLIC
TOASTED BREAD CRUMBS, *page 197*

12-MINUTE SALT AND PEPPER GREEN
BEANS, *page 199*

QUICKEST SAUTÉED SPINACH, *page 199*

GIARDINIERA ROASTED VEGETABLES,
page 202

PARMESAN ROASTED BROCCOLI, *page 204*

GARLIC BREAD, *page 211*

CHEESY GARLIC BREAD, *page 213*

We love meat sauce so much in my house that I decided to try my hand at making a vegetarian version (this can even be vegan!). I wanted something that had the same texture and savory flavor profile, but was cheaper and healthier to make on a regular basis. Many vegetarian substitutes never taste like the real thing; that said, they can be similar enough to satisfy and delicious in their own way. That's how I think of this sauce.

If you want to attempt reducing meat in your diet or you just like the idea of varying your vegetarian dinner options, give this recipe a go. You can serve it as you would traditional meat sauce, over perfectly cooked pasta with a side of Parmesan Roasted Broccoli, Giardiniera Roasted Vegetables, or a salad dressed with Everyday Vinaigrette (page 124). And, of course, with Cheesy Garlic Bread if you feel decadent.

1 teaspoon neutral oil, such as grapeseed or canola, or olive oil

1 cup chopped onion (from 1 medium-size onion)

1 carrot, washed, trimmed, and chopped into ¼-inch dice

1 stalk celery, washed, trimmed, and chopped into ¼-inch dice

1½ teaspoons chopped garlic (from about 1 ½ cloves)

1 (8-ounce) package baby bella or white button mushrooms, wiped clean, trimmed, and cut into ½-inch-thick slices

¼ cup red wine

2 tablespoons tomato paste

1 (28-ounce) can chopped tomatoes

1 (15-ounce) can tomato sauce

½ cup dried brown lentils, rinsed

1 bay leaf

5 fresh basil leaves, torn

Salt, to taste

Freshly ground black pepper, to taste

Olive oil, to finish

Chopped fresh flat-leaf parsley, for garnish (optional)

Grated Parmesan cheese, for serving (optional; skip to keep this vegan)

1. Heat the oil in a large pot set over medium heat. Add the onion, carrot, celery, and garlic, and sauté until the vegetables begin to soften, about 5 minutes. Add the mushrooms and cook for 5 more minutes.

2. Add the wine, if using, and reduce until cooked off by about three quarters. Add tomato paste and toast for 1 minute, stirring so that it doesn't burn.

3. Add the chopped tomatoes, tomato sauce, 1 cup of water (either pasta cooking water or tap water that's been used to clean out the tomato

can), lentils, and bay leaf. Bring to a boil, then reduce the heat to medium-low and simmer until the lentils are cooked through and the sauce thickens to your desired consistency, 35 to 40 minutes. If it thickens too quickly, leaving you with not enough sauce, add up to 1 more cup of water, ½ cup at a time.

4. Remove from the heat and stir in the basil leaves. Season with salt and pepper to taste. Stir in a healthy glug of olive oil. Serve immediately, topped with parsley and Parmesan cheese, if using, or allow to cool completely before storing in a sealed container or resealable plastic bag in the refrigerator for up to 5 days or freezer for up to 3 months.

BUTTERED PASTA *with* RICOTTA AND PEAS
Serves 4-6

MIX-AND-MATCH WITH:

PASTA, *page 28*

FRESH RICOTTA CHEESE, *page 41*

CARAMELIZED ONION (TO TASTE), *page 69*

GARLIC TOASTED BREAD CRUMBS (TO TASTE), *page 72*

BEET AND ORANGE SALAD, *page 129*

SHAVED ASPARAGUS AND FENNEL SALAD, *page 135*

ROASTED CAULIFLOWER WITH GARLIC TOASTED BREAD CRUMBS, *page 197*

12-MINUTE SALT AND PEPPER GREEN BEANS, *page 199*

QUICKEST SAUTÉED SPINACH, *page 199*

GIARDINIERA ROASTED VEGETABLES, *page 202*

PARMESAN ROASTED BROCCOLI, *page 204*

GARLIC BREAD, *page 211*

CHEESY GARLIC BREAD, *page 213*

This is one of those recipes that highlights the difference that great ingredients—homemade, if you can swing it—make. This dish made with your standard supermarket ricotta is just *eh*, but with homemade or fresh ricotta from an Italian specialty or cheese store and *oh my goodness*.

This recipe can be personalized a million ways. Add slivered garlic, red pepper flakes, or even thinly sliced hot pepper to the butter as it melts. Swap out the peas for cut asparagus. Add lemon zest. The possibilities are endless. I also like to top this with Garlic Toasted Bread Crumbs sometimes just because they make everything better.

1 pound pasta

1 cup chicken or vegetable broth, store-bought or homemade (pages 39 and 40) (optional)

8 tablespoons (1 stick) unsalted butter

2 cups cooked fresh or (still) frozen peas

¼ teaspoon salt, plus more to taste

Freshly ground black pepper

Ricotta cheese, fresh or homemade (page 41)

Grated Parmesan cheese

1. Cook the pasta according to the package directions or directions on page 28, being sure to save 1 cup of pasta cooking water.

2. Place the butter in the empty pot in which you cooked the pasta (or, if you've cooked the pasta ahead of time, a pot big enough to hold the pasta) and set over medium-high heat. As soon the butter has melted and the foam begins to subside, add the pasta cooking water. If you forgot to save the pasta cooking water, use the 1 cup of chicken or vegetable broth.

3. Return the cooked pasta to the pot, along with peas and the ¼ teaspoon of salt, and toss to coat. Lower the heat to medium, cover, and cook for 2 minutes. Uncover, toss to coat again, and cook as long as needed for the sauce to take on your desired consistency, 30 to 60 seconds. Remove from the heat and season with pepper and more salt, if desired. Serve immediately topped with dollops of ricotta and grated Parmesan.

PASTA *with* SPINACH PESTO AND GREEN BEANS
Serves 4-6

MIX-AND-MATCH WITH:

PASTA, *page 28*

SPINACH PESTO, *page 58*

BEET AND ORANGE SALAD, *page 129*

SHAVED ASPARAGUS AND FENNEL SALAD, *page 135*

ROASTED CAULIFLOWER WITH GARLIC TOASTED BREAD CRUMBS, *page 197*

QUICKEST SAUTÉED SPINACH, *page 199*

GIARDINIERA ROASTED VEGETABLES, *page 202*

PARMESAN ROASTED BROCCOLI, *page 204*

GARLIC BREAD, *page 211*

CHEESY GARLIC BREAD, *page 213*

Unlike the other pasta sauces in this book, I've put the recipe for Spinach Pesto in the Supermarket Staples section because pesto can be so much more than a pasta sauce. That said, my favorite way to use it—and my kids' favorite way to eat it—is tossed with pasta.

I love the way pesto and green beans pair, and tossing vegetables with pasta makes for a healthy, one-bowl meal, especially given that this pesto is also packed with spinach. If you don't like green beans, asparagus and/or peas work well. Or throw them all in there and make a pesto primavera pasta.

1 pound pasta

8 ounces green beans, washed, trimmed, and cut into 2-inch pieces

1 tablespoon unsalted butter

½ cup spinach pesto, plus more to taste, store-bought or homemade (page 58; about one-half of the recipe as written)

Olive oil, to finish

Salt, to taste

Freshly ground black pepper, to taste

Grated Parmesan cheese, for garnish

1. Cook the pasta according to the package directions or the directions on page 28, being sure to save ½ cup of pasta cooking water before draining.

2. In the meantime, steam the green beans. (You can follow the cooking directions for 12-Minute Salt and Pepper Green Beans on page 299 through step 1.)

3. Place the butter in the empty pot in which you cooked the pasta (or, if you've cooked the pasta ahead of time, a pot big enough to hold the pasta) and set over medium-high heat. As soon as the butter melts and the foam begins to subside, add the pasta cooking water. If you forgot to save the pasta cooking water, use ½ cup of regular water.

4. Return the pasta to the pot along with reserved steamed green beans and at least ½ cup of pesto, or more as desired, and toss to coat. Remove from the heat and finish with a healthy glug of olive oil. Season with salt and pepper to taste. Serve immediately topped with grated Parmesan.

ZITI *with* CORN AND ROASTED TOMATOES

Serves 4-6

MIX-AND-MATCH WITH:

PASTA, *page 28*

FRESH RICOTTA CHEESE, *page 41*

ROASTED CHERRY TOMATOES, *page 67*

BEET AND ORANGE SALAD, *page 129*

SHAVED ASPARAGUS AND FENNEL SALAD, *page 135*

ROASTED CAULIFLOWER WITH GARLIC TOASTED BREAD CRUMBS, *page 197*

12-MINUTE SALT AND PEPPER GREEN BEANS, *page 199*

QUICKEST SAUTÉED SPINACH, *page 199*

GIARDINIERA ROASTED VEGETABLES, *page 202*

PARMESAN ROASTED BROCCOLI, *page 204*

GARLIC BREAD, *page 211*

CHEESY GARLIC BREAD, *page 213*

I love this pasta most in summer when both in-season corn and tomatoes are gorgeous and sweet. That said, it can be made all year-round. Cherry or grape tomatoes are nearly always available, and though never quite like fresh, frozen corn can be quite good. Every once and a while, it's nice to pull this out in the middle of winter for a little taste of summery goodness, even if fleeting.

1 pound ziti or favorite cut of pasta

6 tablespoons salted butter

2 cups fresh or 1 (10-ounce) bag (still) frozen corn kernels

2 teaspoons tomato paste

3 cups roasted cherry tomatoes (page 66; three times the recipe as written)

1 cup chicken or vegetable broth, store-
  bought or homemade (pages 39 and 40)
  (optional)
3 tablespoons grated Parmesan cheese, plus
  more for garnish
Salt, to taste
Freshly ground black pepper, to taste

1. Cook the pasta according to the package directions or the directions on page 28, being sure to save 1 cup of pasta cooking water.

2. Melt 5 tablespoons of the butter in your empty pasta pot (or, if you've cooked the pasta ahead of time, a pot big enough to hold the pasta) over medium heat. Add the corn and cook until tender, about 5 minutes, being sure to keep the butter from browning; lower the heat if necessary.

3. Stir in the tomato paste and toast, 1 to 2 minutes.

4. Add the roasted tomatoes, along with their cooking juices, the remaining tablespoon of butter, and about ½ cup of the pasta cooking water. If you forgot to save the pasta cooking water, use ½ cup of chicken or vegetable broth or regular water. Stir to bring the ingredients together and cook until the sauce thickens slightly, 4 to 5 minutes.

5. Add the cooked pasta and stir to coat well. Continue to cook for 2 to 3 minutes, at which point your sauce should be glossy and, though thin, not watery. If it's too thin, cook for another couple of minutes. If it's not thin or saucy enough, add a bit more cooking water or regular water, ¼ cup at a time.

6. Remove from the heat and stir in the Parmesan. Season with salt and pepper to taste. Serve immediately with more Parmesan on top, if desired.

EASY FOOD PROCESSOR PIZZA DOUGH

Makes enough for one 12-inch pie

———

MIX-AND-MATCH WITH:
CLASSIC MARGHERITA PIZZA, *page 192*
5 UNEXPECTED PIZZA TOPPINGS, *page 194*

Like marinara and meat sauce, people take pizza dough very seriously, as they should. The only problem with that for busy home cooks is that it's hard to find a simple recipe that turns out great dough with minimal planning, or more to the point, in a short amount of time.

Even I find it hard to prioritize making homemade pizza dough when buying it fresh is so easy, especially when I have to plan way ahead to make homemade happen. But then there are those times when I can wait a couple of hours for a single rise. Like when we decide on a cold weekend morning that we should stay in all day and have a pizza and movie night. Or when the kids want to help make pizzas from scratch—it's a great kitchen project and the fact that you only have to wait a couple of hours and not all day makes it easier for them. Not to mention the fact that they—and you—can top homemade pizza with any toppings you can dream up.

¾ cup very warm tap water
2¼ teaspoons (1 packet) active dry yeast
1¾ cups all-purpose flour (see measuring
  tip, page 217)
2 teaspoons salt
1 tablespoon olive oil, plus more for bowl

1. In a small bowl, sprinkle the yeast over the water; set aside.

2. In the bowl of a food processor, pulse the flour and salt until combined. Add the yeast mixture and olive oil. Process for 2 full minutes. If you have a BREAD or DOUGH setting on your processor, set it on that.

3. Transfer the ball of dough from the food processor to a well-oiled medium bowl. Cover with a kitchen towel and allow to rest in a warm spot for 2 hours before using or wrapping in plastic wrap to store in the refrigerator for up to 3 days or in the freezer for up to 3 months.

CLASSIC MARGHERITA PIZZA
Makes one 12- to 15-inch pie

START WITH:
PIZZA SAUCE, *page 183*
PIZZA DOUGH, *page 191*

MIX-AND-MATCH WITH:
BEET AND ORANGE SALAD, *page 129*
SHAVED ASPARAGUS AND FENNEL SALAD, *page 135*
ROASTED CAULIFLOWER WITH GARLIC TOASTED BREAD CRUMBS, *page 197*
12-MINUTE SALT AND PEPPER GREEN BEANS, *page 199*
QUICKEST SAUTÉED SPINACH, *page 199*
GIARDINIERA ROASTED VEGETABLES, *page 202*
PARMESAN ROASTED BROCCOLI, *page 204*

If you're going to make pizza dough, you have to know how to throw together a classic margherita pie! With a round of dough and delicious pizza sauce, it's impossible to go wrong. Start by mastering a plain pie, then start experimenting with toppings. The possibilities are truly endless.

Oil, for baking sheet (optional)

1 round pizza dough, store-bought or homemade (page 191)

Cornmeal or all-purpose flour, for dusting

1 cup Pizza Sauce (page 183; one-third of the recipe as written)

1 small ball fresh mozzarella cheese

¾ cup shredded mozzarella cheese

4 to 5 fresh basil leaves, torn

Additional toppings, as desired (see Make It Tastier, page 194)

1. If the dough has been made ahead of time, bring it to room temperature before working. When ready, put a pizza stone in the oven and preheat to 400°F. If you don't have a stone, pre-heat the oven to 400°F and oil a rimmed baking sheet that you set aside on the counter.

2. If using a pizza stone, sprinkle cornmeal or flour on a pizza peel or a large, wooden cutting board that you can lift; set aside. If you don't have a pizza stone, move on to step 3.

3. On a lightly floured work surface, use your hands to gently ease the dough into a 12- to 15-inch round that's relatively even except for the edges, which should be a little bit thicker to make a crust. Carefully transfer the dough to prepared pizza peel or cutting board or place on the oiled baking sheet, reshaping as necessary to fit.

4. Top the pizza with the sauce, using the back of a spoon to spread it evenly, then with the fresh mozzarella, followed by the shredded mozzarella. Add the basil leaves (and any other desired toppings) and very carefully slip the pie from the peel or cutting board onto the preheated pizza stone or place the baking sheet in the oven and bake until the crust is golden and the cheese is bubbling, 20 to 23 minutes. Remove from the oven and allow to cool for at least 2 to 3 minutes before cutting and serving.

♥ Make It Tastier: 5 awesomely, unexpected pizza topping combinations

1. Pizza Sauce (page 183), sliced Italian Turkey Meatballs (page 156), and Garlic Toasted Bread Crumbs (page 72; added in the last 5 minutes of cooking)

2. Pizza Sauce (page 183), pepperoni, thinly sliced chile peppers, and honey (drizzled on top once out of the oven)

3. Mozzarella cheese, Fresh Ricotta Cheese (page 41), and Maple-Glazed Bacon (page 84) (finish by cracking a couple of eggs on top in the last 10 minutes of cooking)

4. Roasted Cherry Tomatoes (page 66), crumbled or sliced Italian sausage, and Caramelized Onions (page 69)

5. Fresh Ricotta Cheese (page 41), chorizo, Quick Pickled Red Onions (page 70), and fresh cilantro (add the last two toppings after the pizza comes out of the oven, right before serving)

Side Dishes

I often spend so much time planning dinner—or scrambling to make one happen—that just when I think I'm out of the woods and everything is going to be all right, I remember: side dishes.

Unless entertaining, I'm not making side dishes to put out a multicourse spread. Rather, I'm serving two very basic purposes: to fill bellies and meet a veggie quota. When I can do this with one-bowl meals, such as Asian Steak Salad (page 141), Cold Soba Noodle Salad (page 179), Ziti with Corn and Roasted Tomatoes (page 190), or a Classic Margherita Pizza (page 192) topped with veggies, believe me, I do. Those kinds of meals are a lifeline. But I often need something on the side of my main to make sure that my crew is sated with plenty of healthy vegetables.

Given my not very lofty goals, the two categories that my everyday side dishes fall into are vegetables and carb. (Creative, huh?) The sides in this chapter are easy, go-to recipes that you can match with the mains in this book to make complete meals week after week without needing much more. These are the side dishes you keep in heavy rotation.

You might notice a theme to my sides. Most veggies are steamed or roasted because that's how you make tasty vegetables quickly and easily. It's also how you can make them ahead. When I have time on the weekend, especially in the colder months when we spend more time inside, I'll roast a big pan or two of veggies with nothing more than oil, salt, and pepper. I'll also steam green beans, broccoli, and carrots ahead of time. Then, the day of, I can reheat and top with oil and vinegar, a proper vinaigrette, or even browned butter. Simple and delicious.

I'll also make rice and quinoa in big batches so that I can cook once and feed twice. Sometimes I even freeze them—quinoa freezes especially well—so that, by the time they thaw, all I have to do is quickly reheat on the stove or in the microwave. You can dress rice, quinoa, or even orzo a million ways, but I usually use a salad dressing that matches our meal. Sometimes I throw in drained and rinsed canned beans for extra protein.

With these tricks up my sleeve, it takes a lot for me to justify keeping a long list of elaborate sides. Between my simple prep ahead habits and the handful of quick and tasty vegetable and carb dishes I included here, I've got weeknight sides covered, and so can you. Phew.

VEGETABLE SIDES

Most of these recipes are for roasted veggies and that's because making roasted vegetables is easy—cauliflower, squash, broccoli are all here. That said, it can take time. When you don't have time, I find that throwing together a Country-Style Greek Salad (page 132), Beet and Orange Salad (page 129), or Mango Slaw (page 133) is easier than taking to the stove. The exceptions are 12-Minute Salt and Pepper Green Beans (page 199), which I make constantly, and Quickest Sautéed Spinach (page 199).

If you're looking for an even easier side, it's avocado to the rescue. For so many weeknight dinners, you can simply slice up an avocado and serve it with a drizzle of olive oil and good salt (I save crunchy Maldon salt for this). Or make a proper avocado salad in just minutes: between my Avocado and Edamame Salad (page 128) and Avocado and Hearts of Palm Salad (page 129) you can cover most meals. And there's always guacamole (pages 64–65).

If avocado doesn't fit the bill, don't feel bad throwing down a plate of cut-up, raw veggies. When I do this, I often put them out before dinner so that my hungry kids eat them without distraction from things like rice and bread. If I put out a little bowl of Hummus (page 50) or Hearts of Palm Dip (page 99), too, they're in heaven. In fact, they can eat so much that they'll eat less dinner, but I don't mind them getting full on vegetables. And, anyway, this is also a good way to keep me from overeating at dinner, too!

ROASTED CAULIFLOWER *with* GARLIC TOASTED BREAD CRUMBS

Serves 4

Although I could eat plain roasted cauliflower day and night, we eat it enough that varying it is essential. Sometimes that's by roasting cauliflower with a can of rinsed chickpeas, other times it's by tossing still-warm roasted cauliflower with Spinach Pesto (page 58) thawed from the freezer or Everyday Vinaigrette (page 124) waiting in the refrigerator. The tastiest way, though, is to toss roasted cauliflower with Garlic Toasted Bread Crumbs that not only add flavor, but the perfect crunchy texture, too.

1 head cauliflower, trimmed and cut into bite-size florets

3 tablespoons olive oil

Salt, to taste

½ to 1 cup Garlic Toasted Bread Crumbs (page 72), to taste

¼ cup chopped fresh flat-leaf parsley

1. Preheat the oven to 425°F. In a large bowl, toss the cauliflower with the olive oil. Spread the cauliflower on a rimmed baking sheet in a single layer and sprinkle generously with salt (set the empty bowl aside to keep cleanup to a minimum). Roast until the cauliflower is cooked through and browned in spots, about 40 minutes, tossing halfway through the cooking time.

2. Remove the cauliflower from the oven and carefully transfer it to the bowl you've set aside. While still hot, toss the cauliflower with the bread crumbs. Season with more salt to taste, if desired, and sprinkle with the parsley. Toss one more time and serve immediately.

12-MINUTE SALT AND PEPPER GREEN BEANS

Serves 4-6

MIX-AND-MATCH WITH:
THESE HONESTLY GO WITH ANY DINNER YOU CAN MAKE FROM THIS BOOK.

When I only have a few minutes to cook vegetables, I'm prone to avoiding the stove and opting for a salad. This quick-prep green bean recipe, though, is an exception.

This recipe is so forgiving that you can really freestyle it. The measurements for salt and pepper here are fairly conservative so that they suit most palates, so think of it as a baseline. I, for one, like to jack up the black pepper to give my beans a little bite.

2 pounds fresh green beans, trimmed

2 tablespoons unsalted butter

¼ teaspoon salt, plus more to taste

¼ teaspoon freshly ground black pepper, plus more to taste

1. Fill a large, deep pan with a lid with enough water to cover the bottom and come up the sides about ⅛ inch. Place the green beans in the pan, cover, and set over medium heat. Steam until the beans are just tender and bright green, 7 to 9 minutes. Drain, setting the beans aside.

2. Return the empty pan to medium-high heat and melt the butter. Once the foam subsides, return the beans to the pan and season with salt and pepper. Toss to coat the beans well and cook, untouched, until blistered in spots, 3 to 4 minutes. Toss once more, remove from the heat, and adjust the salt and pepper to taste. Serve immediately.

QUICKEST SAUTÉED SPINACH

Serves 4

MIX-AND-MATCH WITH:
AS WITH THE GREEN BEANS, THIS GOES WITH NEARLY ANY DINNER YOU CAN PUT TOGETHER.

I almost didn't include this recipe, but even after testing all sorts of sautéed greens—from kale with red wine vinegar to chard with yogurt—I realized that night after night, when I wasn't working on recipes for the book, I was quickly sautéing spinach.

It's no wonder: when life is busy and you have just a few minutes to make dinner, washing and chopping kale or chard, though easy enough, feels like a major chore. Baby spinach, on the other hand, which comes prewashed and ready to go, takes zero effort. And it's good for you, too.

I encourage you to expand your greens repertoire, but do it when you have time to dress them up. The tastier you can make dark, leafy greens, the more likely your kids—and you!—will come to enjoy them. But when you're busy, grab some mild, healthy, and fresh baby spinach to quickly sauté with lemon, garlic, and oil for the busy weekday win.

3 tablespoons olive oil, plus more to taste

1 tablespoon finely chopped garlic (from about 3 cloves)

Pinch of red pepper flakes (optional)

15 ounces fresh baby spinach, washed

½ teaspoon salt, plus more to taste

2 tablespoon freshly squeezed lemon juice (from about 1 juicy lemon), plus more to taste

1. Place 2 tablespoons of the oil, all the garlic, and the red pepper flakes, if using, in a large pan set over medium heat. As soon as the oil is hot and garlic fragrant, after about 2 minutes, add 10 ounces of the spinach (two thirds of the total amount).

2. Using tongs or a silicone spatula, toss the spinach to coat all the leaves with oil and expose them to the heat at the bottom of the pan. Keep tossing and cooking until only a handful of leaves haven't yet wilted, about 1½ minutes. Add the remaining spinach and salt, and continue tossing until all the spinach has *just* wilted.

3. Add the lemon juice and cook for another 30 seconds before removing from the heat. Plate the spinach, allowing any excess water and lemon juice to remain in the pan, and finish the spinach with the remaining 1 tablespoon of oil. Taste and adjust the salt, lemon juice, or oil as desired. Serve immediately.

ROASTED SQUASH *with* GINGER SHALLOT BROWNED BUTTER

Serves 4

MIX-AND-MATCH WITH:

KEBABS, *page 34*

LENTIL SOUP WITH SAUSAGE, *page 120*

NO-FUSS PAN-ROASTED PAPRIKA CHICKEN, *page 146*

THAI CHICKEN BURGERS WITH QUICK PICKLED CARROTS, *page 147*

CHICKEN CURRY, *page 150*

CHICKEN CUTLETS WITH ARUGULA AND PARMESAN, *page 151*

INDIAN-STYLE MEATBALLS, *page 157*

STEAK WITH SWEET-AND-SOUR PEPPERS, *page 159*

MISO AND SWEET CHILI GLAZED PORK, *page 164*

SLOW COOKER HOISIN PULLED PORK, *page 166*

PORK CHOPS WITH MAPLE BUTTERED APPLES, *page 169*

HOISIN-GLAZED SALMON, *page 172*

I could happily eat plain roasted squash on a regular basis. Its natural sweetness paired with a sprinkle of salt and wrapped in a crisp-on-the-outside, soft-on-the-inside bite is near perfection. But since I like to make it easy to spice things up, I often dress my roasted squash in ginger shallot browned butter. And boy, is it mouthwateringly good.

In fact, this recipe could easily hold its own on your holiday table. The crazy thing is that it's also easy enough to make every week.

About 6 cups peeled, seeded, and cubed butternut squash, cut into 1 to 2-inch pieces (from 1 medium-size squash or 2 (20-ounce) packages precut squash)

2 tablespoons olive oil

¼ teaspoon salt, plus more to taste

Freshly ground black pepper

4 tablespoons (½ stick) unsalted butter

½ cup thinly sliced shallots

2 teaspoons chopped fresh ginger

Chives, chopped, for garnish (optional)

1. Preheat the oven to 425°F. In a large bowl, toss the squash with the olive oil, the ¼ teaspoon of salt, and a pinch of pepper. Spread the squash in a single layer on a rimmed baking sheet (set the empty bowl aside to keep cleanup to a minimum) and roast until tender all the way through and caramelized in spots, about 40 minutes. (Make sure that the squash can hold its shape well enough to be handled without getting mushy.)

2. In the meantime, in a small pan, melt the butter over medium heat. Once the butter has melted completely and begins to foam, start swirling the pan continuously. Watch carefully as the butter cooks and turns color: once you see it turn chestnut brown, remove the pan from the heat and add the shallots and ginger. Swirl the pan a couple more times and return to the heat.

3. Continue to cook, stirring constantly, until the ginger is fragrant and the shallots are soft and caramelized in spots, about 3 minutes. Take off the heat for good and set aside.

4. Remove the squash from the oven and carefully transfer it to the bowl you've set aside. Pour the ginger shallot browned butter over the squash and gently toss. Season with more salt and pepper to taste, if desired, and garnish with chives, if using. Serve immediately.

♥ *Make It Easier:* Get help from the store—or a very sharp knife.

Let's be honest, dealing with butternut squash can be a total drag. Although you don't always get the same vibrant flavor out of the precut kind you can find in most supermarkets nowadays, I find the shortcut totally worth it, especially when roasting will coax out so much delicious flavor. If you can't find or just refuse to buy precut (hey, we all choose the hard path for something!), make it easy by using a sharp knife and sharp peeler.

Start by cutting off each end of the squash, then peel—with a peeler, not your knife. Once you've removed all the skin, stand the squash upright on one of the cut ends. It should be stable so that you can cut the vegetable in half lengthwise. Once split open, you can scoop out the seeds with a spoon and cut each half where the neck meets the body. The neck will be solid; cut it into slices at whatever thickness you like (1½ to 2 inches is good), then cut each slice into strips and, after that, cubes. Cut each remaining half in slices and each slice into cubes. You did it.

GIARDINIERA ROASTED VEGETABLES

Serves 4

MIX-AND-MATCH WITH:

KEBABS, *page 34*

LENTIL SOUP WITH SAUSAGE, *page 120*

NO-FUSS PAN-ROASTED PAPRIKA CHICKEN, *page 146*

CHICKEN CUTLETS WITH ARUGULA AND PARMESAN, *page 151*

EASY ITALIAN TURKEY MEATBALLS, *page 156*

STEAK WITH SWEET-AND-SOUR PEPPERS, *page 159*

BEEF AND LENTIL SLOPPY JOES, *page 161*

PASTA WITH MARINARA SAUCE, *pages 28 and 183*

PASTA WITH MEAT SAUCE, *pages 28 and 184*

PASTA WITH MUSHROOM AND LENTIL "BOLOGNESE" SAUCE, *pages 28 and 185*

BUTTERED PASTA WITH RICOTTA AND PEAS, *page 186*

PASTA WITH SPINACH PESTO AND GREEN BEANS, *page 188*

ZITI WITH CORN AND ROASTED TOMATOES, *page 190*

CLASSIC MARGHERITA PIZZA, *page 192*

This recipe was inspired by (you guessed it!) giardiniera, an easy and sometimes spicy Italian pickle typically served as a condiment or antipasto—at least in New Jersey. To be honest, I'm not sure if it's served in Italy at all or if it's just an Italian American thing. All I know is that, growing up in New Jersey, you get this stuff at the deli, in your sandwiches, and on every antipasto platter. And I love it.

I wanted to find a way to bring the flavors of giardiniera to something we could enjoy on a more regular basis. By roasting giardiniera vegetables, namely, cauliflower and peppers, and finishing them with red wine vinegar, you get the right vibe and a tasty side dish, all in one.

If you're brave, don't seed or devein the hot peppers—or add more of them. I serve this with mostly Italian dishes but these veggies pair well with so much.

- 1 head cauliflower, trimmed, and cut into bite-size florets
- 6 small carrots, peeled and halved lengthwise
- 4 Cubanelle peppers, seeded and cut into 1½- to 2-inch-thick strips (you can use sweet Italian or green bell peppers in a pinch)
- 1 to 2 fresh hot cherry peppers, seeded and deveined for mild, cut into 1-inch pieces
- ¼ cup olive oil
- ½ teaspoon salt, plus more to taste
- 2 to 3 teaspoons red wine vinegar
- Chopped fresh flat-leaf parsley, for garnish (optional)

1. Preheat the oven to 425°F. In a large bowl, toss the vegetables with the olive oil and salt. Spread the vegetables in a single layer on a rimmed baking sheet (set the empty bowl aside to keep cleanup to a minimum) and roast until the heartier vegetables (the cauliflower and carrots) are tender all the way through and smaller ones (the peppers) are caramelized in spots, 40 to 45 minutes.

2. Remove the vegetables from the oven and carefully transfer to the bowl you've set aside. Toss with red wine vinegar to taste. Season with more salt and pepper to taste, if desired. Sprinkle with parsley, if using. Toss one more time and serve immediately.

PARMESAN ROASTED BROCCOLI

Serves 4

If the families I've worked with are any indication, broccoli has become a go-to family vegetable—it certainly is in my home. I have to admit that, in a pinch, I'll throw broccoli florets into a bowl with enough water to fill the bottom by an inch, cover it with plastic wrap, poke a few holes, and steam it in the microwave. Once cooked, I'll dress it with salt, olive oil, and fresh lemon juice or, if I have some in the refrigerator, Everyday Vinaigrette (page 124). It may not be an elegant preparation, but it turns out to be a very healthy one.

It doesn't get easier than that, but it does get tastier with this Parmesan Roasted Broccoli. It takes a little extra time, but the good news is that broccoli roasts faster than many other vegetables—in some cases, in half the time.

With only 20 minutes in the oven, you can serve this side anytime you have a half hour or more to prep dinner. The rest of the time, it's microwave steaming to the rescue.

1½ pounds broccoli (about 1 large head), cut into florets

¼ cup olive oil

2 teaspoons finely chopped garlic (from about 2 cloves)

Pinch of crushed red pepper flakes (optional)

½ teaspoon salt, plus more to taste

¼ cup grated Parmesan cheese

2 tablespoons freshly squeezed lemon juice (from about 1 juicy lemon)

Freshly ground black pepper, to taste

1. Preheat the oven to 425°F. In a large bowl, toss the broccoli with the olive oil, garlic, red pepper flakes, if using, and the ½ teaspoon of salt. Spread the broccoli in a single layer on a rimmed baking sheet (set the empty bowl aside to keep cleanup to a minimum) and roast until tender all the way through, 20 to 25 minutes.

2. Remove the broccoli from the oven and carefully transfer to the bowl you've set aside. Toss with the Parmesan and lemon juice. Season with more salt and pepper to taste, if desired, and toss one more time. Serve immediately.

CARB SIDES

EASY "REFRIED" BEANS

Makes 2 cups beans

MIX-AND-MATCH WITH:

RICE, *page 30*

QUINOA, *page 31*

KEBABS, *page 34*

SMALL-BATCH CHICKEN BROTH, *page 39*

SMALL-BATCH VEGETABLE BROTH, *page 40*

TORTILLA CHIPS, *page 47*

FIRE-ROASTED SALSA, *page 62*
(mix a little bit into the beans to make a dip)

CHORIZO MIGAS, *page 90*

VEGETARIAN TORTILLA SOUP, *page 116*

AVOCADO AND HEARTS OF PALM SALAD,
page 129

CHILI-RUBBED STEAK TACOS, *page 160*

SLOW COOKER CARNITAS, *page 165*

FISH TACOS, *page 175*

VEGETABLE FAJITAS, *page 180*

BEAN AND CHEESE ENCHILADAS, *page 182*

I cook with beans like they are going out of style. Although you'll often see me add them straight from the can to salads, my kids' lunchboxes, rice, orzo, and quinoa, it's good to have a way to switch things up.

These beans aren't actually refried but, rather, quickly cooked with a handful of ingredients that lend big flavor, then mashed. This isn't a double cook or otherwise involved process, but still they manage to have great taste.

I mostly use black beans to make this recipe, but pinto beans work well, too. You can even use white or kidney beans in a pinch.

> 2 (15-ounce) cans black beans, drained and rinsed
>
> ⅔ cup chicken or vegetable broth, store-bought or homemade (pages 39 and 40)
>
> 2 tablespoons neutral oil, such as grapeseed or canola
>
> 2 teaspoons finely chopped garlic (from about 2 cloves)
>
> ¼ teaspoon salt, plus more to taste
>
> 20 (or so) full sprigs cilantro, washed, with only the root cut off

1. Place the beans, broth, oil, garlic, and the ¼ teaspoon of salt in a medium-size pot set over medium heat and stir to combine. Nestle the cilantro in the beans and cook until the liquid thickens, 8 to 10 minutes.

2. Remove the beans from the heat and pick out the cilantro sprigs, allowing any leaves that fall in to remain. Using a fork or a potato masher, mash the beans to your desired consistency. Season with more salt to taste. Serve immediately or allow to cool completely before storing in an airtight container in the refrigerator for up to 3 days. (Add a splash of broth to reheat.)

RICE AND LENTIL PILAF

Serves 4

MIX-AND-MATCH WITH:

KEBABS, *page 34*

CARAMELIZED ONIONS, *page 69*

CURRIED CAULIFLOWER AND RED LENTIL SOUP, *page 121*

NO-FUSS PAN-ROASTED PAPRIKA CHICKEN, *page 146*

GREEK-STYLE KEBABS, *page 162*

INDIAN-STYLE MEATBALLS, *page 157*

PORK CHOPS WITH MAPLE BUTTERED APPLES, *page 169*

With a number of ingredients and multiple pans on the stove, this is a more involved recipe than most in this book BUT, if you can plan well enough to make it ahead of time, it pays off, especially since it can double as a light vegetarian meal or pair up with very quickly and simply cooked protein, such as grilled chicken or roasted salmon. In other words, this superflavorful and very affordable combination of rice and lentils takes some work, but can be the star of the meal.

1 cup dried brown lentils, rinsed and sorted

5 whole peppercorns

2 whole cloves

1 bay leaf

1 teaspoon salt, plus more to taste

1 cup uncooked rice

1 tablespoon unsalted butter

1 whole star anise (optional, but recommended)

Freshly ground black pepper, to taste

Olive oil, to finish (optional)

1 cup Caramelized Onions (page 69), to serve

½ cup plain Greek-style yogurt, for garnish (optional)

2 tablespoons chopped fresh mint, for garnish (optional)

1 tablespoon freshly squeezed lemon juice (from about ½ a juicy lemon), to finish (optional)

1. Place 2½ cups of water and the lentils, peppercorns, cloves, and bay leaf in a medium-size pot set over medium heat. Bring to a boil, then lower the heat to maintain a gentle simmer. Cook, uncovered, until the lentils are cooked through but not mushy, 20 to 30 minutes. (You may need to add water along the way to ensure that the lentils remain just barely covered with water as they cook.) Drain, picking out the peppercorns, cloves, and bay leaf; season with ½ teaspoon of the salt and set aside.

2. In the meantime, place the rice in another medium-size pot along with 2 cups of water and the butter, star anise, and remaining ½ teaspoon of salt. Cook according to the package directions or the directions on page 30 and set aside.

3. When ready to serve, transfer the lentils and rice to a large serving bowl and gently stir to mix well. Season with salt and pepper to taste; I also like to add a teaspoon of good olive oil. Top with the caramelized onions. If desired, combine the yogurt with a drizzle of olive oil (up to 1 teaspoon), mint, lemon juice, salt, and pepper to taste and dollop on top of each serving.

GREEN CHILE CHEESY RICE

Serves 4

MIX-AND-MATCH WITH:

KEBABS, *page 34*

VEGETARIAN TORTILLA SOUP, *page 116*

CHICKEN CUTLETS WITH QUICK AVOCADO TOMATO RELISH, *page 154*

CHILI-RUBBED STEAK TACOS, *page 160*

SLOW COOKER CARNITAS, *page 165*

FISH TACOS, *page 175*

VEGETABLE FAJITAS, *page 180*

BEAN AND CHEESE ENCHILADAS, *page 182*

Although another hearty rice dish, this Green Chile Cheesy Rice is a bit of a departure from my healthy Rice and Lentil Pilaf. It is decadent, creamy, cheesy, and though I hate to admit it, without all that much nutritional value, unless you swap in brown rice (which is good, but not quite the same, if you ask me). But, boy, is it delicious. And it's sure to fill everyone up and keep them happy. Kids especially love this dish and it's a potluck party pleaser, too. Just double the recipe and be prepared for more invites (or just pass this book along!).

You can make the rice up to three days ahead of time, to make this recipe go fast.

1 tablespoon salted butter, plus more for baking dish

1 cup uncooked rice

1 cup chopped onion (from about 1 medium-size onion)

1 (4-ounce) can mild green chiles

2 cups shredded Cheddar and/or Jack cheese

1 cup (8 ounces) sour cream

Scant cup (½ pound) cottage cheese (low-fat is fine)

¼ teaspoon salt, plus more to taste

Chopped fresh cilantro, for garnish (optional)

1. Preheat the oven to 350°F and butter a 3-quart baking dish. Cook the rice according to the package directions or directions on page 30. You can do this up to 3 days ahead of time and then start at step 2.

2. Melt the tablespoon of butter in a medium-size pan set over medium heat. Add the onion and chiles and sauté until the onions are fragrant and translucent and most of the liquid from the green chiles has cooked off, about 5 minutes.

3. In a large bowl, mix together the cooked rice, onion mixture, 1 cup of the shredded Cheddar, sour cream, cottage cheese, and the ¼ teaspoon of salt, using a silicone spatula or wooden spoon, until well combined. Adjust the salt to taste. Spread the rice into the prepared baking dish and sprinkle the remaining cup of shredded Cheddar on top. Bake until the cheese is melted and bubbly, about 30 minutes. Remove from the oven, allow to cool for a few minutes, and serve, garnished with cilantro, if desired.

COLD ORZO SALAD

Serves 6

MIX-AND-MATCH WITH:

LENTIL SOUP WITH SAUSAGE, *page 120*

EVERYDAY VINAIGRETTE, *page 124*

BUTTERMILK DILL (OR RANCH!) DRESSING, *page 127*

NO-FUSS PAN-ROASTED PAPRIKA CHICKEN, *page 146*

CHICKEN CUTLETS WITH ARUGULA AND PARMESAN, *page 151*

CHICKEN CUTLETS WITH QUICK AVOCADO-TOMATO RELISH, *page 154*

EASY ITALIAN TURKEY MEATBALLS, *page 156*

STEAK WITH SWEET-AND-SOUR PEPPERS, *page 159*

SLOW COOKER BBQ PULLED PORK, *page 167*

BBQ SALMON, *page 173*

LEMONY OREGANO SHRIMP, *page 174*

Just as with rice and quinoa, orzo can be dressed up a million and one ways to serve as a side dish with nearly any meal. One of my favorites is to just toss it with butter and salt—it's fast and totally delicious. If I'm going to do anything more, though, I'm going to make this cold salad. Packed with vegetables, it serves as a carb *and* a vegetable side, which makes it *really* easy, especially if you make it ahead of time.

This is also great for potlucks and picnics.

1 (16-ounce) box orzo, cooked per the package instructions (5 cups cooked)

1 cup fresh corn cut off the cob or thawed frozen corn kernels

1 cup halved or quartered cherry tomatoes, depending on size

1 cup Buttermilk Dill (or Ranch!) Dressing (page 127)

½ cup cubed fresh mozzarella or crumbled feta cheese

Salt, to taste

Freshly ground black pepper, to taste

1. In a large bowl, combine all the ingredients, adding salt and pepper to taste, and toss to combine well. Taste and adjust the salt and pepper. Serve immediately or store in a sealed container in the refrigerator for up to 3 days. If making this ahead, dress the pasta with only ½ cup of dressing before storing in the refrigerator, then toss with the remaining dressing right before serving.

♥ *Make It Easier:* Turn any grain into a deliciously filling warm side or cold salad in minutes.

It's easy to amp up the health and taste of simply cooked grains by pairing them with fresh chopped or thawed frozen vegetables and a sauce or dressing. Cheese and nuts are great additions, too.

An important thing to remember when combining grains with other ingredients is to make everything a uniform(ish!) size. So, for quinoa or rice, chop peppers and quarter cherry tomatoes. For soba noodles, cut carrots into strips and just halve snap peas.

Here are some of my favorite combinations:

- rice + butter + drained, rinsed canned chickpeas
- rice + thawed green peas + Everyday Vinaigrette (page 124) or Spinach Pesto (page 58)
- rice + edamame (thawed frozen or crunchy) + red pepper + cucumber + Ginger Lime Vinaigrette (page 125)

- rice or orzo + Buttermilk Dill (or Ranch!) Dressing (page 127) + thawed, frozen corn + halved cherry tomatoes
- quinoa + Fire-Roasted Salsa (page 62) + drained and rinsed canned black beans
- quinoa + red pepper + mango + cilantro + Everyday Vinaigrette (page 124)
- quinoa or barley + Roasted Cherry Tomatoes (page 66) with some of the oil in which they've been cooked + chickpeas + crumbled feta
- quinoa + chopped Sweet-and-Sour Peppers (page 68) + Everyday Vinaigrette (page 124)
- quinoa or soba noodles + Ginger Lime Vinaigrette (page 125) + chopped cucumber and avocado

If you want to turn any of these into a full-blown meal, you can add meat, as well. You'll end up with something similar to my Salmon Rice Bowl (page 170). This approach is an especially great way to use up leftovers or throw together a quick lunch. Ideal options include leftover meat from kebabs (page 34), steak from Steak with Sweet-and-Sour Peppers (page 159) or Chili-Rubbed Steak Tacos (page 160), Easy Italian Turkey Meatballs (page 156), Indian-Style Meatballs (page 157), Slow Cooker Carnitas (page 165), Slow Cooker BBQ Pulled Pork (page 167), Hoisin-Glazed Salmon (page 172), or Sesame-Crusted Salmon (page 172).

GARLIC BREAD, 2 WAYS

I'm not big into serving bread with dinner—probably because I would eat it all myself—but it can be a great way to fill out an otherwise light, quick meal. Although delicious on its own, crusty bread slathered with garlicky butter is food of the gods. Then melt cheese on top? Yup, I go there sometimes—usually for a vegetarian meal such as Pasta with Mushroom and Lentil "Bolognese" Sauce (page 185)—and I'm not sorry.

Garlic bread is especially great at a dinner party and especially, *especially* great if some of your dinner party guests are small. If serving more than four people, you'll need to buy larger loaves of bread. I suggested cutting full-size loaves in half and treating each half like a full loaf per the directions below.

You can serve garlic bread with anything. Seriously, with nearly every recipe in this book. I have proof and it's in my belly.

GARLIC BREAD
Serves 4

4 tablespoons (½ stick) salted butter

4 cloves garlic, peeled and smashed

1 demiloaf Italian bread, cut in half lengthwise

Fresh flat-leaf parsley, chopped, for garnish (optional)

1. Preheat the oven to 350°F. Melt the butter in a small saucepan set over medium-low heat. Add the smashed garlic and reduce the heat to low. Cook the butter for 5 minutes to infuse it with a strong garlic flavor. You don't want to brown

the butter, though the garlic may start to turn golden brown around the edges by the end of the 5 minutes. Remove from the heat and discard the garlic.

2. Brush the garlic butter on the cut side of the bread, dividing it evenly between the two halves. Put the halves together and wrap the loaf in aluminum foil. Bake for 10 minutes. Remove the bread from the oven and allow to cool for 2 minutes before sprinkling the parsley, if using, on the cut side of each half-loaf and cutting into serving-size pieces. Serve immediately.

3. Remove the bread from the oven and set the broiler to HIGH. Very carefully open the foil, separate the halves, and lay each half on a baking sheet, cut side up. Top with the mozzarella and broil the bread until the cheese just melts, 2 to 3 minutes. Remove from the oven, allow the bread to cool, sprinkle with parsley, if using, and cut into serving-size pieces. Serve immediately.

CHEESY GARLIC BREAD
Serves 4

4 tablespoons (½ stick) salted butter

4 cloves garlic, peeled and smashed

1 demiloaf Italian bread, cut in half lengthwise

4 or 5 slices fresh mozzarella cheese

Fresh flat-leaf parsley, chopped, for garnish (optional)

1. Preheat the oven to 350°F. Melt the butter in a small saucepan set over medium-low heat. Add the smashed garlic and reduce the heat to low. Cook the butter for 5 minutes to infuse it with a strong garlic flavor. You don't want to brown the butter, though the garlic may start to turn golden brown around the edges by the end of the 5 minutes. Remove from the heat and discard the garlic.

2. Brush the garlic butter on the cut side of the bread, dividing it evenly between the two halves. Put the halves together and wrap the loaf in aluminum foil. Bake for 10 minutes.

Dessert

No matter how healthy my eating becomes—and it has gotten *much* healthier over the years—I still love a good dessert. My philosophy is that if it's homemade with wholesome ingredients, it's okay. And you've burned calories making it, so there's that.

All right, maybe not so much on the burning calories front but, if you're in good health, generally watch sugar in your diet, and keep most of your treats wholesome, you're in pretty good shape to indulge in brownies every once and a while.

Making dessert from scratch may seem like a tall order. I suspect that most families end up eating less than wholesome and overly sugary store-bought desserts because, with dinner-making a necessity, there's no time to also make desserts from scratch. I get it, but also think that forcing yourself to go homemade will naturally help you enjoy dessert in moderation. If there's no time to cook it, maybe you don't need it—serve yogurt with honey and fruit or some all-natural pops instead.

If that just won't fly in your house and you're going to keep buying store-bought dessert foods, do yourself and your crew a favor by getting in the habit of quickly checking food labels (see page 14). Also, I encourage you to reconsider diet desserts—more and more research shows that they do more harm in the long run, without even helping people lose weight in the first place.

I've broken this chapter into two parts. It isn't a neat split by any means—when is dessert ever?—but the recipes generally divide between Everyday Desserts and Bake Sale Goodies and Special Occasions. The recipes in Everyday Desserts may take some advance planning, but are truly easy and can be made ahead to have on hand to swap in for less wholesome store-bought desserts. I think that some of the bake sale desserts fit the bill, too, but if you're not used to baking, you may disagree. I'll leave it up to you.

As for Special Occasions desserts, well, I find that most people like having a small handful of stellar recipes that they can whip out for a special occasion. Otherwise, they like perusing the web or cookbooks for new ways to experiment and impress their family and friends. I'm no different, so the handful of special occasion recipes here are my go-to stash.

SAUTÉED BANANAS

Serves 4, as a topping

MIX-AND-MATCH WITH:
FRUITY FROZEN YOGURT, *page 108*
MAPLE CINNAMON WHIPPED CREAM,
page 216

As a fan of fruity desserts, such as pie, crisps, and crumbles, and someone who easily overeats pie, crisps, and crumbles, I had to figure out a way to get my fix of warm, bubbling fruit without quite so much decadence. And faster, too, because, let's be honest, making a pie is no joke. I realized that I could get the same effect in just minutes by sautéing fruit in a pan with a little sugar and butter.

Bananas are my favorite sautéed fruit because, when I eat them, I don't miss the crust; like Bananas Foster, these Sautéed Bananas are perfect as is. If you don't like bananas or just want to experiment, try apples, pears, plums, or peaches instead. They all cook up beautifully.

Serve this with ice cream and, if you're feeling really decadent, Maple Cinnamon Whipped Cream on top. For a healthier version, use these to top yogurt or Fruity Frozen Yogurt made with banana.

2 tablespoons unsalted butter
4 ripe to slightly overripe bananas (they shouldn't be completely mushy), cut into 1½-inch pieces
1 tablespoon light brown sugar
1 teaspoon pure vanilla extract

1. Melt the butter in a medium pan set over medium heat. Once the foam subsides, add the banana pieces and brown sugar. Stir gently until the sugar dissolves, 1 to 2 minutes.

2. Add the vanilla and sauté for 30 more seconds. Remove from the heat and serve warm.

♥ *Make It Easier: 3 delicious ways to build a quick everyday sundae* If you're a dessert family like we're a dessert family, you have ice cream in the freezer at all times. These easy recipes make the perfect toppings to turn a plain bowl of ice cream (or Fruity Frozen Yogurt, page 108) into an exciting everyday sundae. Because why shouldn't we eat ice cream sundaes whenever we want?

- Quick Berry Jam (page 53)
- All-Purpose Strawberry Sauce (page 73)
- Sweet and Salty Granola Cereal (page 78)
- Maple Cinnamon Whipped Cream (page 216)
- Homemade Chocolate Shell (page 217)
- Sautéed Bananas, see above

APPLE CIDER GELATIN

Serves 4

MIX-AND-MATCH WITH:
MAPLE CINNAMON WHIPPED CREAM,
see next recipe

Gelatin is sort of old school, but still a kid favorite. When made from scratch without artificial flavor and color, I like it a lot, too, especially topped with Maple Cinnamon Whipped Cream. Make this ahead and keep it sealed in the refrigerator for up to two weeks. It makes the easiest grab-and-serve dessert and is good for a fun snack, too, when paired with fresh fruit, Trail Mix (page 96), or your favorite granola bar (pages 104–105).

2 cups apple cider
1 (1.25-ounce) packet (3 teaspoons)
  unflavored gelatin
1 tablespoon honey, plus more to taste

1. Put 1 cup of the cider in a large bowl, ideally one with a pour spout, and sprinkle the gelatin over the top. Allow to sit for 2 minutes.

2. In the meantime, heat the remaining cup of cider in a small pot set over medium heat. Take it off the heat as soon as it starts to boil.

3. Add the honey to the hot cider and stir to dissolve.

4. Pour the sweetened hot cider into the gelatin mixture and stir until the gelatin dissolves completely. Divide the liquid among four serving cups and place, uncovered, in the refrigerator until firm, at least 3 hours. If not serving the same day, cover the cups with plastic wrap after 3 hours and store in the refrigerator for 5 to 7 days.

MAPLE CINNAMON WHIPPED CREAM

Makes 2 cups whipped cream

MIX-AND-MATCH WITH:
FRUITY FROZEN YOGURT, *page 108*
SAUTÉED BANANAS, *page 215*
APPLE CIDER GELATIN, *see previous recipe*
GINGERED PEACH CRISP, *page 222*
CHERRY CLAFOUTIS, *page 224*
PINEAPPLE UPSIDE-DOWN CAKE, *page 230*
SWEET POTATO PIE, *page 234*

Making whipped cream is dead easy. You can even just put heavy whipping cream and some sugar in a jar, seal, and shake. *That's* how easy it is. There's really no excuse not to make it yourself, given how hard it is to find all-natural whipped cream at the store. This has natural sweetness from the maple syrup and the cinnamon adds a warm note. I'm not going to say that you'll never go back to whipped topping, but (you may never go back to whipped topping).

Oh, and if you don't like the sound of exercising your arms (um, best exercise results ever), put the kids to work or use a mixer fitted with a whisk attachment or an electric handheld mixer.

1 cup heavy whipping cream
2 tablespoons pure maple syrup
½ teaspoon ground cinnamon

1. Combine all the ingredients in a medium-size bowl (ideally a metal bowl that's been refrigerated for 20 minutes, though this isn't absolutely necessary) and whisk until stiff peaks form, 3 to 5 minutes if whisking constantly. Use immediately or store in a sealed container in the refrigerator for up to 3 days.

CHOCOLATE AND PEANUT BUTTER CHIP BANANA MUFFINS

Makes 1 dozen muffins

Although we like to serve muffins at breakfast and for snack time, many muffin recipes call for an amount of sugar and sweet mix-ins that make them more like a dessert. These indulgent bites are a prime example.

If you'd like to adjust the sweetness of these to make them a better snack-time treat, resist the urge to reduce the granulated sugar in the batter and, instead, add just half a cup of chips, either all chocolate, all peanut butter, or a combination of the two. If you're fine with a full cup of chips but prefer to stick to just one type, you can do that, too. At your own risk, of course.

- 4 tablespoons (½ stick) unsalted butter
- Neutral oil, such as grapeseed or canola, for pan (optional)
- 1 cup all-purpose flour (see measuring tip, page 217)
- 1 cup whole wheat pastry flour (or another cup of all-purpose flour)
- ½ cup granulated sugar
- 1 tablespoon baking powder
- 1 teaspoon salt
- 1 cup milk
- 1 large egg, ideally at room temperature
- 1 large, ripe banana
- ½ cup chocolate chips
- ½ cup peanut butter chips

1. In a small saucepan or in the microwave, melt the butter and set aside to cool.

2. Preheat the oven to 400°F. Line a 12-cup muffin tin with paper or silicone cups or lightly grease with oil.

♥ *Make It Tastier:* Learning how to measure flour properly is not just a fussy cooking technique; it can also impact the flavor and texture of your pancakes, waffles, and baked goods. So, what's the trick? Instead of scooping a measuring cup into the bag of flour, use a spoon to transfer the flour from its package or container into your measuring cup, tapping the bottom of the measuring cup on your counter every few spoonfuls. Then, once full, use a straight edge (maybe the handle of your spoon or a butter knife) to even out the surface. This process helps make sure that you don't get a packed cup of flour, which may be too much for the recipe.

3. In a medium-size bowl, whisk together the flours, sugar, baking powder, and salt; set aside.

4. In a separate medium-size bowl, whisk together the melted and cooled butter, milk, and egg. Add the wet ingredients to the dry and, using a silicone spatula or wooden spoon, mix until just combined.

5. Cut the banana in half lengthwise and then crosswise into ½-inch pieces. Stir in the banana pieces and chips until well combined.

6. Divide the batter evenly among the prepared muffin cups and bake for 18 to 20 minutes, or until a toothpick inserted into the middle of the muffin comes out clean. Remove from the oven and allow the muffins to cool in the pan for 3 to 5 minutes before transferring them to a wire rack or the counter to finish cooling completely. Serve immediately or store in a sealed container at room temperature for up to 2 days or in the freezer for up to 3 months.

HOMEMADE CHOCOLATE SHELL

Makes 1 cup sauce

MIX-AND-MATCH WITH:

10 SNACK IDEAS YOU CAN MAKE WITHOUT A RECIPE, *page 94*

DELICIOUS WAYS TO BUILD A QUICK, EVERYDAY SUNDAE, *page 215*

Yup, this is a homemade version of Magic Shell: that chocolate sauce that magically hardens as soon as it hits cold temperatures. It's one of my favorites and I make no excuse—especially since I've learned that the stuff in the bottle is strangely wholesome. Except for the soy lecithin, it's not that far off from homemade. So then, why make it?

Besides the fact that making this magical sauce at home is just plain fun (kitchen project!), you can make it with higher-quality chocolate, which means higher-quality taste. You can also add flavors using pure, all-natural flavor extracts, which is fun, too. And, if you're dairy-free, you can use dairy-free chocolate. It works!

1 cup of your favorite semisweet chocolate chips or chopped pieces of your favorite chocolate

½ cup coconut oil (both refined and unrefined work, though the latter may give your sauce a slight coconut flavor)

1. To make in the microwave: combine the chocolate chips and coconut oil in a microwave-safe bowl and melt on high power in 15- to 20-second intervals, mixing between each interval, until the chocolate is 85 percent melted. Remove the bowl from the microwave and use a fork or whisk to stir—this will complete the melting process.

To make on the stovetop: combine the chocolate chips and coconut oil in a small saucepan set over medium heat. Cook until the mixture is 85 percent melted, whisking every 30 seconds or so. Remove the pot from the heat and continue to stir until completely melted.

2. Allow the sauce to cool slightly before using. To store: pour the sauce into a glass jar or storage container, seal, and keep at room temperature. If the sauce hardens and your container is microwave safe, place it in the microwave and heat for a few seconds at a time until it loosens. Alternatively, place the container in a warm water bath until it liquefies. This will keep for up to 2 weeks.

♥ Make It Tastier: Give your Chocolate Shell extra magic!

For every cup of chocolate chips that you use, add ¼ teaspoon of all-natural flavor extract. I love using peppermint for candy cane sundaes around the holidays, and though it's not always easy to find, pure strawberry extract added to Chocolate Shell made with white chocolate chips is killer for strawberry ice-cream sundaes in the summer months. Frontier brand makes a natural, alcohol-free version and, generally, Nielsen Massey makes high-quality pure flavor extracts—but they aren't cheap!

ONE-BOWL LEMON RICOTTA POUND CAKE

Makes one 9 x 5-inch loaf

MIX-AND-MATCH WITH:
FRESH RICOTTA CHEESE, *page 41*

I originally made this recipe to use up a last bit of homemade Fresh Ricotta Cheese before it went bad but, as it turns out, adding ricotta cheese to pound cake turns out a supermoist cake with the perfect crumb. This cake manages to be dense, as a pound cake should be, but also soft and silky. Except for the outside, which has the perfect dark golden brown crust to hold thick slices together.

As with all pound cakes, this is most delicious served the day of, but will stay good up to three days. On the second and third days, I like to toast fat slices and slather them with butter. Or even better, fresh ricotta and a drizzle of honey.

8 tablespoons (1 stick) unsalted butter, at room temperature, plus more for pan

1 cup granulated sugar

½ cup ricotta cheese, store-bought or homemade (page 41)

1 teaspoon lemon zest (from about 1 lemon)

4 tablespoons freshly squeezed lemon juice (from about 2 juicy lemons)

1 teaspoon pure vanilla extract

½ teaspoon salt

4 large eggs, ideally at room temperature

2 cups all-purpose flour (see measuring tip, page 217)

¾ teaspoon baking powder

½ teaspoon baking soda

1. Preheat the oven to 350°F. Butter a 9 x 5-inch loaf pan and line with parchment paper; set aside.

2. In a large bowl that works well with a hand mixer or in the bowl of a stand mixer fitted with the whisk attachment, combine the butter, sugar, ricotta, lemon zest, lemon juice, vanilla, and salt on low speed until just combined.

3. Mix in the eggs, one at a time, making sure to fully incorporate each egg before adding the next.

4. Add the flour, baking powder, and baking soda to the same bowl. Use a wooden spoon or silicone spatula to mix until just well incorporated.

5. Pour the batter into the prepared loaf pan and smooth out the top. Bake for about 60 minutes, until a toothpick inserted into the center comes out clean. Remove from the oven and allow the cake to cool in the pan for 5 minutes before removing from the pan to finish cooling on a wire rack. Serve the same day or, once cooled completely, wrap tightly all around in plastic wrap and store on the counter for 2 to 3 days or in the freezer for up to 3 months.

GINGERED PEACH CRISP

Makes one 10-inch crisp; serves 6–8

MIX-AND-MATCH WITH:

MAPLE CINNAMON WHIPPED CREAM,
page 216

Another example of a recipe that can fit into either section of this chapter; I chose Everyday Desserts since this is the kind of laid-back baking that's perfect for lazy summer weekends. Sure, there's prep and measuring and baking, but it's all gloriously fluid. There's no need to stress over exact measurements—a great reason to have the kids help with this one—or even exact ingredients. If you can't find perfectly ripe peaches or the season has passed entirely, use plums. Or apples. Or pears. Throw in some berries, too, if you're feeling sassy.

The most important thing is to flavor the fruit with a little lemon juice and spice, and to add some flour as a thickener. And, of course, having a killer crisp topping is important, too. This one works with any fruit.

- 6 ounces (1½ sticks) unsalted butter, cold and cut into small pieces, plus more for baking dish
- 4 cups peeled, sliced peaches (from 6 to 8 small to medium-size fresh, ripe peaches; you can substitute 4 cups thawed frozen peach slices, drained of their juice, or fresh nectarine, plum, apples, or pears)
- 1 cup light brown sugar
- 2 tablespoons freshly squeezed lemon juice (from about 1 juicy lemon)
- 2 teaspoons pure vanilla extract
- 1 to 2 teaspoons minced fresh ginger, to taste

- 1 cup plus 2 tablespoons all-purpose flour (see measuring tip, page 217)
- 1¼ cups old-fashioned rolled oats
- ½ teaspoon salt

1. Preheat the oven to 375°F. Butter a 2-quart baking dish and set aside.

2. To make the filling: place the peaches in a large bowl and toss with ½ cup of the brown sugar and the lemon juice, vanilla, ginger, and 2 tablespoons of the flour; set aside.

3. To make the topping: combine the remaining ½ cup of brown sugar, remaining cup of flour, the oats, and the salt in a medium-size bowl. Scatter the cold pieces of butter across the flour mixture and, using your hands or a pastry cutter, work the butter into the dry ingredients until clumps of varying sizes form. Some crumbs will be big, others small, and much of the mixture will turn into the texture of coarse sand.

4. Pour the peach mixture into the prepared baking dish and cover evenly with the topping. Bake until the topping is crisp and golden brown, about 45 minutes. Remove from the oven and allow to cool before serving warm, ideally with a scoop of vanilla ice cream and Maple Cinnamon Whipped Cream.

CHERRY CLAFOUTIS

Makes one 10-inch dessert; serves 6-8

MIX-AND-MATCH WITH:

MAPLE CINNAMON WHIPPED CREAM,
page 216

Clafoutis, a French dessert of fruit baked in a thick, custardy batter, is divine and ridiculously simple to make. You throw ingredients into a blender, whiz them up, and pour the resulting batter over fruit waiting in a baking dish. An hour later, you'll be in heaven.

But, yes, it takes an hour to cook and you probably don't have that time to spare on busy work nights. You may have time on a weekend, though, even if it's packed with sports, birthday parties, and other fun. It's a lovely Sunday night dessert or you can make it on Sunday night to serve on Monday or Tuesday. It won't be quite the same at room temperature or rewarmed, but it will still be good. Very, very good.

This is also a great dinner party dessert, since the last thing you want to do is bake a special occasion cake after making dinner for a crowd. Blend the batter before guests arrive, and depending on how you want to pace dinner, you can throw it into the oven around the time that you sit down to eat. It will impress which, let's be honest, we always want to do when we cook for people.

- 3 tablespoons unsalted butter, melted and cooled, plus more for pan
- 3 large eggs
- 1¼ cups milk
- ¾ cup all-purpose flour (see measuring tip, page 217)
- ½ cup light brown sugar
- 1 teaspoon pure vanilla extract
- ¼ teaspoon ground cardamom (optional)
- ¼ teaspoon salt
- ¼ teaspoon lemon zest (from about ¼ lemon)
- 2 cups pitted cherries, fresh or thawed frozen and drained of juice

1. Preheat the oven to 350°F. Butter a 10-inch round baking dish and set aside. Place all the ingredients, except the cherries, in a blender and whiz on low speed until well combined, 20 to 30 seconds.

2. Pour the batter into the prepared dish and scatter the cherries evenly across the surface. Bake for 40 to 45 minutes, until puffed and golden brown. When you jiggle the dish, the center should look just firm; if it's still very jiggly, return to the oven and bake for another 4 to 5 minutes. Remove from the oven, allow to cool for at least 5 minutes, and serve warm.

DEEP CHOCOLATE LAYER CAKE

Makes one 9-inch double-layer cake or 24 cupcakes

MIX-AND-MATCH WITH:
EASY CREAM CHEESE FROSTING, *page 226*

I tested a lot of cake recipes for this book trying to find one that is easy, practical, and can fit as effortlessly into a bake sale or casual get-together as it can a special occasion. In the end, I came back to the fact that so many of us love the flavor of boxed cake. Yes, even some organic-buying, all-natural-eating, scratch-cooking folks have admitted to it.

The key? Use excellent cocoa, such as Dutch-processed, or even better, Double Dutch Dark Cocoa.

Yep, that's the catch: unlike most of the other recipes in this book, this one calls for a harder-to-find ingredient. Oh, and Dutch-processed cocoa is expensive, too. In this case, though, I really believe it's worth it. I wouldn't have bothered otherwise.

8 ounces (2 sticks) unsalted butter, at room temperature, plus more for pans

2 cups all-purpose flour (see measuring tip, page 217)

¾ cup unsweetened cocoa powder (see Make It Tastier, page 226, for other tasty cocoa options)

1 teaspoon salt

1 teaspoon baking powder

½ teaspoon baking soda

1½ cups light brown sugar

½ cup granulated sugar

3 large eggs, ideally at room temperature

1½ teaspoons pure vanilla extract

1¼ cups buttermilk

½ cup warm brewed coffee

1. Preheat the oven to 325°F. Butter two 9-inch round cake pans and line with parchment. If making cupcakes, grease 12 muffin wells with butter or line with cupcake liners.

2. In a medium-size bowl, whisk together the flour, cocoa powder, salt, baking powder, and baking soda; set aside.

3. Place the butter, brown sugar, and granulated sugar in a large bowl that works well with a hand mixer or in the bowl of a stand mixer fitted with the whisk attachment and, at medium speed, cream together until light and fluffy, 3 minutes. Add the eggs, one at a time, making sure to mix in each one before adding the next. Add the vanilla, and mix until just incorporated.

4. Add half of the dry ingredients to the wet and, using a silicone spatula or wooden spoon, gently mix. Stir in the buttermilk and add the remaining dry ingredients. Once just incorporated, mix in the coffee and combine until the batter comes together, being careful not to overwork it.

5. Divide the batter evenly between the two baking pans or among the muffin wells and bake until a toothpick inserted into the center of the cake or cupcakes comes out clean; the cupcakes take 20 minutes, and the cake takes 30. Remove from the oven and allow to cool for 5 minutes before removing the cake or muffins from their baking pan and finish cooling on a rack or the counter. Once cooled completely, frost and serve. If making ahead, store unfrosted cakes wrapped tightly all around in plastic wrap or unfrosted cupcakes in a plastic bag on the counter for 2 to 3 days or in the freezer for up to 3 months.

♥ *Make It Tastier: Splurge on good cocoa!* There are real differences between sweetened cocoa, unsweetened cocoa, Dutch-processed cocoa, black cocoa, and, my favorite, Double Dutch Dark Cocoa, a combination of Dutch-processed cocoa and black cocoa. Both my Deep Chocolate Layer Cake, previous page, and Fudgy Brownies, next page, can be made with regular unsweetened cocoa for a delicious version of everyday brownies and cake. But if you want to make them special, splurge on Dutch-processed, or even better, Double Dutch Dark Cocoa (which I get from King Arthur). Especially if you use the latter, you'll end up with a rich, deep taste and super dark color (think Oreos!) that take both treats to another level.

EASY CREAM CHEESE FROSTING
Makes 2½ cups frosting

MIX-AND-MATCH WITH:
DEEP CHOCOLATE LAYER CAKE, *page 225*

I have a confession: I don't like most frostings. Buttercream is way too rich and most other frostings are excessively sweet, at least for my taste. The only frosting I can get down with is a simple, slightly tangy, just-sweet-enough cream cheese frosting like this one. It's the perfect way to ice my Deep Chocolate Layer Cake and, really, most any cake. It's particularly good at balancing rich, spiced, or super sweet batters.

I go light with frosting on my cakes and, given that I'm not into fancy cake decorating, I don't usually do a crumb coat. With that in mind, the 2½ cups that this recipe yields is enough for one 9-inch double layer cake or two dozen cupcakes in my house. That said, if you want to go about this more formally and/or you like a lot of icing, I'd double the recipe, which, if you need a gauge, will yield more like two tubs of store-bought frosting.

2 (8-ounce) blocks cream cheese, softened
8 tablespoons (1 stick) unsalted butter, at room temperature
¾ cup confectioners' sugar
1 teaspoon pure vanilla extract (optional)
¼ teaspoon salt

1. Place all the ingredients in a medium-size bowl that works well with a hand mixer or in the bowl of a stand mixer fitted with the whisk attachment and beat until everything comes together in a frosting consistency, about 3 minutes. Use immediately or store in an airtight container in the refrigerator for up to 5 days.

FUDGY BROWNIES

Makes one 8-inch square pan brownies;
serves 4-6

Of all the recipes in this book, this might be my favorite. Isn't it funny? Even with all my recipe testing and experimenting over the years, it comes down to simple, fudgy brownies.

It was hard not to put this recipe in the Everyday Desserts section because it's really easy to make and even easier to eat every day. But I suppose that's not the best idea. Instead, save this for a fun weekend treat or the school bake sale. Once you see how quickly these insanely rich and delicious brownies come together, you'll be tempted to put this recipe in heavy rotation. And maybe you should for a while. But, then, walk away slowly and keep this treat in its rightful, occasional place.

(I don't really believe what I'm saying to you, but also don't want to feel responsible for your brownie addiction.)

4 tablespoons (½ stick) unsalted butter, at room temperature, plus more for pan

¾ cup unsweetened cocoa powder (see Make It Tastier, page 226, for other tasty cocoa options)

½ cup all-purpose flour (see measuring tip, page 217)

¼ teaspoon salt

6 tablespoon neutral oil, such as grapeseed or canola

1¼ cups granulated sugar

2 large eggs, ideally at room temperature

1½ teaspoon pure vanilla extract

1. Preheat the oven to 325°F. Butter an 8-inch square baking pan and line with parchment paper; set aside.

2. In a medium-size bowl, whisk together the cocoa powder, flour, and salt until very few, if any, clumps remain.

3. In a large bowl that works well with a handheld electric mixer or in the bowl of a stand mixer fitted with a whisk attachment, whisk together the 4 tablespoons of butter and the oil. Add the sugar, eggs, and vanilla. Beat until well incorporated, 30 to 60 seconds.

4. Add the dry ingredients to the wet and, using a silicone spatula or wooden spoon, stir together until mixed thoroughly.

5. Pour the batter into the prepared pan and spread evenly. Bake until a toothpick inserted into the center comes out batter free, 30 to 33 minutes; the toothpick should still have very moist crumbs if you want these to be fudgy, but it shouldn't look like liquid batter. Remove from the oven and allow the brownies to cool in the pan for 10 minutes. Remove from the pan, with the parchment paper still attached, and finish cooling on a wire rack on the counter before removing the paper and cutting the brownies into squares for serving. Serve immediately or store in a sealed container on the counter for up to 4 days.

PEANUT BUTTER *and* JAM THUMBPRINT COOKIES

Makes 24 cookies

There is not a better—or easier—kid-friendly cookie than peanut butter thumbprint cookies. The dough comes together in a single bowl with just a few ingredients and bakes up in less than ten minutes. These are such simple business that you can easily get little ones to help, especially with the thumbprint part.

You can fill these all-purpose, naturally gluten-free bites with anything that you like with peanut butter. I've used chocolate hazelnut spread and marshmallow crème but, as you can imagine, my older son's favorite is jam. Yup, even more than Nutella. I guess PB&J is a classic for a reason. And you don't mess with classics for a reason, too.

1 cup smooth peanut butter, store-bought or homemade (page 51)

1 cup granulated sugar, plus more for coating the cookies

1 large egg, lightly beaten

1 teaspoon baking powder

1 teaspoon pure vanilla extract

½ teaspoon ground cinnamon

Berry jam, store-bought or homemade (page 53)

1. Preheat the oven to 350°F. Line a baking sheet with parchment paper and set aside.

2. In a medium-size bowl, combine the peanut butter, sugar, egg, baking powder, vanilla, and cinnamon. Stir with a silicone spatula or wooden spoon to combine well.

3. Place the coating sugar in a small bowl. Using a tablespoon measure to scoop up the batter, shape into a ball, and roll the ball in the sugar. Place on the prepared baking sheet and press down in the middle with your thumb to make a thumbprint. Continue to shape and coat the cookies, placing them 2 inches apart on the prepared baking sheet.

4. Bake for 7 minutes. Remove the cookies from oven, but keep the oven set at 350°F. Your thumbprint will have puffed up, but will still be there. Using the back of the small spoon, press the thumbprint back down and fill the depression with jam. Return the cookies to the oven and continue to bake for another 3 minutes.

5. Remove the cookies from the oven and allow to cool on the cookie sheet for 1 to 2 minutes. Transfer to a wire rack to finish cooling completely. To store, layer the cookies between sheets of waxed paper; they will keep in an airtight container for up to a week.

PINEAPPLE UPSIDE-DOWN CAKE

Makes one 9-inch cake

MIX-AND-MATCH WITH:
MAPLE CINNAMON WHIPPED CREAM,
page 216

If you love cooked fruit and cinnamony, brown sugary flavors as much as I do, you're sure to love this upside-down cake. I mean, does it get any better than a lightly spiced, buttery cake covered in gooey brown sugar and cooked fruit? It really doesn't. That said, the true beauty of this cake is how easy and adaptable it is.

I like making mine with pineapple most, but you can add any fruit you want. On my site, One Hungry Mama, you'll find a holiday version with pears and cranberries. I've also made it with apples in the fall, mixed berries in the summer, and nectarines whenever I can get my hands on them. The batter is always the same and you need just enough fruit to cover the bottom of your pan either in a pretty pattern or with total messy abandon. Either way, this cake comes out beautiful and delicious.

½ pineapple, cored and cut into five
   ½-inch-thick rings

6 ounces (1½ sticks) unsalted butter

¾ cup light brown sugar

1¼ cup all-purpose flour (see measuring
   tip, page 217)

1¼ teaspoons baking powder

¼ teaspoon salt

¼ teaspoon ground ginger

¼ teaspoon ground cinnamon

⅛ teaspoon ground cloves

1 cup granulated sugar

2 large eggs, ideally at room temperature

1 teaspoon pure vanilla extract

½ cup milk

1. Preheat the oven to 350°F. Cut one of the pineapple rings into quarters and set all the fruit aside.

2. Melt 4 tablespoons (½ stick) of the butter in a 9-inch round cake pan set over very low heat. (Leave the remaining butter on the counter to come to room temperature.) Add the brown sugar to the pan and allow it to dissolve, 1 to 2 minutes. Remove from the heat and, using a silicone spatula, spread the melted sugar to cover the entire bottom of the cake pan; set aside to cool.

3. In a medium-size bowl, whisk together the flour, baking powder, salt, ginger, cinnamon, and cloves.

4. In a large bowl that works well with an electric mixer or in the bowl of a stand mixer fitted with a whisk attachment, beat remaining 8 tablespoons of butter and the granulated sugar until light and fluffy, 1 to 2 minutes. Add the eggs, one at a time, making sure to mix in each one fully before adding the next. Add the vanilla and mix until incorporated.

5. Add half of the dry ingredients to the wet and, using a silicone spoon or spatula, fold in until just combined. Add the milk, mix until well incorporated, and then add the remaining flour mixture. Gently stir until just combined, being careful not to overwork the batter.

6. Arrange the pineapple rings in the pan on top of the cooled sugar, using the four smaller pieces to fill in empty spaces. Spread the batter evenly on top of the fruit. Bake until a toothpick inserted into the center comes out clean, 45 to

50 minutes. Remove the cake from the oven and allow to cool in the pan for 20 minutes.

If serving immediately, gently run a knife around the edges of the pan and invert onto a serving plate. Otherwise, leave the cake in the pan—uncovered for a few hours, covered with plastic wrap if longer—and warm it up before removing from pan and serving. Alternatively, you can invert it onto a microwave-safe plate after 20 minutes of cooling and warm the cake for a short time in your microwave before serving. *The point is to serve this cake warm!*

PIE DOUGH

Makes enough for one 9-inch double-crust pie

MIX-AND-MATCH WITH:
SWEET POTATO PIE, *page 234*

There are so many recipes for pie dough, with a crazy array of ingredients. This one is a simple, everyday recipe that balances solid technique with accessible ingredients and a simple process. In other words, this is how you make pie dough when you want to make it easy and would rather not buy a store-bought crust.

Although it's getting easier to find all-natural options (page 240), store-bought doesn't compare to even the most basic homemade pie crust, except that maybe it has a more perfectly decorated edge. And let's talk price: the all-natural crusts aren't inexpensive, certainly not when compared to the price of flour, sugar, salt, and butter, all of which you probably have in your pantry right now.

Because this comes together in a food processor, you can pretty much make this pie dough whenever you're feeling up to washing the parts. And when that happens, I suggest you make a double batch—this freezes well, which makes throwing together a pie when you're ready a cinch.

- **3 cups all-purpose flour, plus more for rolling (see measuring tip, page 217)**
- **1 tablespoon granulated sugar**
- **2 teaspoons salt**
- **12 ounces (3 sticks) unsalted butter, very cold and cut into pieces**
- **½ cup ice-cold water**

1. Place the flour, sugar, and salt in the bowl of a food processor and pulse to combine. Add the butter, one piece at a time, pulsing after each piece. (Tip: Keep half of the pieces in the freezer to stay very cold while you combine the first half.) Continue until all the butter has been added and the dough resembles coarse sand.

2. Sprinkle the dough with about ¼ cup of the cold water and pulse again until the dough is crumbly but holds together when rolled with your hands. If necessary, add the remaining cold water, 1 tablespoon at a time. Only add as much water as you need to get the dough to a place where it holds together when rolled (but still looks like coarse sand; it will not form a ball on its own in the food processor).

3. Transfer the dough to a lightly floured work surface; you'll have to pack it together using your hands, since it should still be crumbly. Patiently pat and roll the dough into a ball, then cut in half. Roll each half into a ball and, one at a time, gently flatten each to form a disk about ¾ inch thick. Wrap both disks very tightly in plastic wrap and refrigerate until firm, at least 30 minutes and up to 3 days. If not using immediately, freeze the disks for up to 3 months, making sure to thaw before using.

4. When ready to use, remove the dough from refrigerator, one disk at a time, and place on a lightly floured surface. Lightly flour your rolling pin as well, and roll the disk into a 13-inch round with even thickness throughout, turning, flipping, and lightly flouring the dough as necessary as you go. Transfer the rolled dough to a pie plate, gently easing it into the bottom and up the sides. Trim any excess overhang with kitchen shears or a paring knife. If making a double-crust pie, place the dough-lined pie plate in the refrigerator and repeat the rolling process with a second disk to top the filling when ready.

♥ *Make It Easier: Freeze your fat.*

There are a million "secrets" to perfect pie dough, from vodka to egg yolks, but I've found that very cold butter is most important. The colder your butter is as you blend, pat, and roll your pie dough, the more likely it is to keep from melting into the dough. The more pockets of solid butter you achieve, the flakier your pie dough.

I tend to use half refrigerated and half frozen butter for my dough. I very carefully cut the butter straight from the freezer, using a very sharp chef's knife. The butter will crack into chunks or break into shards. Throw them both in; as long as the pieces are relatively small and cold, cold, cold, you're good to go.

SWEET POTATO PIE

Makes one 9-inch single-crust pie

MIX-AND-MATCH WITH:

MAPLE CINNAMON WHIPPED CREAM,
page 216

Fruit pies are great, but I'm always changing them up. Once you land on a good recipe, you can pretty much start experimenting with different fruit and spice combinations on your own. In that way, it's hard to have just one that you make all of the time. At least for me.

This recipe, on the other hand, is the kind that you go back to over and over, especially over the winter holidays. I admit that it's not easy to think of making it the rest of the year, but if you get over thinking of sweet potato pie as a holiday-only treat, you'll be happy you did. Because, honestly, there is no better way to end a summer cookout than with this pie topped with Maple Cinnamon Whipped Cream. Plus, it's a delicious pie made with a vegetable. Take that, kids.

2 large sweet potatoes

Pie dough for a 9-inch single-crust pie, store-bought or homemade (page 232; one-half of the recipe as written)

10 ounces evaporated milk

4 tablespoons (½ stick) unsalted butter

¾ cup light brown sugar

¼ cup granulated sugar

3 eggs, ideally at room temperature

1 tablespoon pure vanilla extract

1 teaspoon lemon zest (from about 1 lemon)

¾ teaspoon ground cinnamon

½ teaspoon ground allspice

½ teaspoon ground nutmeg, preferably freshly grated

¼ teaspoon ground coriander

1. Preheat the oven to 425°F. Wrap the sweet potatoes in aluminum foil and place on a small baking sheet. Roast until very tender all the way through, 50 to 60 minutes. Remove the potatoes from the oven and, if baking the pie right away, lower the oven temperature to 375°F. Once the potatoes are cool enough to handle, unwrap and peel them, and puree the flesh in a food processor until very smooth. Measure out 2 cups of puree and set aside.

2. If using homemade dough, line a 9-inch pie plate with the dough and set aside in the refrigerator.

3. In a medium-size pot set over low heat, combine the evaporated milk, butter, and both sugars. Cook, whisking all the while, until the butter and sugars melt and the smooth mixture just begins to bubble. Remove from the heat and allow the mixture to cool in the pot.

4. In a large bowl that works well with a hand mixer or in the bowl of a stand mixer fitted with a whisk attachment, mix together the sweet potato puree, eggs, vanilla, zest, and spices at low speed. Add the cooled evaporated milk mixture and continue to mix until all the ingredients are well combined.

5. Pour the filling into the chilled crust and bake for 45 to 50 minutes, until the sweet potato filling is just set in the middle. Check on the pie after 30 minutes and if the crust is getting too brown, cover it loosely with aluminum foil for the remaining baking time. Remove the pie from the oven and allow to cool for at least 30 minutes before serving. If not serving immediately, cover with plastic wrap and store in the refrigerator for up to 2 days. Be sure to return to room temperature before serving.

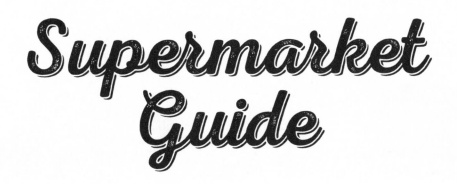

PART III

Supermarket Guide

Food shopping can be a maddening task, especially with a crew in tow. Navigating packed aisles, meltdowns, opinions, cravings, and the power of marketing is no small task—every week. So, here's a cheat sheet that helps you find delicious, healthier products that can help make feeding yourself and your family easier without sacrificing health.

While I mention products and brands on this list, I urge you to keep your own eye out and, if you're really particular, to follow food news. New products and brands are popping up all the time, some big brands are starting to change how they formulate their foods for the better, and, of course, they are also buying up the notable organic brands. Annie's is owned by General Mills and now Applegate is owned by Hormel—these are just two examples.

It's yet to be seen whether the organic brands have sold out or the conglomerates are buying into the organic food movement. Even taking all of that into account, this list is far from exhaustive. All those great, small, local, and new-but-growing brands? Most aren't listed here, but you should look out for them.

As you look over this list, keep in mind that I'm a food writer and recipe developer, not a nutritionist. My choices aren't based on nutrition label diligence as much as nutritional common sense balanced by a parental eye, taste, and performance in the kitchen.

One last thing: not every product by a single brand is created equal. If you're curious about a brand recommended here, use my method for quickly analyzing the nutrition labels (see page 14) of each of their products to see which suits your needs.

Fresh Basics

PRODUCE

If you don't want to buy all-organic produce, check out the Dirty Dozen list (see page 9) for the produce that you really want to buy organic. If you're buying fresh, look no further than the organic produce at your grocery store or talk to farmers at your local farmers' market for fresh, seasonal produce.

For the rest? These national brands of packaged fresh and frozen produce help me keep my fridge well stocked all year-round and also give me easy shortcuts when I need them. The noted products of these brands are organic and/or non-GMO.

FRESH
Bunny-Luv (organic carrots)
Cal-Organic
Earthbound Farm Organic (greens, fruits, vegetables)
Love Beets (organic varieties)
Sunset (organic varieties of tomatoes, cucumbers, and bell peppers)

FROZEN
Alexia (organic varieties)
Cascadian Farms

Earthbound Farm Organic (fruits and vegetables)
Seapoint Farms (organic edamame)
Stahlbush Island Farms
Woodstock

DAIRY

To get the full run-down on dairy, check out pages 240–242. The only thing to add is that not all organic dairy is created equal. One of the major organic brands, for example, produces milk on a mega industrial dairy farm. The same goes for some of the organic private labels. If you want to avoid factory farm milk, stick only to the following brands. Otherwise, you should be able to find a couple of other organic options at your market or farmers' market.

Here I discuss butter, cow's milk, dough, cheese, ice cream, and yogurt. Looking for cream cheese, sour cream, and cottage cheese? Between the brands listed here, you'll have a good sense of which products to consider buying.

BUTTER

Given that it takes about 11 quarts of milk to make a single pound of butter, buying organic butter is even more important than buying organic cow's milk if that's something that matters to you. Also, grass-fed makes more nutritious and delicious butter—and not all organic dairy is grass-fed dairy—so that's a factor as well. Put them together and, well, the options are limited—and more expensive. Still, I find these brands, most of which make you choose between organic or grass-fed, worth it.

Quick note to butter aficionados: President is not listed here because it is not organic and it is unclear whether it is made from grass-fed cows. That said, it is undeniably among the best tasting butters, so you may want to grab it if none of these brands are available.

Anchor (nonorganic, excellent -quality grass-fed)
Kerrygold (nonorganic, excellent-quality grass-fed)
Organic Valley (organic grain-fed except for its pasture butter, which is both organic and grass-fed)
Smjör (non-organic, excellent-quality grass-fed)
Stonyfield (organic, grain-fed)

COW'S MILK

Amish Country Farms
Clover Organic
Natural by Nature
Organic Valley
Stonyfield
Wegman's
Whole Foods 365

CHEESE

These brands cover most everyday uses, except for Parmesan. Please buy high-quality, imported Parmesan cheese. Please, please. It's worth it. And if it's just not affordable—I admit that it can be expensive—look for imported Grana Padano. It was recommended as a less expensive substitute by a famous Italian chef and I've been happily using it for everyday use ever since!

Also, let's talk feta. I list options, but if you can get important feta for a good price, please do. The flavor is far superior to the prepackaged brands. French will be mild and creamy; Greek or Bulgarian, gamier.

Green Field Farms
Organic Creamery (including feta)
Organic Valley (including feta)
Rumiano Cheese
Sierra Nevada Cheese Company (including feta)

DOUGH AND PIE SHELLS

Keep in mind that even all-natural refrigerated dough is highly processed and packed with oils and sugar. Consider buying them as treats, as opposed to everyday foods.

Annie's cookies, crescent rolls, biscuits, and cinnamon rolls
Dufour puff pastry and shells
Immaculate Baking Company biscuits, scones, sweet rolls, crescent rolls, pretzel dough, and piecrusts
Pillsbury Simply . . . line of biscuits and cookies
Sweet Loren's cookie dough
The Fillo Factory (note: tricalcium phosphate)
Trader Joe's fresh pizza dough (plain and whole wheat)
Trader Joe's puff pastry
Wholly Wholesome piecrust

ICE CREAM

There are so many wonderful small ice cream brands, many locally based, with more popping up every day. Since you're probably buying ice cream in small (or maybe smallish?!) quantities, I suggest that you look for high-quality brands making awesome ice cream in small batches with great ingredients. A favorite of mine on the East Coast is Phin & Phebes, which is available via mail order. Three other amazing mail-order options are Salt & Straw, Jeni's Splendid, and McConnell's. And, honestly, these brands are just the tip of the iceberg. You'll want to look for simple, recognizable ingredients: milk, sugar, eggs, et cetera. No funny five-syllable words out of high school chem class.

If you're looking to feed a crowd and a big-brand ice cream is best, here are some labels to look out for. Not all of them are organic—because we eat ice cream in smaller quantities, I worry more about overall quality and taste than certified organic milk.

One last note about ice cream: if you're concerned about what's in it, you're best sticking with simple flavors like vanilla and chocolate. The crazier the flavor, the more likely you'll find things like fillers and thickeners, even with some of these generally trustworthy brands.

  Alden's Organic
  Ben and Jerry's
  Clover Organic
  Häagen-Dazs (especially its basic flavors and
    Five line)
  Steve's Ice Cream
  Stonyfield Organic (yogurt)
  Three Twins

YOGURT

From Greek to Icelandic, premixed to fruit-on-the-bottom, yogurt options are seemingly endless. With a reputation for being über-healthy, this should be good news. In reality, though, most of the yogurts available in the supermarket are made with tons of sugar, fillers, and even artificial ingredients.

Your best bet is to look for local brands, read labels, or check out these more widely available brands.

Keep in mind that some of these brands have vast product lines and not every single item may fit the bill. Also, some contain natural thickeners and stabilizers; when I can't find yogurt without, I stick with the simplest flavors of these brands because they are organic or made from milk produced by the highest standards and taste good without out too much else added, especially sugar.

  Clover Organic
  Erivan Yogurt
  Nancy's
  Seven Stars Farm
  Smári
  Stonyfield Organic
  Wallaby Organic
  Whole Foods 365

EGGS

Eggs are particularly tricky in an already confusing dairy market. Also, not many great brands are shipped nationwide (though there are a few including Handsome Brook Farm, Vital Farms, and Organic Valley). Instead of providing brands, here's a quick guide to making sense of the many labels you may find on your egg packaging. Just keep in mind that regulations that govern labels often change.

If your eggs are not labeled with any of these, chances are they are from chickens raised on conventional feed (nonorganic, possibly GMO) in cages on industrial farms.

And, of course, regardless of labels, fresh, local eggs that come straight from a farmer you know and trust are going to taste better than anything you can pick up at the market.

Organic: Eggs from noncaged chickens raised on organic feed that are supposed to have access to the outside, though they may be primarily raised inside. This is a USDA certified label.

Nonorganic pasture-raised: Eggs from birds that typically seem to be raise in wide open green space. Pasture birds may get to eat some grass and worms (like real birds!), though they are raised on nonorganic feed. This is a voluntary label.

Organic pasture-raised: Eggs from outdoor birds that are raised and fed according to USDA organic guidelines (see above).

Cage-free: Eggs from birds not kept in cages, but often raised indoors where they don't see the light of day. There are no regulations on how much space cage-free birds get, so many are packed in very tightly. Still, they often get marginally more room and freedom to graze on food compared to caged chickens. This is a voluntary label.

Free-range: Eggs from birds that are raised indoors, but are free to go outside, though there are no regulations on how long they are allowed to stay outdoors. This is a voluntary label.

Free-range certified humane: Eggs from free-range birds (see above) that are left to be outside for up to 6 hours a day on at least 2 square feet of outdoor space. This is a voluntary label.

Vegetarian: Eggs from chickens fed exclusively vegetarian feed. Sometimes this voluntary label signifies indoor-raised chickens since

pasture-raised ones may eat worms and other foraged insects on their own, which makes them ineligible for the label.

MEAT

I—or, I should say, *one*—could write an entire book just on the state of animal protein production in our country. In fact, someone has. If you really want to dig in (and, honestly, I encourage you to), check out *Good Meat: The Complete Guide to Sourcing and Cooking Sustainable Meat*. For here and now, though, to keep it easy, I'm going to make bold-stroke suggestions.

1. Stay away from industrial meat. The easiest way to attempt this is to buy organic meat, though doing that alone is far from fail proof, as many organic meat producers have become quite large productions. Still, organic is a regulated label that requires animals to be raised on 100 percent organic and vegetarian feed, have year-round access to outdoors, and may not be treated with antibiotics or hormones. For chicken especially, if you're shopping at a conventional market, "organic" is the most comprehensive label.

For beef, pork, and lamb, grass-fed and pasture raised is thought to be an even better choice. The problem is that the label has serious flaws. Grass-fed meat is best when you can buy it directly from a farmer. "Free-range," "natural," and "antibiotic-free" labels, it turns out, don't mean much and meat labeled as such can easily be from factory farms.

When buying beef and lamb, organic is not necessarily the best option. Look for meat raised *entirely* on grass that is also hormone-free and raised on vegetarian feed (on the off-season when grass is not available).

With some estimates claiming that over 90 percent of domestic pork is produced on factory farms, it's hard to suggest anything other than finding small local pork producers that raise pasture pork.

2. Stop buying meat at conventional markets. This is an extreme suggestion in a book full of moderate ones aimed at making healthy compromises, but it's by far the easiest way to ensure that you're feeding your family sustainable, healthy, happy meat. Instead, hit the farmers' market or find a butcher who you can talk to and trust. And, yes, be prepared to pay more and possibly eat less (to make up for the extra cost).

Although a handful of nationally distributed meat brands are better than the rest, I hope you'll look for local purveyors. One way to find them is to plug in your zip code at the Eat Well Guide (www.eatwellguide.org) or at Local Harvest (www.localharvest.org). Also, don't be afraid to buy meat online! Some of the larger farms sustainably raising meat ship their meats nationwide.

A note on deli meat and hot dogs. I've long been a devotee of Applegate, which has been purchased by Hormel, a company with very different values. It may be that Applegate will influence Hormel for the better (or at least be left alone to continue operations as usual) or that Hormel will shift the way Applegate does business. For now, I'm sticking to Applegate's organic meats (versus the just "natural" options), which covers hot dogs, chicken hot dogs, turkey hot dogs, deli ham, and Sunday Morning bacon. And, most important, I'm feeding them in moderation since the most recent research links even "better" processed meats with disease.

SEAFOOD

There are two primary concerns when buying seafood: sustainability and mercury. Sustainability is an environmental issue more than anything else. Seafood is being overfished and there is urgent concern about the health of our oceanic ecosystems—like, will our children have the same access to seafood as us and worse. Mercury is a personal health issue that is of particular concern if you are pregnant, breastfeeding, and/or sharing your fish with young eaters.

Since I am concerned with both issues, I tend to cross-reference the two, using two resources I cannot live without: the Monterey Bay Aquarium Seafood Watch (www.seafoodwatch.org) and Natural Resources Defense Council (www.nrdc.org). You can hop onto the Seafood Watch site to reference or download consumer buying guides or, if you have a smart phone, download their app. It provides a list of the best ocean-friendly choices, good alternatives, and fish to avoid completely. The NRDC site ranks fish from least to highest mercury and, between the two, I have the info I need to make smart seafood choices.

One last resource: The Environmental Defense Fund Seafood Selector (seafood.edf.org) gives every fish on a list of commonly eaten seafood a red, yellow, or green light rating for both environmental impact and mercury contamination on one list that you can pull up on a computer or smartphone.

You may notice that these resources don't mention organic fish. For fish to be certified organic, it must be farmed (i.e., the feed must be controlled). The problem is that, as of now, there are no official federal standards for fish farm feed. So, not only can you not be guaranteed that the fish is actually organic, but you can also bet it's farmed—not always the best choice. And while speaking of farmed versus wild, given that wild Atlantic salmon populations are near extinct, the likelihood that Atlantic salmon is farmed is very high, as well.

The list of options is long, especially if you're open to moderate mercury (which isn't as bad as it sounds if you eat only six servings or less per month, for example). Refer to lists depending on what matters to you. And, if both matter, here's a quick list of some of the better options of the more commonly available seafood.

Atlantic cod
Atlantic pollock (US, Canada)
Catfish (domestic US)
Crab (domestic US)
Dover sole
English sole
Salmon (fresh wild from Canada, California, Oregon, and Washington)
Scallops (farmed or wild)
Shrimp (farmed or wild)

Pantry and Fridge Basics

BEANS

While canned beans are super easy, dried beans are less expensive and do not come in a package of any concern. All you have to consider is organic or not.

If you're looking for canned beans, see the section on canned products (page 250) for suggestions on which canned beans to buy; for dried, pick these up.

Arrowhead Mills
Eden
Whole Foods 365

BROTH

I use chicken and vegetable broth so much that I'm constantly stocking my pantry with packaged broth and my freezer with homemade broth.

I exclusively use low-sodium broth because it's better for your health and also for your cooking. You want to control the amount of salt in every dish and the high levels of salt in regular broth can interfere with that. Also, I usually opt for organic chicken broth the same way that I opt for organic chicken meat. I'm more willing

to go conventional with vegetable broth, though if the price is right, I prefer organic. I almost never use beef stock and didn't take it into consideration for this list of go-to brands.

I exclusively buy broth packaged in Tetra Pak cartons. They are reliably BPA-free, which canned broth is not. They also come in what I find to be a more convenient package size.

Last note: your eyes do not deceive you. I have only recommended two brands, which is limiting, I know. I've made a point of balancing eco, packaging, values, and health criteria with good old-fashioned quality and taste for other products, but chicken broth poses a challenge. Most store-bought brands don't taste great and, the one I've found that does is produced by a large food company with questionable meat sourcing practices (and lots of products in its line that include MSG, additives, and/or "flavoring"). Given that, I don't feel comfortable recommending it.

The two brands that I recommend live up to the rest of the store-bought options—which is to say they are all mediocre—and are organic. That's the upside. The down is that organic is more expensive.

If you don't like these brands or are comfortable buying conventional, it may be worth trying a few to see which you like best.

Imagine (Chicken, Vegetarian No-Chicken, Vegetable)
Swanson (Organic Vegetable only)

NUT AND SEED BUTTER

The best kind of peanut butter is packed with protein and not much else bad (especially if you make it homemade [page 53]) and is easy to use. The wrong kind, though, may contain partially hydrogenated oil, stabilizers, and lots of added sugar, not to mention be made with GMO nuts. The same goes for peanut butter alternatives.

Since, as so often is the case, the *natural* label doesn't mean all that much, the best option when buying any nut or seed butter is to read the label closely looking for the things that matter to you, whether organic or non-GMO. I urge you to also look for a sign that your peanut butter is made without hydrogenated oil, which may come in the form of a label or if your peanut butter doesn't need to be stirred (in natural nut butters without any additives, the oil often separates so you need to stir it).

Also, don't just stick with peanut butter. Cashew, almond, and other tree-nut and seed butters have hit the market and they are delicious. They also offer varying nutritional benefits. We like to switch it up to get the best of all worlds!

Artisana Organics
Barney Butter
Justin's
NuttZo
Santa Cruz Organic

Smucker's (specifically, it offers a natural option without hydrogenated oil and an organic option)
Sneaky Chef No-Nut Butter
SunButter (organic or no sugar added)
Tree of Life
Woodstock

JAMS AND JELLIES

When it comes to jam, the major considerations are whether it is made with organic fruit and its sugar content. Although many of my favorite jams are made with fruit that repeatedly land on the Dirty Dozen list (e.g., berries), I'm less concerned about buying organic since I use jams and jellies in such small quantities. Sugar, though, is a big one, and there's not much to do about it: jams and jellies are packed with sugar by nature. In the end, I use them in moderation and go with taste and also brands that don't pack their spreads with high-fructose corn syrup and fillers.

Bonne Maman
Crofter's Organic
Santa Cruz Organic
Smucker's
Tree of Life

PLANT-BASED MILKS

Plant-based milks aren't simple business, sorry to say; along with nuts, seeds, or soybeans and water, many brands include pesky carrageenan, a seaweed derivative that has caused some controversy.

While there's no clear final word on carrageenan, I avoid it as much as possible—I figure why bother taking it in if I don't have to. That said, it's not all that easy to find a plant-based milk without it.

I've listed a few overall better options, but none stands out a clear winner. The WestSoy plain unsweetened soy milk is the closest I've found to pure. Of the rest, some have carrageenan, and others oil and additives.

The brands listed here have vast product lines with everything from almond to hemp and oat milks, sweetened and unsweetened varieties, plain and vanilla flavors, so be sure to check labels.

Califia Farms (in process of going carrageenan free; this is the coconut almond milk combination I use, page 77)
New Barn (almond milk)
Organic Valley (soy milks)
Rice Dream (refrigerated original has no carrageenan, but oils and tricalcium phosphate)
Silk (unsweetened coconut milk)
So Delicious (unsweetened coconut milk and culinary coconut milks for cooking)
Trader Joe's (varies greatly product by product, but some are carrageenan free)
WestSoy (many products are carrageenan-free; plain organic unsweetened variety doesn't contain anything but water and soybeans)

CEREAL

The key to a healthier breakfast cereal is for it to be low in sugar and high in dietary fiber. When looking at a cereal label, start with the sugar. There is a difference between naturally occurring and added sugar. Sugar is naturally found in fruits and grains, which are considered part of a healthy, balanced breakfast. Too much added sugar, though, can be detrimental to our health. The exact amount of sugar intake for a healthy person varies by age and size, but it may be helpful to keep in mind that every 4 grams of sugar on the label translates to 1 teaspoon of sugar.

It's also good to be mindful of the total carbohydrate-to-sugar ratio, which should be no less than four to one. So, for example, if the "Total Carbohydrate" line on a nutrition label says 24 grams, the "Sugars" should have a value of 6 grams or fewer. If it does, this tells you that most of the carbs come from the grain and fibers, not from the added sugars. Super nutritious cereals have a carb-to-sugar ratio of six or seven to one.

Another quick guide to help you determine whether a cereal (or other breakfast food like instant oatmeal or breakfast bars) has enough fiber is the Five and Five rule: look for foods with less than 5 grams of sugar and at least 5 grams of fiber.

The best breakfast cereal is plain, hot oatmeal that you can flavor with whatever you like. Of the packaged cold cereals, here are a few better options. Please note that not all are organic and/or GMO-free. If either matter to you, please refer to the label.

Arrowhead Mills
Back to Nature
Barbara's
Cascadian Farms
Erewhon
Farm to Table
Kashi
Nature's Path
Post Grape-Nuts

SANDWICH BREAD

Many brands of sandwich bread are formulated with high-fructose corn syrup or what I consider excessive sugar. Also, those pillowy soft slices that remain soft even after a week and a half on the shelf? Not natural; check the label to make sure that your supersoft bread is preservative free.

Your best bet for all-natural bread is to hit a local bakery and ask them to slice you up a loaf. Just beware: if that bakery is part of a mega chain store or even a conventional market, you're likely to end up with a parbaked loaf that's been shipped to the store. That doesn't have to be a big deal, though it may mean that the bread is less wholesome than it seems.

My choices for the best breads on the market may take some getting used to. Since they lack dough conditioners, preservatives, and other ingredients that give store-bought bread its signature soft texture, these options may seem dense at first. The good news is that they are tasty and you'll get used to it. Given how frequently kids eat sliced bread (at least if you're packing their lunch), I think switching to these brands is worth it.

> Alvarado Street Bakery
> Dave's Killer Bread (great option; soft and delicious)
> Food for Life Ezekiel 4:9 breads
> The Baker breads
> Vermont Bread Company

TORTILLAS

It's surprisingly hard to find tortillas made without preservatives, even in the refrigerator section. Here are a few brands that make all-natural tortillas. And, of course, if you live near a Mexican grocery store that sells fresh-made, go for that!

Keep in mind that some of these tortilla brands might not keep as long as you're used to. Also, some may contain ingredients like palm fruit oil that are controversial; if it isn't something on my Ingredients to Avoid list (see page 15) or a proven concern, it may show up in one or more of these products. Check the label to know for yourself.

> Food for Life Ezekiel Sprouted Grain Tortillas (these may take some getting used to!)
> Garden of Eatin' (flour)
> La Tortilla Factory, Sonoma All Natural line (corn and flour)
> Mi Rancho's organic line (corn and flour)
> Stacey's Organic (wheat flour tortillas)
> Trader Joe's (corn, flour, whole-grain)

RICE

There is growing concern over the amount of arsenic found in rice. Ugh. The issue is bigger than we're going to get into here, but I want to go over a few basics so that you can be smart about your choices and *enjoy* rice. It's one of the great comforts and a lifesaver for any busy family cook.

If you're concerned about arsenic intake (and, really, it's just the inorganic arsenic that's a problem), you should consider reducing your overall consumption. This is particularly true if you have small kids or even babies. And although healthier in some ways, brown rice has been found to have higher levels of arsenic. I say, go for white and keep the rest of your diet healthy. Or eat more quinoa.

When you do buy rice, it's thought that white basmati from California, India, and Pakistan is best, along with sushi rice from the United States. And, so long as your tap water is low in arsenic, rinsing your rice really well before cooking reduces the amount of arsenic you'll take in, too.

SNACKS

This is a huge category that spans a wide variety of foods from applesauce to dehydrated fruit, crackers to pretzels. The same general rules apply to snack foods as to all other packaged foods. Organic is a consideration for snacks made of fruits, veggies, and dairy, but does not necessarily equal healthy; reading labels is important; the less sugar and salt, the better; the fewer ingredients the better; and so on (see page 94).

This far-from-exhaustive list is a nice overview of snack brands that can help round out your pantry. Also, consider buying simple, organically grown dried and dehydrated fruits, baked fruit chips, and nuts to have around.

18 Rabbits
Angie's
Annie's
Back to Nature
Barbara's
Bare Fruit
Beanitos
Bearitos
Brad's Organic
Crispy Green
Food Should Taste Good
Garden of Eatin'
GoGo squeeze
Harvest Snaps
Health Warrior
Just Tomatoes Etc. (organic fruits and vegetables)
Justin's
Kashi
Kettle Chips
KIND
Late July
LesserEvil
Lucy's
Lundberg

Made in Nature
Nature's Path
Peeled
Peter Rabbit Organics
Popcorn Indiana
Quinn Popcorn
Rhythm Super Food Chips
Seasnax
Simple Squares
Simply Balanced
SkinnyPop
Slammers (organic)
Stretch Island Fruit Co. / FruitaBu
The Better Chip
Way Better
Whole Foods 365
Woodstock

SPICES

When shopping for spices, concern yourself less with organic than with freshness. Although ground spices have a long shelf life, those bottles that have been in your cabinet for years need to go. Not only do the spices lose their potency, but they can also go rancid. They generally won't make you sick—but your cooking will suffer.

Stock your pantry with whatever spices you use frequently and consider buying smaller bottles for more frequent turnover. Consider going beyond garlic powder and oregano. Try ground cardamom (see page 151 for ideas on how to use it!), experiment with a mild (or spicy!) curry powder, or do something new with ground coriander.

Buying spices from your supermarket is the easiest way to shop; however, those supermarket bottles have been sitting for a long time, especially the ones filled with less frequently used spices. A serious commitment to freshness will have you shopping at local ethnic markets or even online at such merchants as Penzy's (https://www.penzeys.com) or World Spice Merchants (https://www.worldspice.com/s), where you can buy fresh spices in smaller quantities. And if you're committed to all things grown organically, Frontier Co-op and McCormick's both offer lines of organic spices.

One more thing. Although it's expensive, I urge you (implore you!) to buy a box of crunchy Maldon sea salt. Use it sparingly to finish dishes, the way you do your good olive oil. It adds great flavor, good crunch, and just looks great, too.

CANNED FOODS

The major issues with canned foods are typically taste quality and packaging safety. Taste quality depends on the food: canned tomatoes and canned fish can be great, canned beans quite good (especially given their ease of use), and canned fruits and vegetables not good at all. Packaging safety, on the other hand, is more universal.

Bisphenol-A (BPA) is a chemical commonly used in the lining of cans. Increasingly, brands are removing BPA from their packaging (which, for me, raises a question about what is being added in its place?). Here are a few things that are important to keep in mind.

• BPA is more difficult to remove from cans used to package highly acidic foods, such as tomatoes. That said, there are companies that have successfully done it.
• A 2015 report from the Environmental Working Group suggests that many companies that have removed BPA from their lining have not publicized it or do not indicate "BPA-free" on their package. If you have strong ties to a brand and are concerned with BPA, check its website or contact the company to learn more.

• Glass food packaging is BPA-free except, in some cases, for the lining of the cap. Tetra Paks are also BPA-free.
• Some companies have removed BPA from the lining of some canned foods, but not others. A few companies have successfully removed BPA from cans across their entire product line, including the following, many of which are available for mail order through their own sites or Amazon:

> American Tuna
> Amy's Kitchen
> Annie's Homegrown
> Bearitos
> Bionaturae
> Earth's Best
> Farmer's Market
> Healthy Valley
> Juanita's
> Jyoti
> Lucini Italia
> Muir Glen
> Native Forest
> Raincoast Trading
> Tyson
> Westbrae Natural

BEANS

Because of ease of use, I use canned beans more frequently than I use dried. The beans by these companies are packaged in BPA-free cans and I find their quality comparatively high. If you're concerned about salt, be sure to look at the nutrition label, especially when buying bean products, such as refried beans or soup.

> Amy's Kitchen (tasty, all-natural, vegetarian refried beans are among the best you'll get from a can)
> Eden Foods

Trader Joe's (most, but not all beans are in BPA-free cans; they disclose specifics on their site)
Westbrae Natural

BROTH

Given how easy it is to find broth packaged in Tetra Pak packaging (i.e., cartons; see page 245) I don't ever buy canned broth anymore.

If you share my concern over BPA and have a favorite brand of canned broth that you don't want to give up, check the company's website or contact them to see if their cans are BPA-free.

COCONUT MILK

For the full story on coconut (and other plant-based) milk, see page 246. Overall, canned coconut milk tends to be more pure without nearly as many additives as the kind that comes in a carton, but there's that pesky BPA lining, except for in these brands.

Native Forest
Trader Joe's

FISH

High-quality packaged tuna is nice to have around. Sometimes, I'll pick up a can of salmon, as well, as an alternative. Besides packaging, seafood has a lot of concerns (see page 243)—it's already hard to choose safe seafood without throwing in BPA-lined cans. The easiest way to keep it simple is to stick with jarred tuna, which tends to be (though isn't exclusively) higher quality.

If you want canned fish, though, these brands marry high-quality product, effort toward environmentally friendly practices, and safe packaging. They are also more expensive because, well, all that stuff I just mentioned. For the record,

Trader Joe's offers BPA-free tuna at a more conventional price point.

American Tuna
Oregon's Choice (select products)
Wild Planet Foods

FRUIT

As with vegetables, there are only a couple of canned fruits you'll ever see me buy. Actually, make that one: crushed pineapple, which is useful for baking and batter, as in the recipe for Hummingbird Muffins (page 101). Along with all other canned fruit, pineapple rings and chunks are usually too sweet and bloated, even when packed only in their own juice. They can also taste tinny and be packed with added sugar. If you can't find fresh, frozen fruit is a far superior option. That said, if you really need or want canned fruit, try this brand.

Native Forest (which even offers organic pineapple)

TOMATOES

There is huge discrepancy in taste, texture, and color across canned tomatoes and, at the end of the day, though there are standouts, it's a matter of taste. Although there are surely other brands of tomatoes that are tasty and responsibly packaged, these are my favorites (prices vary quite a bit across this short list).

Lucini Italia
Muir Glen (a stand out when you consider all factors: safe packaging, organic, taste)
Pomi (which come in Tetra Paks; any other tomatoes you find in Tetra Pak packaging should be BPA-free, as well)
Trader Joe's
Whole Foods 365

VEGETABLES

There are very few veggies that I recommend buying canned, though one that you should definitely pick up for baking is canned pumpkin and/or sweet potato. The following offer BPA-free options.

> Farmer's Market
> Trader Joe's
> Whole Foods 365

I like to keep canned hearts of palm and artichokes (hearts or bottoms) in my pantry. I've only found one brand that is reliably BPA-free. Both artichokes and hearts of palm are also available in glass packaging, which is always a safe choice.

> Nature's Forest

CHILES

Given how much my family and I love Mexican food, I often used canned chiles. Although Trader Joe's is clear that it packages hatch chiles in cans that contain BPA, it's unclear if they offer other green chiles in BPA-free packaging anywhere in the country. Hatch Chile Company makes good-tasting green chiles (and enchilada sauces, for the record), but its cans contain BPA linings. If you don't mind, they are a great choice. As for chipotles, I haven't been able to identify a single brand commonly found in US markets that is reliably packaged in BPA-free cans, so go for taste, which is comparable across most brands. I like La Morena.

A quick note on dried chipotles: if you want to avoid the canned stuff, dried chipotles or even ground chipotle chile powder is great, but it's no substitute in a recipe that calls for chipotles in adobo, which is a sauce that has onions, vinegar, and other ingredients that lend a uniquely rich and complex flavor.

CONDIMENTS, OIL, AND DRESSINGS

Some condiments and sauces just have to be purchased, and that's where this list comes in.

OIL, VINEGAR, DRESSINGS, AND SAUCES

Oil: Oil is among the most important condiments in my pantry. I like to keep a smaller, more expensive bottle of great olive oil for finishing, alongside bigger bottles of supermarket brands for cooking and everyday use. My favorite good (but not insanely expensive) olive oil is Frantoia, which, if you can't find it at a market near you, you can buy online. In addition to Frantoia, I stock a cheaper organic olive oil; coconut oil; and neutral oil, such as grapeseed or canola.

Vinegar: Supermarket brands do the trick here. I like to keep a white wine or champagne, balsamic, and red wine vinegar on hand at all times.

Packaged dressings: Not only do they not taste great, but they tend to be packed with sugar and sometimes additives, too. If you're going to buy bottled dressing, definitely look at the nutrition label as well as the ingredients list. More than that, give my Everyday Vinaigrette (page 124) at least one try. I swear you'll be a convert as soon as you see how easy homemade can be.

Cooking sauces: I find it very difficult to find natural *and* tasty versions of the sauces I use most commonly: hoisin, BBQ, enchilada, and curry sauces.

I haven't found an all-natural brand of hoisin that doesn't also contain caramel color, at best, so there's no suggestion for hoisin below.

Annie's (salad dressings)
Artisana Organics (coconut oil)
Bragg (oil, vinegar, dressings)
California Olive Ranch (oils)
Eden (tamari, soy sauce, and mirin)
Hatch (green and red enchilada sauce; cans
have traces of BPA)
Lucini (oil and vinegars)
Marukan (organic rice vinegars)
Maya Kaimal (curry simmer sauce)
Miso Master (miso pastes)
Spectrum (organic oils and vinegars)
Stubb's (BBQ sauce)
Tree of Life (oils)
Whole Foods 365

HUMMUS

Most store-brought brands of hummus contain preservatives. To be fair, the most common (though not the only) preservative found in hummus, potassium sorbate, is widely considered safe. Still, two studies possibly linked it to birth defects and though that's far from causal, if even reliable, I figure why not avoid it.

These brands aren't the most widely available, but the plain variety of each is made without preservatives (so it's possible!). Please note that the crazier the flavors, the more likely that you'll run into funky ingredients.

Cava
Engine 2
Hope Foods
Ithaca Hummus
Tribe Organic
Whole Foods brand

GUACAMOLE

I have yet to find a packaged guacamole that I can stand behind. If you really want/need to buy guac, check the dairy or deli section of your supermarket for guacamole that is made in-house. Check the label: it should be nothing more than avocado, lime juice, and some veggies.

SALSA

There has been an explosion of gourmet salsas made with care and wholesome ingredients that seem to be popular. Here are a few brands that you might want to look for (you should also keep an eye out for small, local brands or other organic, all-natural brands not listed here that you may like).

Desert Pepper
Frontera
Green Mountain Gringo
Salpica
Xochilt

PASTA AND PASTA SAUCE

For the most part, buying dried pasta is a straightforward charge, at least if you eat gluten.

I admit to being loyal to De Cecco. It's great quality, reasonably priced, and widely available. It makes a line of organic products, but if that's not your concern, pasta might be a good place to consider saving money and go nonorganic. If you're interested in GMO-free pasta, Ronzoni is a widely available option, and Whole Foods 365 offers both organic and GMO-free options.

Quite a few high-quality jarred pasta sauces are available. That's the good news, but the bad is that they are crazy expensive. If you feel strongly about having a jar of sauce around, I urge you to spend the extra money on a good, wholesome option. Also, don't bother with flavors and cheese and all that jazz. Go for regular marinara and, if you really want to, doctor it at home however you like.

One more thing: if you're looking for pesto, skip anything that can live on an unrefrigerated shelf for months and hit the refrigerator section instead, where you'll find fresh pesto, or make your own (page 58).

Classico Marinara with Plum Tomatoes and Olive Oil (though note the "natural flavors")
Lucini
Rao's

BAKING SUPPLIES

While I often opt for organic flours, I generally focus on performance when shopping for baking supplies. I have strong brand loyalty that I'll share here, but most major brands of flour, sugar, yeast, baking soda, and so on work well. Instead of focusing on brands here, it's more about deciding if you want organic and/or GMO-free, then picking brands that are affordable and work well in your kitchen.

COCOA POWDER

I always keep regular unsweetened cocoa powder in my cupboard for making brownies, but I also keep something else—something more special—around: Dutch-processed cocoa. In short, Dutched cocoa lends a smooth, mellow, earthy flavor and deep, dark color that reminds me of one of the great chocolate confections of all times, Oreos.

Buying Dutch-processed cocoa is a splurge—but so worth it. Use it sparingly when it really

matters, like when you make a birthday cake—your little one's or your own. Or, even better than Dutch-processed cocoa (yes, there is such a thing), go all out and treat yourself to a combination of Dutch-processed and black cocoa, a precious baking ingredient that will turn any old chocolate baked good into something sublime. (It's all I use to make my Deep Chocolate Layer Cake, page 225). You can buy it online (my favorite brand is below). Go now. Do that.

Droste Cocoa (Dutch-processed)
Hershey's Natural Unsweetened Cocoa
Hershey's Special Dark Cocoa (a blend of natural and Dutch-processed)
King Arthur Dutch-processed cocoa
King Arthur Double Dutch Dark Cocoa (a blend of Dutch-processed and black cocoa)

FLOUR

I love King Arthur Flours, but will often buy whatever is priced right at the market. More than the brand, though, I want to urge you to pick up some whole wheat pastry flour, as well as all-purpose. The two are interchangeable and using whole wheat pastry adds a little bit of whole grain to your baked goods. It's a small change, but why not.

ORGANIC FLOUR:
Hodgson Mill offers both all-purpose and whole wheat pastry in organic and GMO-free.
King Arthur Flour's line of organic products

FOOD COLORING AND FLAVOR EXTRACTS

Artificial food coloring and flavorings are on my list of ingredients to avoid in packaged food, but sometimes it's hard to avoid when making a special baked good at home. Like when your little one insists on a fire engine cake for his birthday (true story). Then what's a busy mom to do?

The good news is that natural food coloring, have gotten better, and several great brands make natural flavor extracts. I stock up on this stuff and then have it around for whenever I find myself making treats.

Beanilla (online)
Color Garden (food coloring)
Frontier Co-op
J. R. Watkins
Nature's Colors by India Tree (liquid food coloring, sprinkles, and sanding sugar)
Nielsen Massey
Penzey's (online)

SUGAR

You've heard a lot about sugar, I've heard a lot about sugar . . . let's make it easy with a bottom line shared with me by a nutritionist. Once in the body, sugar behaves as sugar does regardless of what form it has come in. Given that, the best one to use is whichever allows you achieve the flavor you want with the least amount of added sweetener.

With that in mind, and also an eye towards using the least processed kind, I stick with honey, maple syrup, granulated sugar, and brown sugar. Though granulated sugar and brown sugar are processed, they strike a balance between being effective sweeteners and predictable, which is especially important for baking. Other popular sweeteners, such as agave nectar, don't perform as well and cannot be substituted into conventional recipes easily. (Plus, they are not proven any better for our health—or the environment. Some even believe that agave is bad for our health and, while I can't say for sure one way or the other, there is some evidence that makes me wonder. Plus, it's *highly* processed.)

Domino Sugar: some GMO-free options including its Baker's Special Granulated Sugar, Medium Fine Granulated Sugar, Light and Dark Brown Sugars
Whole Foods 365 and C&H: GMO-free lines of conventional and organic sugars, from cane to light brown

Honey is something that you should try to buy local, and not just to be hip. Honey produced in your area offers regionally specific health benefits, especially to those with allergies. Plus, buying it locally—or splurging on artisanal honey from a single known source—helps ensure that you're not getting cheap imported honey. The EU has banned honey from certain countries and even our government has expressed concern about traces of heavy metals and even antibiotics found in honey imported from certain international sources.

If you live close to where maple syrup is made, be sure to buy that local as well. Otherwise, whatever you do, buy pure maple syrup, which you can find by looking for the word "pure" on the label. The grading system for maple syrup has recently changed in the United States, but grades refer only to color and taste—not quality—with Grade A being lighter in both, and Grade A Amber, Grade A Dark, or Grade B having a progressively darker color and deeper flavor.

METRIC CONVERSIONS

The recipes in this book have not been tested with metric measurements, so some variations might occur. Remember that the weight of dry ingredients varies according to the volume or density factor: 1 cup of flour weighs far less than 1 cup of sugar, and 1 tablespoon doesn't necessarily hold 3 teaspoons.

GENERAL FORMULA FOR METRIC CONVERSION

Ounces to grams	multiply ounces by 28.35
Grams to ounces	multiply grams by 0.035
Pounds to grams	multiply pounds by 453.5
Pounds to kilograms	multiply pounds by 0.45
Cups to liters	multiply cups by 0.24
Fahrenheit to Celsius	subtract 32 from Fahrenheit temperature, multiply by 5, divide by 9
Celsius to Fahrenheit	multiply Celsius temperature by 9, divide by 5, add 32

VOLUME (LIQUID) MEASUREMENTS

1 teaspoon	= ⅙ fluid ounce	= 5 milliliters
1 tablespoon	= ½ fluid ounce	= 15 milliliters
2 tablespoons	= 1 fluid ounce	= 30 milliliters
¼ cup	= 2 fluid ounces	= 60 milliliters
⅓ cup	= 2⅔ fluid ounces	= 79 milliliters
½ cup	= 4 fluid ounces	= 118 milliliters
1 cup or ½ pint	= 8 fluid ounces	= 250 milliliters
2 cups or 1 pint	= 16 fluid ounces	= 500 milliliters
4 cups or 1 quart	= 32 fluid ounces	= 1,000 milliliters
1 gallon	= 4 liters	

WEIGHT (MASS) MEASUREMENTS

1 ounce	= 30 grams	
2 ounces	= 55 grams	
3 ounces	= 85 grams	
4 ounces	= ¼ pound	= 125 grams
8 ounces	= ½ pound	= 240 grams
12 ounces	= ¾ pound	= 375 grams
16 ounces	= 1 pound	= 454 grams

OVEN TEMPERATURE EQUIVALENTS, FAHRENHEIT (F) AND CELSIUS (C)

100°F	= 38°C
200°F	= 95°C
250°F	= 120°C
300°F	= 150°C
350°F	= 180°C
400°F	= 205°C
450°F	= 230°C

VOLUME (DRY) MEASUREMENTS

¼ teaspoon	= 1 milliliter
½ teaspoon	= 2 milliliters
¾ teaspoon	= 4 milliliters
1 teaspoon	= 5 milliliters
1 tablespoon	= 15 milliliters
¼ cup	= 59 milliliters
⅓ cup	= 79 milliliters
½ cup	= 118 milliliters
⅔ cup	= 158 milliliters
¾ cup	= 177 milliliters
1 cup	= 225 milliliters
4 cups or 1 quart	= 1 liter
½ gallon	= 2 liters
1 gallon	= 4 liters

LINEAR MEASUREMENTS

½ inch	= 1½ cm
1 inch	= 2½ cm
6 inches	= 15 cm
8 inches	= 20 cm
10 inches	= 25 cm
12 inches	= 30 cm
20 inches	= 50 cm

ACKNOWLEDGMENTS

It's hard for me to know how to communicate my appreciation on a page like this. I can list names—oh, and I will—but it just doesn't seem enough, especially since I'm sitting at my dining room table, alone and focused, when I'd rather be playing and gallivanting with the people I love and who made this book possible. I guess I just ask anyone mentioned here to please imagine that I'm with you right now hugging you, laughing hard, and, of course, eating.

I have to start with the two people without whom this book would have never happened: Isaac and Oliver. Isaac, you are one of the smartest people I have ever met—and you are only eight. I don't know where you came from but, man, am I blessed that you chose me to be your mom. You challenge and teach me every day, making me a better person. Given how quickly you're sure to surpass me on most every level, I hope that I can at least always teach you a little something about food, cooking, and love. You are already a killer dinner date (yes, even when you're messy) and I look forward to sharing meals with you well into my old age.

Oliver, sometimes I wonder why we didn't listen to Isaac and make your middle name "Brightlight." Although it would have made us sound way more hippie than we actually are, it would have been accurate. I guess it doesn't matter much since everyone can see and feel the brightness you bring to the world from the moment they meet you. When I was pregnant with you I felt tremendously nervous about upsetting our perfect little group of three. You complete our family so fully, so gloriously, that those thoughts

now seem like they belong to someone else. And I guess they do: the me before you. She was good, but now I'm better.

Mike, well, it would pretty much take a whole other book to write all the things I have to say to you. We've grown up together, so this book has nothing on us. You didn't just help make this book possible, you helped make everything that led up to this book possible, and everything before that. I want you to know that, no matter what, I have *always* known that you love and believe in me. Without that, none of this would be happening. There is no greater gift and I'm amazed that you think I deserve it. Thank you. I love you.

My mom, well, though she'll argue that this is totally unfair and wholly untrue: the cooking gene skipped a generation. It's not that she can't cook (I know you can, Mom), but food is not that important to her. In moments, this has frustrated me (like the time when she told me to eat a can of sardines and sliced feta cheese for dinner because she was too tired from work to make anything—I was twelve), but now I realize that it's a gift. As much as I love food, there's a whole other side to me and much of it comes from my mom, including my drive and my belief in myself. She pushed me hard and was clear: it was because I could achieve anything I wanted to. She also pushed herself hard and has led an amazing life. She never stops challenging herself to grow and she's one hell of a grandmother. Thank you for everything, Mom, I love you.

And my dad. With tears in my eyes and a sad, heavy heart, I write this knowing that my dad will never get to hold this book, see the fruits of my labor, understand more fully what I've been working toward all these years and, worst of all, read this. He passed away right as the first draft of this book was due. Heartbreaking. My comfort, though, is that he lives in every page. Every recipe in this book was developed from the heart of my own family's kitchen and it beats the way it does because of who my dad was—doting, gregarious, food-loving, simple cooking, fiery tempered. He taught me, more than anyone, that the table is a place for food, drink, conversation (a good argument, even!) and, of course, love. Not by telling me, but by sitting with me at the table every moment he could, feeding me, and being endlessly interested in talking to me. We had the best talks (and debates, too) and, though they don't play out the same way—and I'll truly never be the same without you here—I know you're with me, Daddy. I'm with you, too.

Sheila. There's so much to thank you for, starting with loving and taking care of Daddy. You remained as dedicated in his last days as you were when you first met him, with so many long, hard years in between. I couldn't have wished for better for him-and for me, too. And, you know, there were many happy years, too. Thank you for so many fun, formative memories. My life wouldn't be the same without you. I love you and look forward to many more happy years again ahead of us.

I've always been one of those "your friends are your family" people but, as I've grown older, I've come to realize that, though true, there is also a difference. My family is special. My maternal grandmother, whom I often refer to as *yiayia* on *One Hungry Mama*, is no longer with us and, honestly, I have complicated feelings toward her. But she helped shape my love affair with food. She's also the one who showed me that no matter the difficulty of family relations, the dinner table can always be a place of joy if you cook with love and feed with abandon. I wish you could have known how much your hard work in the kitchen—and in life—means to me, Yiayia. Hopefully, somehow, you do.

I lost my brother, Steven, years ago and always miss what I hoped we could be. Although I didn't always realize it because of age and distance, my sister has been teaching me what siblings can—and should—be the whole time. Thank you for that, Ellen. And for always eating with me (even when I push bizarre health ingredients on you and your family) and especially for giving me li'l P and his sister, G. I love you all tremendously.

There are so many other people to thank, but I hear that music they play at the Oscars when someone's running long. Thitsa, I love you and know that the busyness of my life gets in the way, but look at what I made! I can't wait to share it with you. Ann, Alan, and Nan, you have each expanded my world in ways beyond which I could have imagined and, in many ways, the belief that I can be someone who writes a book comes from you. Who knew I had it in me? I didn't until you. I feel blessed to have you three—and your families, too—as part of my innermost circle.

To all of my friends and extended family whom I neglected to call, haven't seen, and otherwise dropped out of touch with while writing this book, I hope you're proud of what I've been doing. I would have much rather been playing with you guys, but think this might have been worth the break. Your words of encouragement along the way made a big difference. Now let's make a date STAT.

I cannot write this without calling out one friend in particular. Miss C., your friendship has been a gift for which I'm immeasurably grateful. I love you and have so many times drawn from your deep soul and incredible wisdom. You never cease to amaze me and make me feel like I never cease to amaze you, even when I can't imagine how. Thank you for that. Plus, nothing makes me feel freer than cruising the streets of LA with you, convertible style, singing Katy Perry. Keep your socks weird forever.

Liz, Kristen, and the whole Cool Mom team: you are, hands down, the best group of people with whom I've ever had the pleasure of working. Your work makes me proud, your emails make me laugh, and your support (which I truly needed through this process, especially at the end) humbles me. Plus, you all have some seriously great taste.

Sally and Renée. SALLY AND RENÉE! You both believed in me when I didn't. There is no thank you big or loud enough to convey how deeply grateful I am for this. Sally, I fondly remember the dinner when we first met in Austin as a moment when things shifted. You and I both knew I wasn't ready then, but you stayed steady, present, and available until I was. You could have easily moved along, but didn't. Although I'm not sure why, I hope this book makes you proud that you stuck with me.

And, Renée, there was a call with other people on it before you decided to take a chance on me. I don't often feel the need to "perform," but I did on this call. Something serious. I was *so* nervous and then, suddenly, at one point, I realized that you were someone who saw something in me and, though none of us were exactly sure what it was or how it should take shape in book form, I could stop performing and just be myself. Even when being myself meant not having a clear answer. That's when I knew I wanted to work with you and I appreciate every day that you have continued to nurture and support not some marketable idea of me, but the real-deal me—nerdy, foul-mouthed, enthusiastic, and so

very long-winded. I hope we get to do this again because I can't imagine not.

There are so many other people who go into making a book happen and I'd be remiss not to say thank you to every single person who helped (and will help from this point forward) make this book a reality, but look at how absurdly long this already is. Quickly, though: my photo crew. You guys blew my mind. I know you were just doing a job, something you do day in and day out with people way more experienced than me but, for me, working with you was exhilarating. Naomi, Christina, Cyd, Brett, Karin, and Alex, you are all stunningly talented and I thank you, from the bottom of my heart, for working on this book with me. I hope that you love my part as much as I love yours. Kate, thank you for being a believer from the very beginning. I'm over the moon that we get to work together and, more than anything, hope that you find this book helpful in your own kitchen! Megan, how great that we found each other?! Bringing you onto the team has been such a gift. And to Christine and your dream team: there are no words to express how deeply grateful I am for the tremendously hard work you put into making this book shipshape. (Though you guys could probably think of some.) Thank you also to Jaime and the Lisa Ekus Group team and everyone at Da Capo and Perseus who has touched this project, even in a small way. It might just be your job, but it's my dream and so you matter to me! And, of course, to all of my recipe testers (you guys rocked it!); Sarah S., for helping me rally and organize at the hardest point; and everyone who has helped make *One Hungry Mama* a place worth every single minute I've put into it.

And you, too, reader, thank you. Because without readers, there is nothing worth writing.

INDEX

ABOUT THE AUTHOR

Stacie Billis is a mom of two and the food writer behind the award-winning blog One Hungry Mama, where she serves up original family-friendly recipes and tips for managing life as the family cook. (Wine is involved.) Stacie is also managing editor of Cool Mom Eats, the only dedicated food site that shares recipes, tips, and food finds curated specifically for family cooks from the publishers of Cool Mom Picks.

Stacie's common sense approach stems from her masters degree in child development, as well as from her experience working with families one-on-one to help parents *manageably* feed their children more healthfully on whatever budget, regardless of cooking skill, and on any schedule. But honestly, her popularity might have more to do with her cheesy sense of humor and non-judgy approach. Because it's really time that we stop being so hard on each other over food choices.

Stacie's work has appeared in the Huffington Post, *Parents* magazine, *Every Day with Rachael Ray* magazine, Baby Center, and Babble, to name a few. Stacie and her family live in Brooklyn, New York.

SOCIAL MEDIA: OneHungryMama